IMAGES
of America

NEW BOSTON

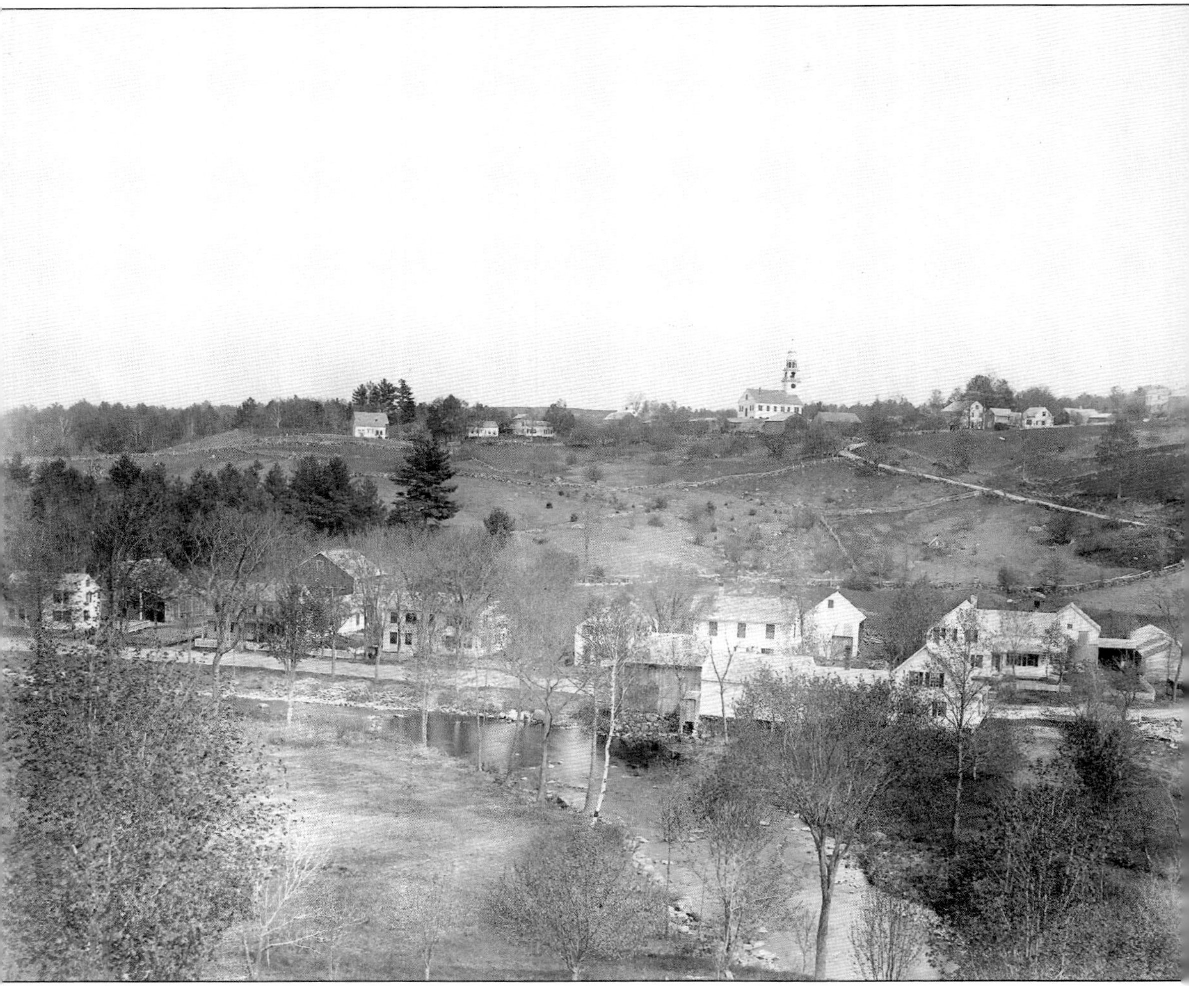

This photograph shows a panoramic view of the town of New Boston in the late 1800s.

IMAGES
of America

NEW BOSTON

New Boston Historical Society

ARCADIA
PUBLISHING

ISBN 978-0-7385-3513-5

Published by Arcadia Publishing
Charleston, South Carolina

Printed in the United States of America

Library of Congress Catalog Card Number: 2004100458

For all general information, contact Arcadia Publishing:
Telephone 843-853-2070
Fax 843-853-0044
E-mail sales@arcadiapublishing.com
For customer service and orders:
Toll-free 1-888-313-2665

Visit us on the Internet at www.arcadiapublishing.com

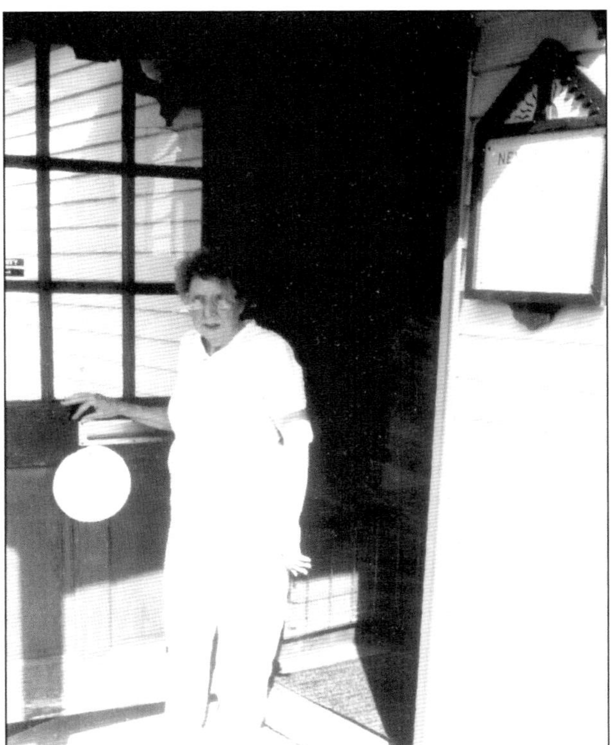

This book is dedicated to the memory of Rena Davis. Rena helped establish the New Boston Historical Society in 1968 and was the driving force behind it for nearly 30 years. She was deeply committed to the community and to the preservation of its history. Without her extensive research and documentation of nearly every aspect of our town's past, this book could not have been written.

Contents

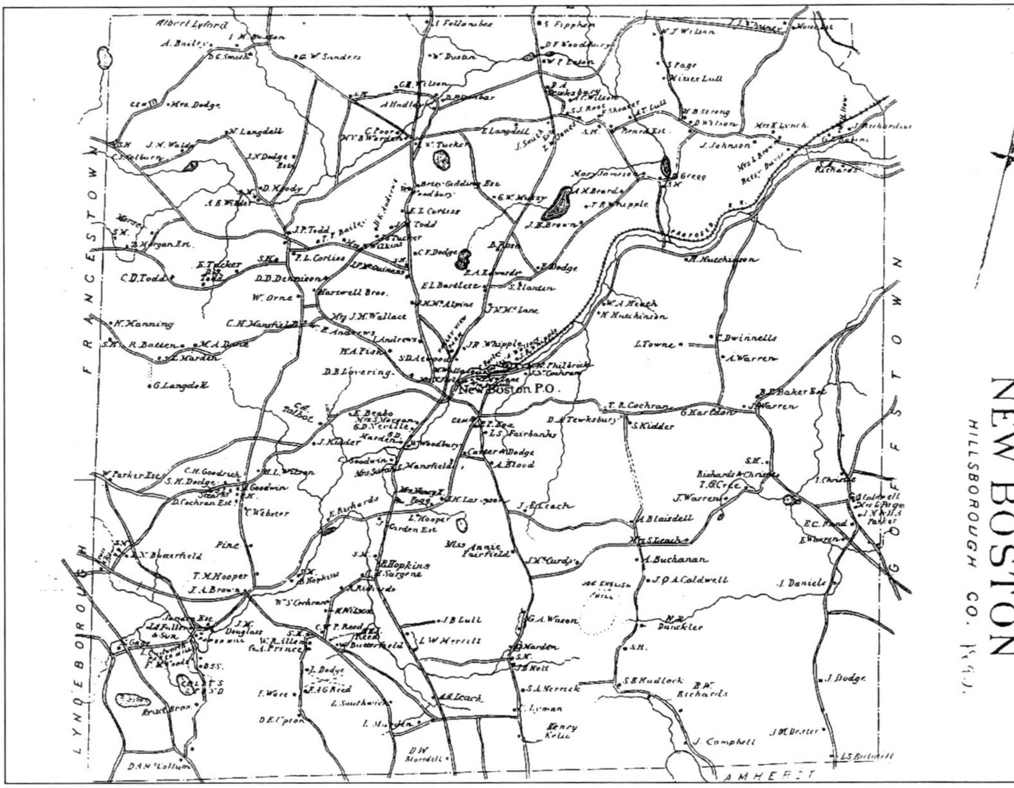

Pictured is an 1892 map of the town of New Boston, Hillsborough County, New Hampshire.

The New Boston Historical Society Book Committee

Sandy Molloy, Chairperson
Bill Brendle
Polly Brendle
Janet Chamberlain
Thomas Lazott
Clem Lyon
Ruth Lyon
Dick Moody
Betty Poltrack
Nonah Poole
Kevin St. John

The committee has relied upon information available at the historical society, as well as that provided by individual citizens. We apologize for any errors or omissions that may exist in our work.

INTRODUCTION

As we look over our beautiful hills and valleys we cannot realize that at the time of the first settlements, supposed to be about the year 1733, our loved town was an unbroken forest, with perhaps, the smoke from an Indian wigwam rising here and there among the lofty trees.

—New Boston resident F. A. D. Atwood, 1902

If you happen to read the hand-painted sign that greets all travelers entering town, you are reminded that New Boston is the home of Joe English Grange and the Hillsborough County fair. But after nearly 250 years of incorporation, is that all? Admittedly, most of New Boston's colorful history is something that in bits and pieces may not warrant its own book. But that is hardly the case when the bulk of New Boston's past is considered. Like a patchwork quilt made for display at the county fair, the collective history of New Boston is often practical but appealing, unique but familiar. Amongst the tapestry, there are more than a few colorful swatches that will catch your eye. So, the New Boston Historical Society has undertaken this book project to attempt a mostly visual appreciation of New Boston's own quilted history through the use of historic photographs (most are published here for the first time) and line art.

On January 14, 1736, the General Court of the Massachusetts Bay Colony granted future New Boston to John Simpson and 52 others of Boston (the 53 soldiers or heirs of the men who perished during the disastrous expedition for Sir William Phipps to Canada in 1690). Of this original group, Thomas Smith of Chester became the first permanent settler of Lane's Town, as New Boston was then known, choosing the northeast part of town called Pine Plain. Following Smith, the earliest settlers were almost entirely Scottish emigrants from Londonderry. Lured by the power and potential of the Piscataquog River, which was named for a Native American term meaning "great deer place," the first settlements that survived were in close proximity to the water.

Pioneer, or frontier, life was characterized by constant hardships for the early settlers. Land had to be first cleared of large trees, most of which were burned, prior to sowing the land with rye or corn. Log homes were constructed with stone chimneys, and pathways were painstakingly cleared of stumps to accommodate sleds. Aside from a straw bed, furniture was rare; even tables and chairs were generally unavailable until there was a sawmill able to produce board lumber. Diets did not include milk until sufficient land was cleared for cows. Eventually, the combination of harsh weather and the true frontier location (skirmishes with Native Americans were a distinct, and usually feared, possibility) proved too much for some of the earliest settlers.

In 1741, New Hampshire became a separate province from Massachusetts Bay Colony. Within 10 years, the first settlers of Lane's Town had successfully petitioned Governor Wentworth and satisfied the Masons that they did in fact have legal rights to the land. On February 18, 1763, New Hampshire province incorporated Lane's Town and it was named New Boston, after the capital of Massachusetts Bay Colony. John Goffe presided over the first official town meeting held within the required 20-day period of incorporation, on March 10, 1763.

Like most New England towns, a condition of the original grant was that New Boston be divided into equal shares and that one share must be reserved for the first settled minister, one share for the ministry, and one share for schools. There were 63 shares for New Boston, and each share represented approximately 400 acres. As New Boston became more established, the hilltops that provided rocky yet fertile soil and commanding views of the river valley were the preferred locales for homesteads, the first meetinghouse, and the first cemetery. In 1752, New Boston had literally doubled in size, as an additional six square miles was granted and called the New Boston addition. But in 1772, the addition was incorporated as neighboring Francestown and New Boston was reduced to its original boundaries.

When the call to arms came during the Revolutionary War, a total of 136 men from New Boston participated on battlefields from Bunker Hill to Bennington. At Bennington, led by Gen. John Stark, the colonists won their first and arguably most pivotal battle against the British. During the battle, numerous arms were captured, including two four-pound cannons—the future Molly Stark (named after John Stark's wife) and a mate. Today, our own "Old Molly" is the most unique heritage associated with New Boston. The cannon is incorporated into the town seal and is fired by the New Boston Artillery Company as a fitting tribute to our fight for independence every Fourth of July holiday.

During the Civil War, New Boston officially celebrated its centennial in 1863. By this time, the town was a thriving locale of industry, as evidenced by the numerous goods that were produced here by both factories and mills. Tragically, nearly 40 buildings that comprised most of the village were destroyed by fire in 1887. However, rebuilding in post–Civil War New Boston was far more manageable and quicker than in the early settlement period, particularly once the railroad was extended to New Boston in 1893. Still, even though J. R. Whipple and his industry bolstered New Boston, the town never fully recovered. For example, by the 1930s, the Baptists had dissolved for good and the new church built after the fire was torn down. However, as a consolation, the former church property was given to the town for perpetual use as a common, which is still used today.

After the fire of 1887 and the passing of J. R. Whipple and his industry in 1912, New Boston was no longer the industrial town it once had been. But it always remained a community. By the late 1920s, Reverend Swanson formed the Playground Association that fostered organized baseball; purchased a motion picture machine that was used for outdoor viewings, drawing hundreds of residents over the course of a summer; coordinated glee clubs; and directed an annual minstrel show. Also, the Playground Association began sponsoring an annual Fourth of July celebration, which, as current residents know, has become an indelible part of the town's heritage to rival the annual Hillsborough County fair. Reminders of the past abound, including former homesteads, schools, landmarks, and other silent but proud testimonies to New Boston's heritage.

One

Clearing the Land

The present generation have but a very limited idea of the amount of labor and hardships endured in clearing the land, erecting buildings and the making of other improvements upon the land by the earliest settlers in the primeval forest.
—From a sermon at New Boston Old Folk's Day, 1895

In 1735, Thomas Smith of Chester became the first permanent settler of the "primeval forest" that would eventually be known as New Boston in the northeast part of town called Pine Plain. Within a year, on January 14, 1736, the General Court of the provincial Massachusetts Bay Colony granted John Simpson and 52 others of Boston "the unappropriated lands of the province, of the contents of six miles square, with one thousand acres added for ponds," allowing for two rods for every 100 acres "for unevenness of surface and swag of chain." It was land specifically described as "lying on the south and middle branches of the Piscataquog River." Initially known as Lane's Town, the name of New Boston was suggested by the grantees and first applied to the grant lands by the proprietors on April 16, 1751.

The first census—recorded on September 25, 1756—reports that 59 persons resided within the township, which by then could boast of 215 cleared acres, 32 completed houses, a barn, a sawmill, a grain mill, and a dam. On February 18, 1763, New Boston was granted its charter of incorporation by the provincial governor, Benning Wentworth, acting on behalf of King George III of England. Within only a few weeks, John Goffe directed the first town meeting at the home of Dea. Thomas Cochran on March 10, 1763. By 1767, the first community church and meetinghouse was completed, situated on the site of the present-day cemetery. New Boston was now an established town experiencing significant population and industry growth.

Within 100 years of the first census, in 1856, updated reports indicated that New Boston was thriving. It consisted of 18 sawmills; 4 gristmills; 1 seraphine factory; 1 door, sash, and blind factory; 1 edged tool factory; 1 tannery; 3 cabinet shops; 2 cooper shops; 2 blacksmith shops; 3 stores; 1 hotel; and 2 meetinghouses. Ironically, it was not long after the 1856 census that residents began to lament the fact that the hardships of the earliest settlers would soon be forgotten, in part a result of the prosperity and modernization of those same settlers' descendants.

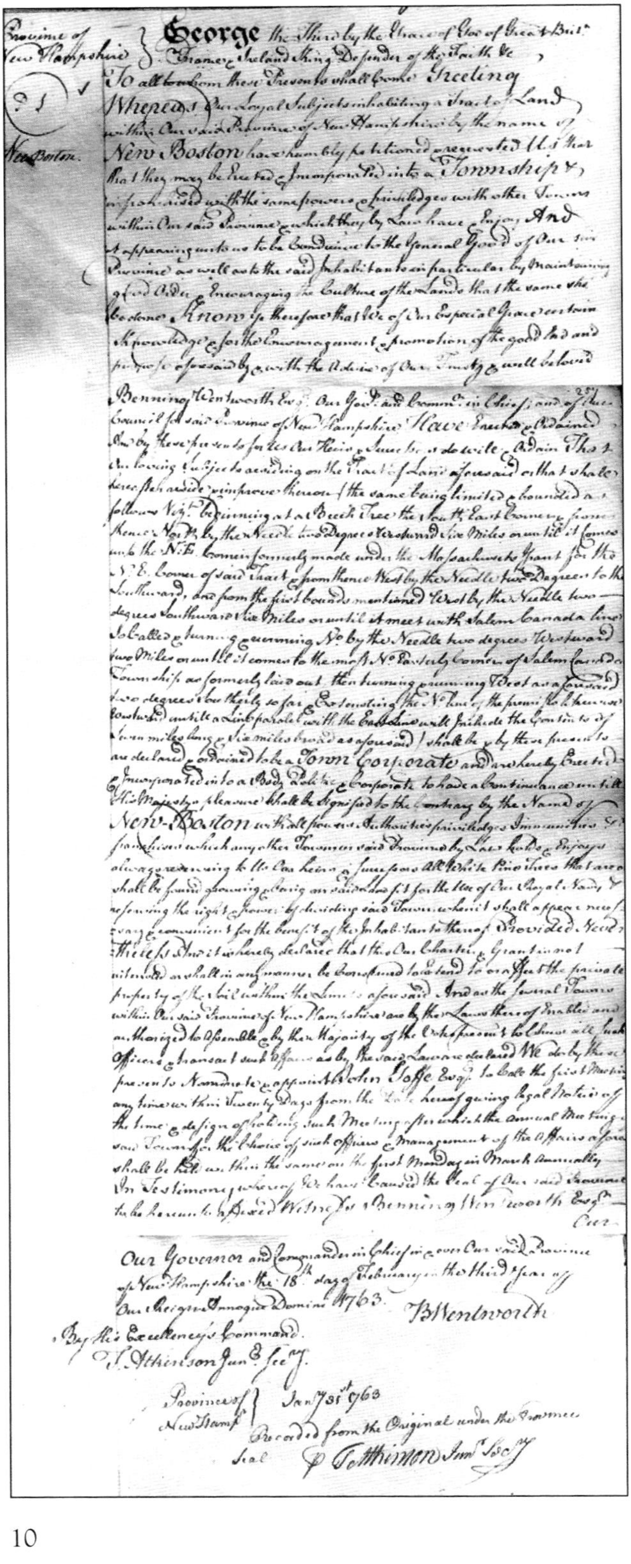
Province of New Hampshire } George the Third by the Grace of God of Great Brit. France & Ireland King Defender of the Faith &c.

To all to whom these Presents shall Come Greeting

Whereas Our Loyal Subjects inhabiting a Tract of Land within Our said Province of New Hampshire by the name of New Boston have humbly petitioned & requested Us that they may be Erected & Incorporated into a Township & infranchised with the same powers & priviledges with other Towns within Our said Province & which they by Law have & Enjoy And it appearing unto us to be Conducive to the General Good of Our said Province as well as to the said Inhabitants in particular by Maintaining good Order & Encouraging the Culture of the Lands that the same sh[oul]d be done Know ye therefore that We of Our Especial Grace certain Knowledge & for the Encouragement & promotion of the good End and purpose aforesaid by & with the Advice of Our Trusty & well beloved Benning Wentworth Esq. Our Gov. and Comm. in Chief and of Our Council for said Province of New Hampshire Have Erected & Ordained and by these presents for Us Our Heirs & Successors do will & Ordain That Our loving Subjects residing on the Tract of Land aforesaid or that shall hereafter inhabit & improve thereon (the same being limited & bounded as follows Viz. beginning at a Beech Tree the South East Corner from thence North by the Needle two Degrees Eastward Six Miles or until it Comes unto the N.E. Corner formerly made under the Massachusetts Grant for the N.E. Corner of said Tract & from thence West by the Needle two Degrees to the Southward, and from the first bounds mentioned West by the Needle two degrees Southward Six Miles or until it meet with Salem Canada line so called & turning & running No. by the Needle two degrees Westward two Miles or until it comes to the most No. Easterly Corner of Salem Canada Township as formerly laid out then turning & running West as aforesaid two degrees Southerly so far Extending the No. line of the premises [illegible] until a Line parallel with the East line will include the Contents of Seven miles long & Six miles broad as aforesaid) shall be & by these presents are declared & ordained to be a Town Corporate and are hereby Erected & Incorporated into a Body Politic & Corporate to have a Continuance until His Majesty's pleasure shall be signified to the Contrary by the Name of New-Boston with all powers Authorities priviledges Immunities & franchises which any other Towns in said Province by Law hold & Enjoy always reserving to Us Our heirs & Successors All White Pine Trees that are or shall be found growing & being on said Tract fit for the Use of Our Royal Navy & reserving the right & power of dividing said Town when it shall appear necessary & convenient for the benefit of the Inhabitants thereof Provided Nevertheless & it is hereby declared that this Our Charter & Grant is not intended and shall in any manner be Construed to extend to or affect the private property of the Soil within the Limits aforesaid And as the several Towns within Our said Province of New Hampshire are by the Laws thereof Enabled and authorized to Assemble & by the Majority of the Voters present to Choose all such Officers & transact such Affairs as by the said Laws are declared We do by these presents Nominate & appoint John Goffe Esq. to Call the first Meeting any time within Twenty Days from the Date hereof giving Legal Notice of the time & design of holding such Meeting after which the annual Meeting in said Town for the Choice of such Officers & management of the Affairs aforesaid shall be held within the same on the first Monday in March Annually In Testimony whereof We have Caused the Seal of Our said Province to be hereunto affixed Witness Benning Wentworth Esq. Our Governor and Commander in Chief in & over Our said Province of New Hampshire the 18th day of February in the third Year of Our Reign Annoque Domini 1763.

B Wentworth

By His Excellency's Command.
T. Atkinson Jun. Secy.

Province of New Hamp. Seal
Jan. 31st 1763
Recorded from the Original under the Province Seal
T Atkinson Jun. Secy.

In 1736, Massachusetts granted the land now known as New Boston to a group of men from Boston named as "John Simpson and 52 others." The town was known at times as Lane's Town and Boston Piscataquog Township. The province of New Hampshire incorporated the town on February 18, 1763. This is a copy of a transcription of the original 1763 charter signed by Gov. Benning Wentworth.

One of the first missions of the settlers was to erect a meetinghouse. New Boston's first church, located on the cemetery grounds on Meetinghouse Hill, "stood in a bleak place and never had means of warming." In 1822, townspeople began to lobby for a new church in a different location, and the Church on the Hill was constructed opposite the Wason house. It was dedicated on Christmas Day 1825 by Reverend Bradford.

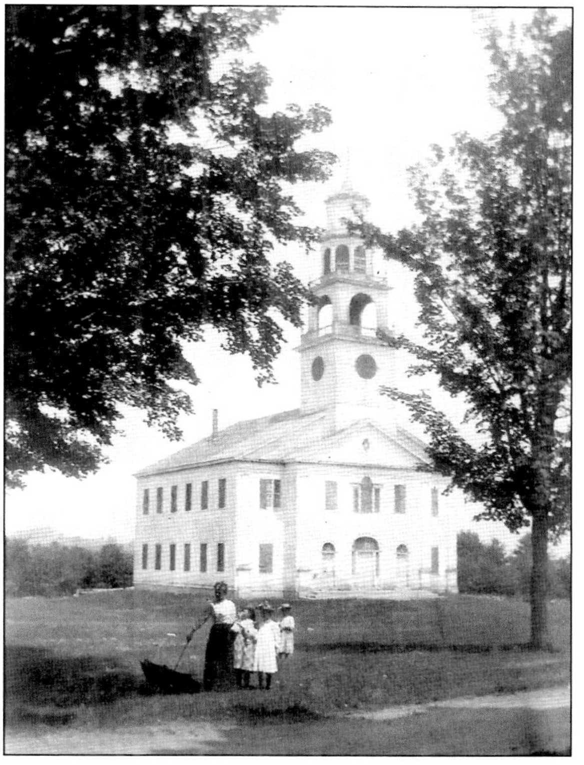

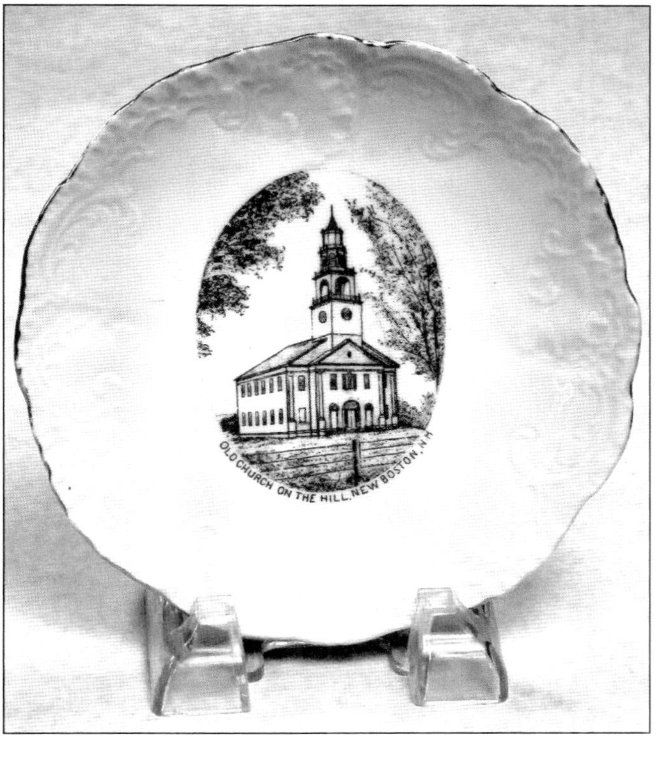

This beautiful and stately church stood on a hill on the corner of Meetinghouse Hill and Bedford Roads. In many old photographs, its steeple can be seen rising above the town. Unfortunately, it was struck by lightning in 1900 and completely destroyed. The church, however, has been memorialized in many ways, including having its image printed on china, as in this decorative collector's plate. (Photograph by J. Hansen.)

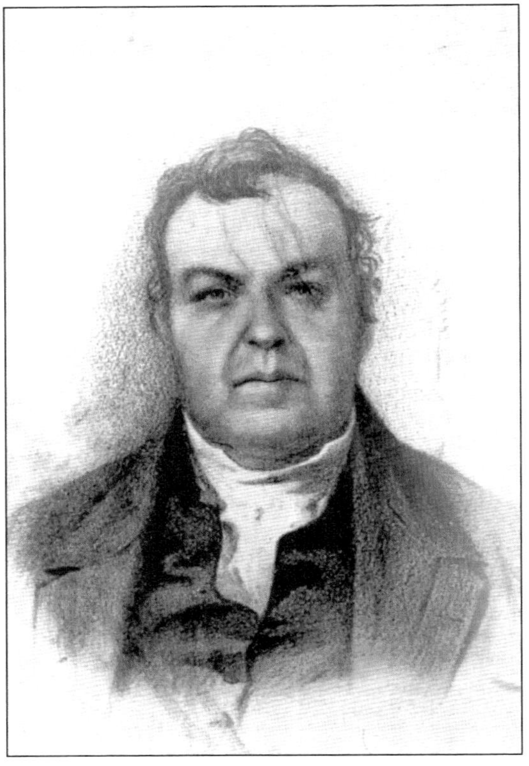

For over 30 years, the Presbyterian church was the only religious organization in town. Rev. Ephraim P. Bradford was its second minister, ordained and installed in 1806 as the successor to Reverend Moor, who had served for 36 years. Reverend Bradford was much loved by his people. He died in 1845 and is buried in the town's cemetery. A marble monument marks the location of his grave.

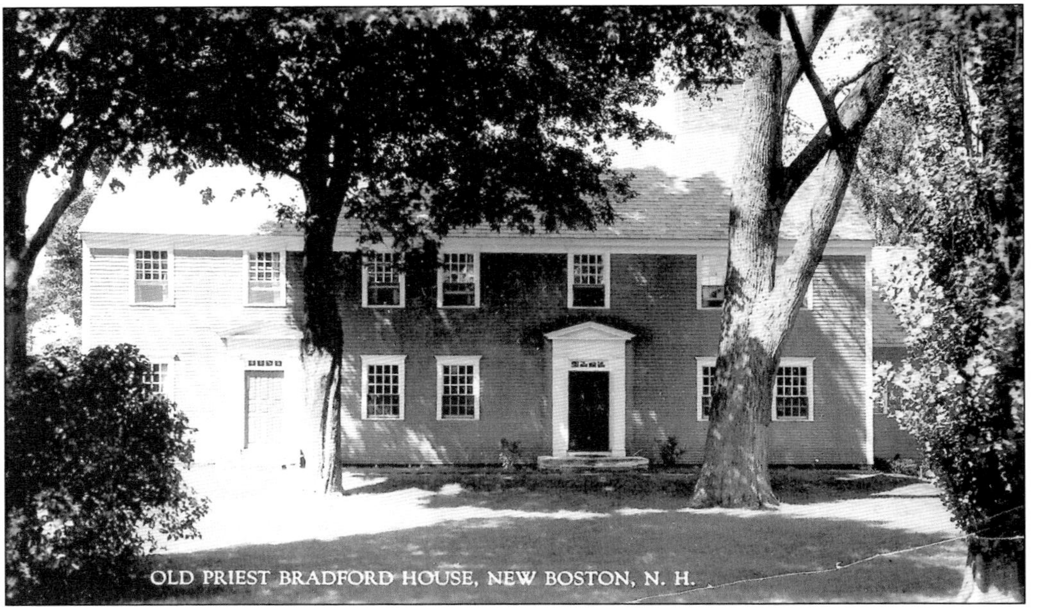

Here is a postcard showing the Bradford house. This house was built before 1763 and is located on Bradford Lane opposite the town's cemetery. Reverend Bradford purchased it in 1805 and occupied it until his death. The town meetings of 1764 and 1765 were held in this house.

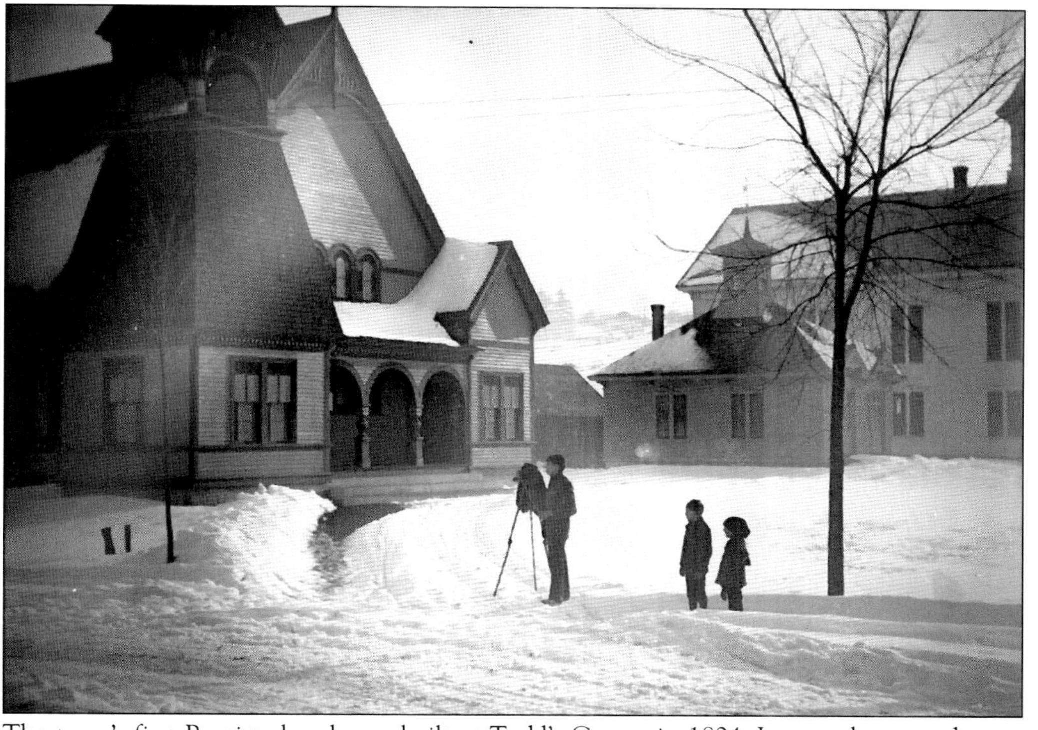

The town's first Baptist church was built at Todd's Corner in 1804. Later, a larger and more centrally located one was erected in the Lower Village, but this building was destroyed during the great fire of 1887. The church pictured here replaced the one that burned and was located on the common where the gazebo now stands. It was torn down in 1943.

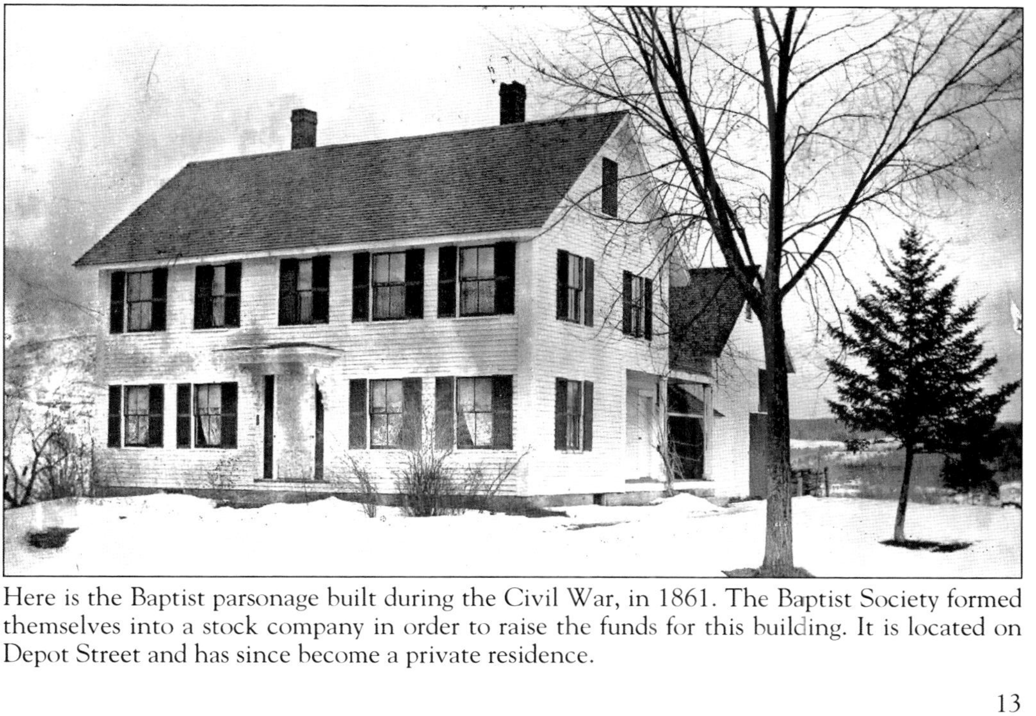

Here is the Baptist parsonage built during the Civil War, in 1861. The Baptist Society formed themselves into a stock company in order to raise the funds for this building. It is located on Depot Street and has since become a private residence.

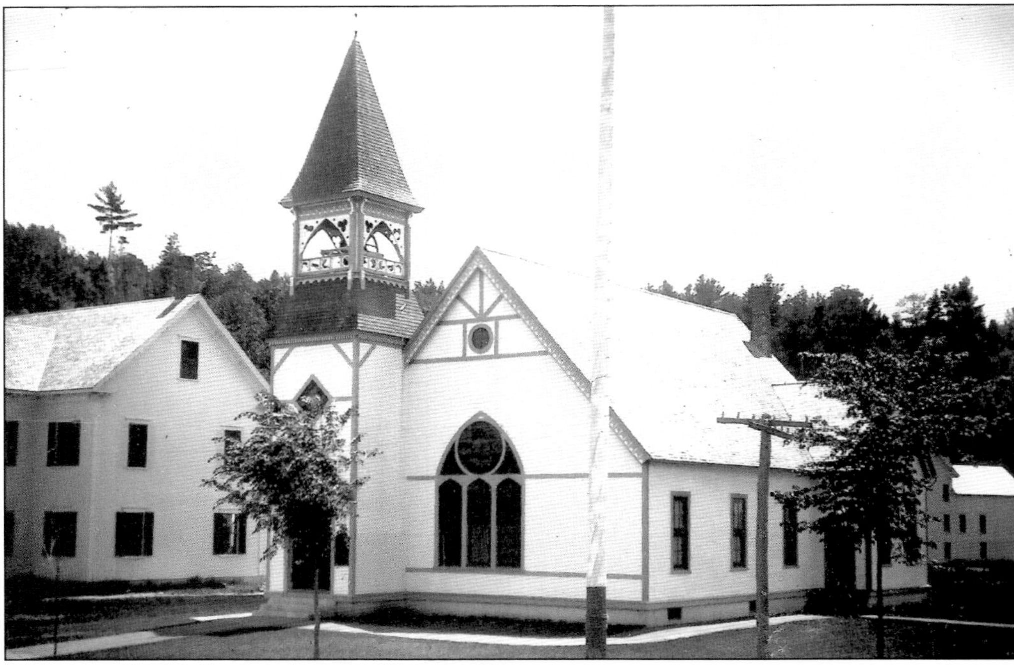

Although the locations have changed, there remains a Presbyterian society here in town. The church pictured here replaced a chapel that was destroyed by fire in 1887. The steeple houses a genuine Paul Revere bell purchased in 1826 and installed here in 1892 after the Church on the Hill was abandoned.

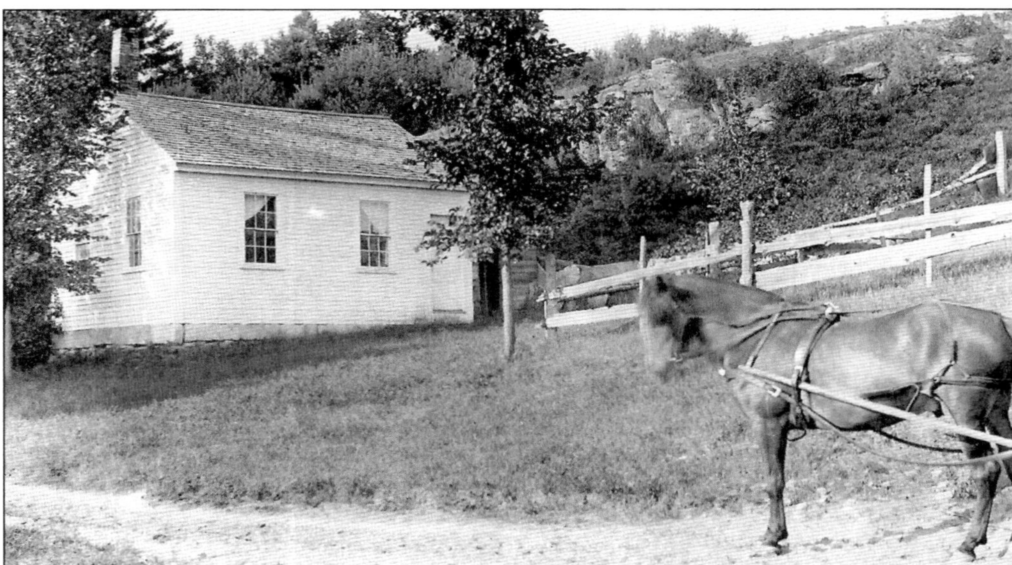

In addition to creating a place to worship, the settlers were faced with the task of educating their children. A small building near the meetinghouse, known as the Session House, was often used as a school, but due to the area's scattered population, 18 school districts were eventually established. The building pictured here shows a typical one-room schoolhouse. (Courtesy of M. Dodge.)

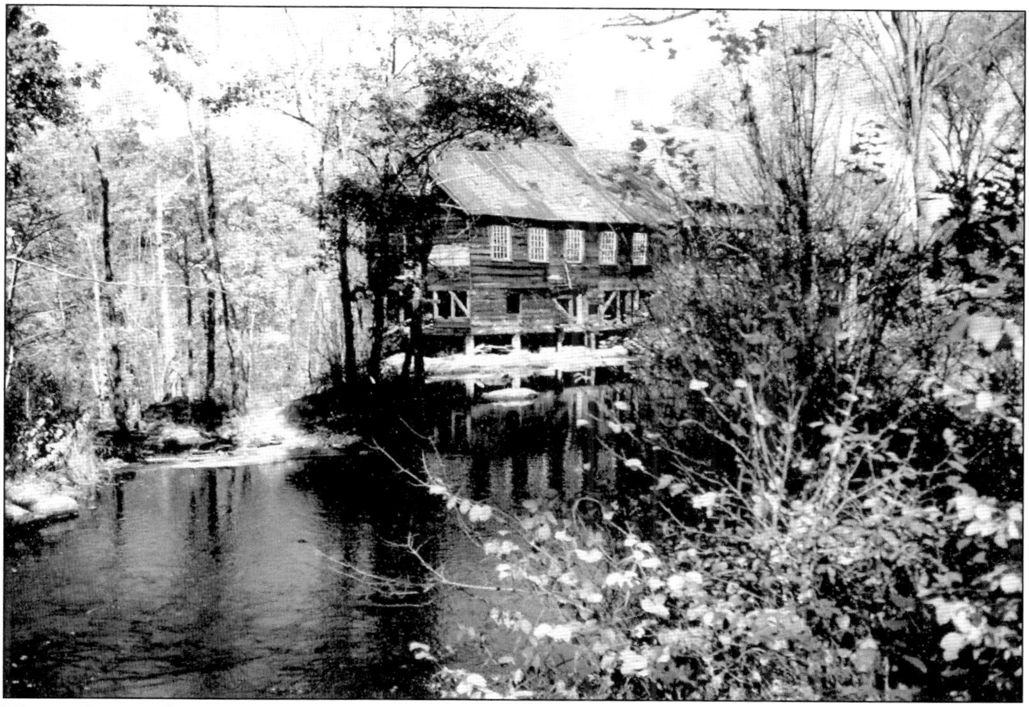

The earliest industries in town were that of milling lumber and grain. The Hadley Mill, pictured here, was New Boston's second sawmill. This mill continued to saw lumber until c. 1950 and, as of this writing, still stands. This photograph was taken in 1951 by Dr. Albert Snay.

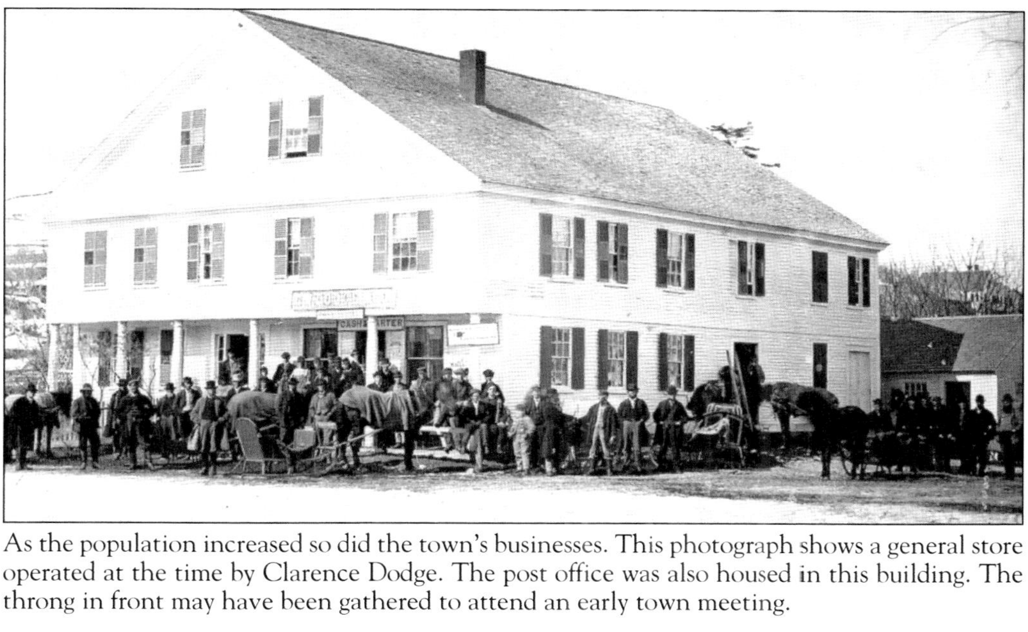

As the population increased so did the town's businesses. This photograph shows a general store operated at the time by Clarence Dodge. The post office was also housed in this building. The throng in front may have been gathered to attend an early town meeting.

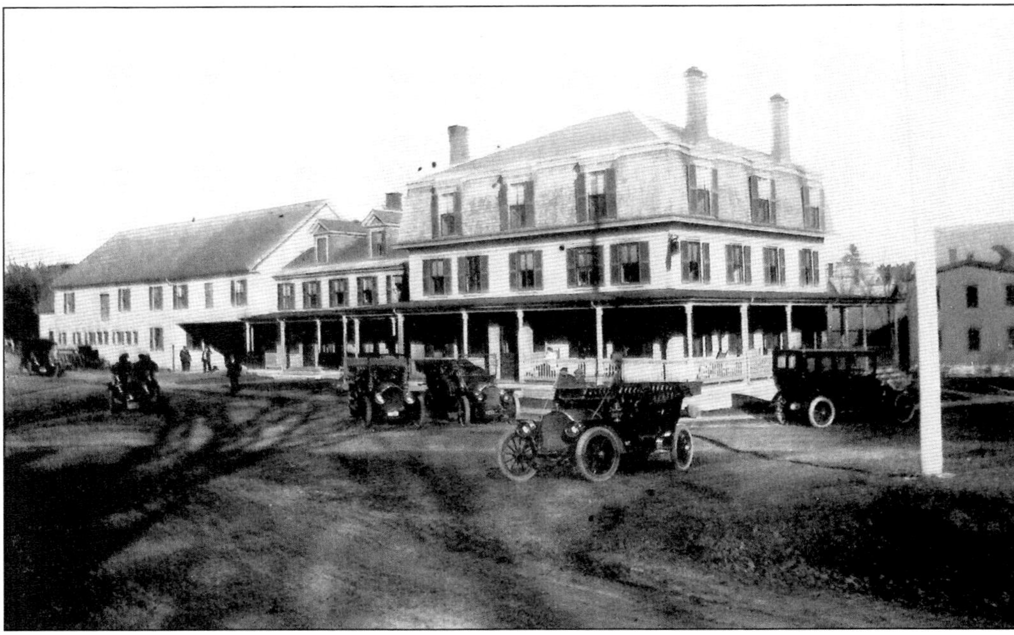

Other businesses that arose in town included a pharmacy, a meat market, and various cottage industries. This photograph shows New Boston's famous Tavern. The arrival of passenger rail service to the area in the late 1800s helped to promote the tourist industry, and the Tavern was a popular destination. Most of this building was torn down in the 1940s.

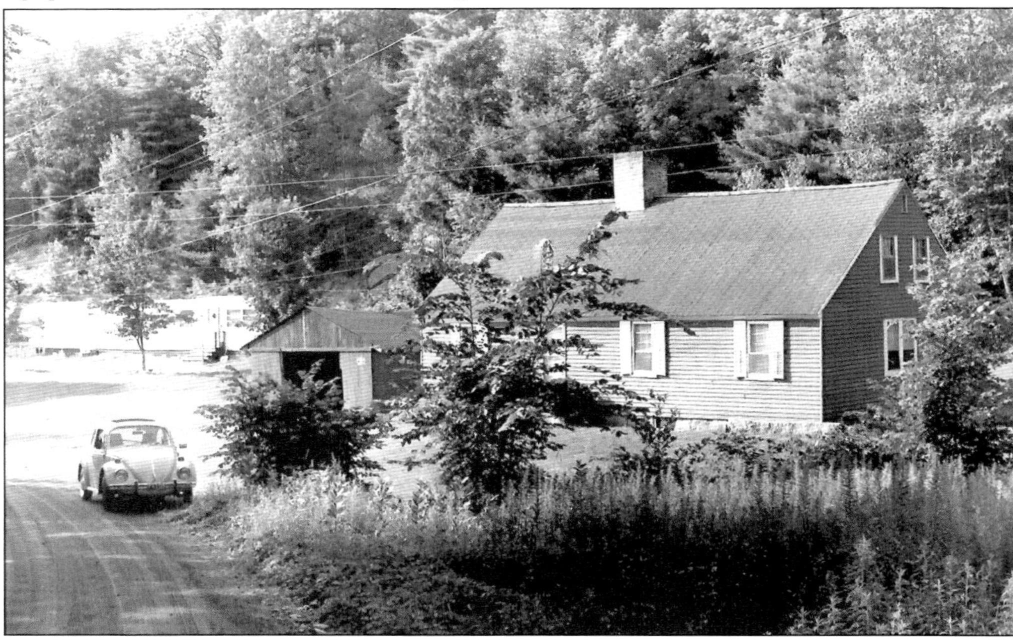

This house is believed to be the oldest house in town still standing. It is located on Meadow Road near Joe English Hill and was built in the 1750s by Dea. Archibald McMillen. Dr. Hugh McMillen practiced medicine here after learning about herbs and drugs from an old medical book that he found. (Courtesy of A. Christoph.)

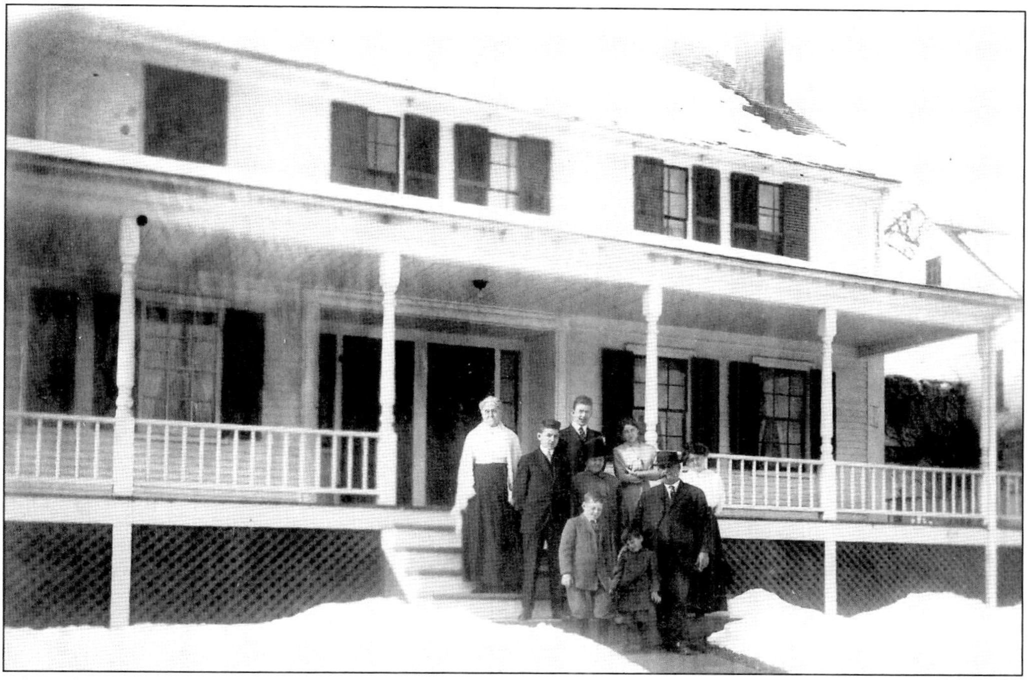

This photograph shows the Whipple Homestead, the former home of Capt. John Whipple. Whipple had eight children, among them James, who ran the Tavern, and J. Reed, who was the famous Boston hotelman. This house is located on High Street.

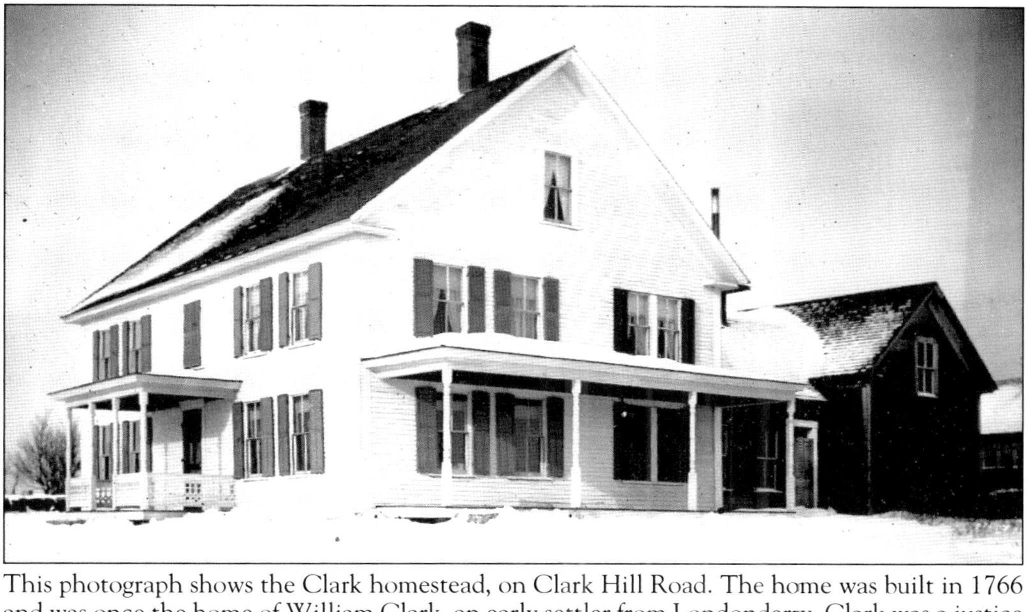

This photograph shows the Clark homestead, on Clark Hill Road. The home was built in 1766 and was once the home of William Clark, an early settler from Londonderry. Clark was a justice of the peace commissioned by the British government. Although he was a Tory, it is reported that he was trusted by his fellow townsmen.

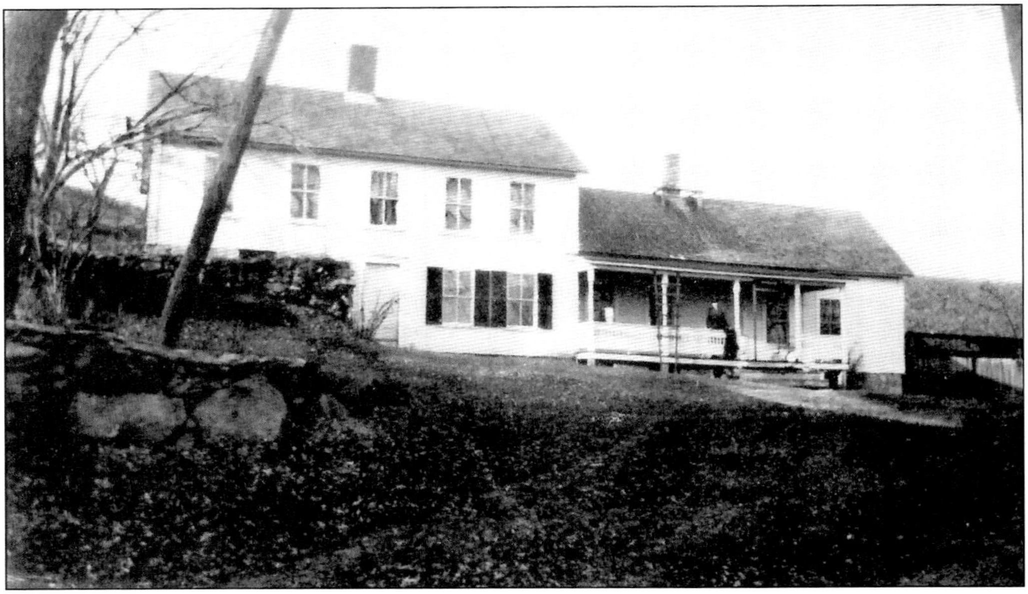

This house, known as the Orrin Waldo house, is located on Colburn Road. It was built in the 1830s by Leonard Colburn and acquired by James Waldo in 1863. It remained in the Waldo family for nearly 80 years. This photograph was taken by Martha Card, who was a teacher at Schoolhouse No. 13 and a boarder at the Waldo home. (Courtesy of R. Silvernail.)

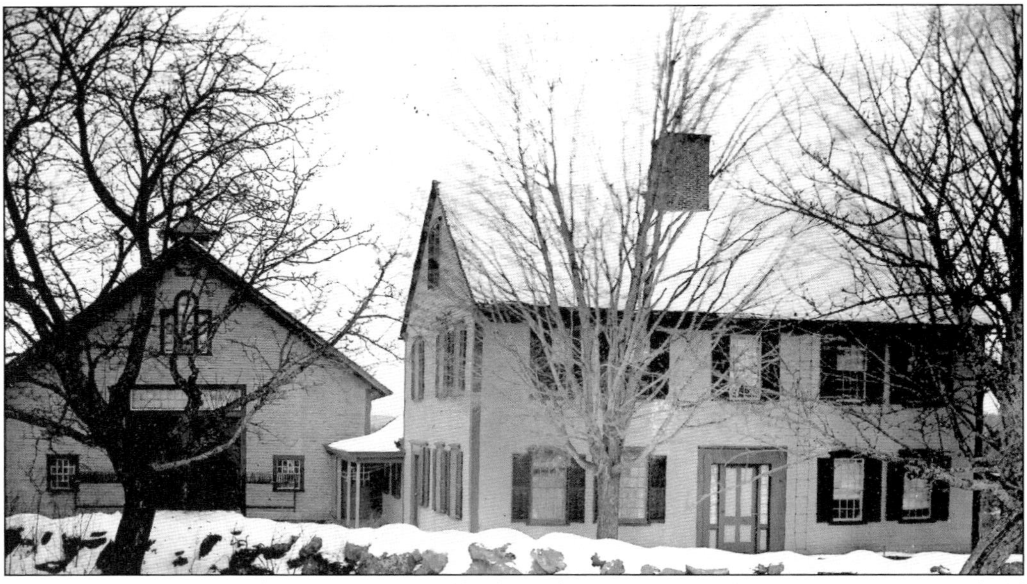

This is the Thomas Cochran place on Bedford Road. New Boston's first town meeting was held at the Cochran home in 1763. However, that house burned down in 1916 as the result of a bad thunderstorm, and this house was built to replace it. A gun reputed to have belonged to Native American Joe English was lost in the fire.

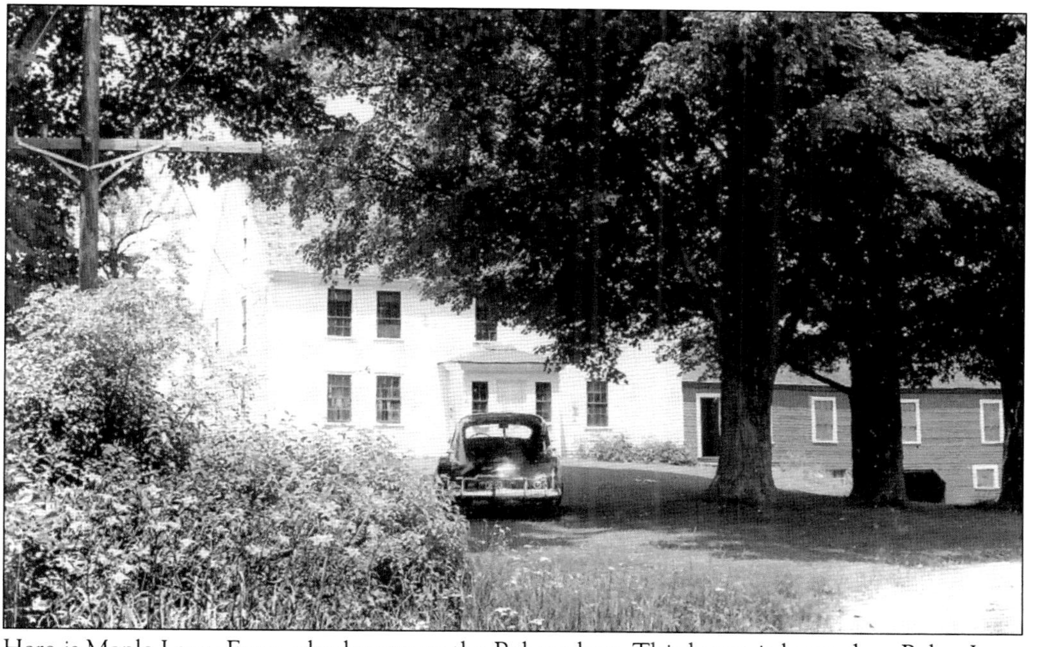

Here is Maple Lawn Farm, also known as the Baker place. This house is located on Baker Lane and once hosted summer boarders. A frame belonging to Abraham Cochran is listed on the 1756 census at this location, but it is unknown if this is that original structure.

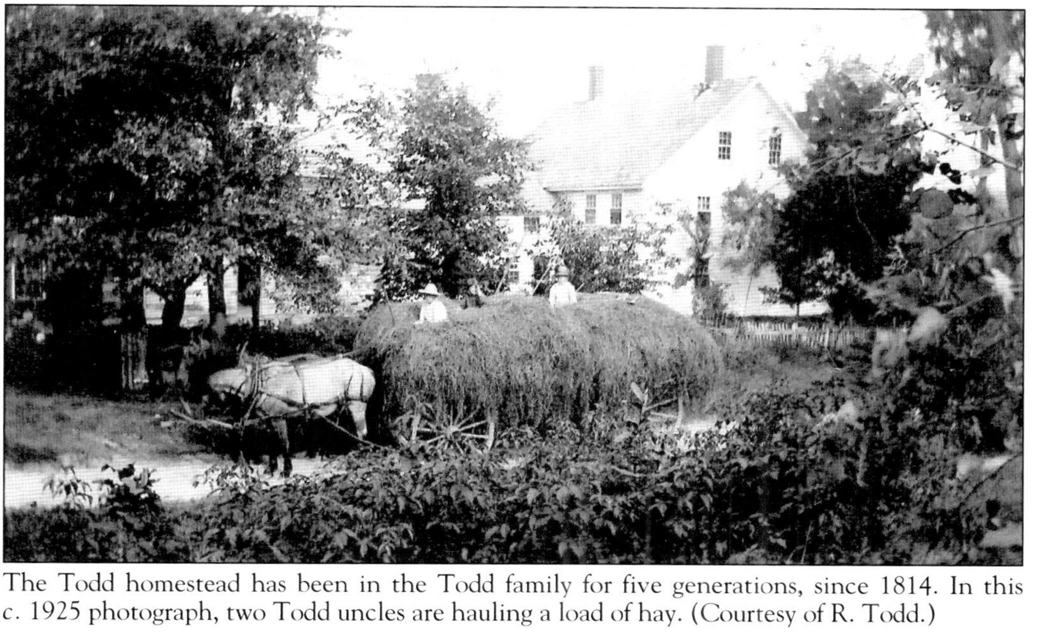

The Todd homestead has been in the Todd family for five generations, since 1814. In this c. 1925 photograph, two Todd uncles are hauling a load of hay. (Courtesy of R. Todd.)

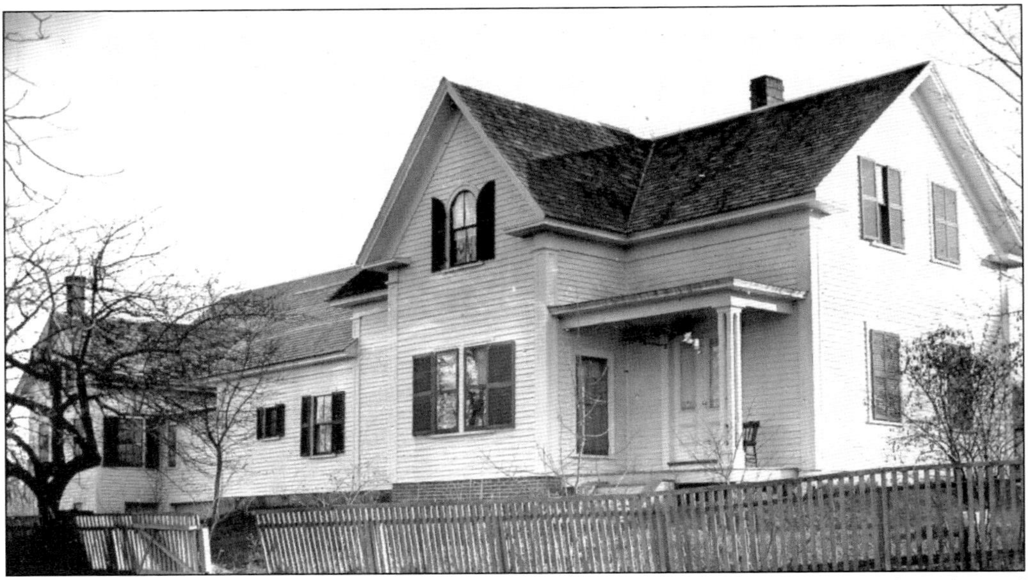

This was once the home of Albert Goodwin on Cochran Hill Road. Unfortunately, it burned down in 1959, when it was owned by John Conley. The fire was caused by a power surge in the attic, and the house was never rebuilt.

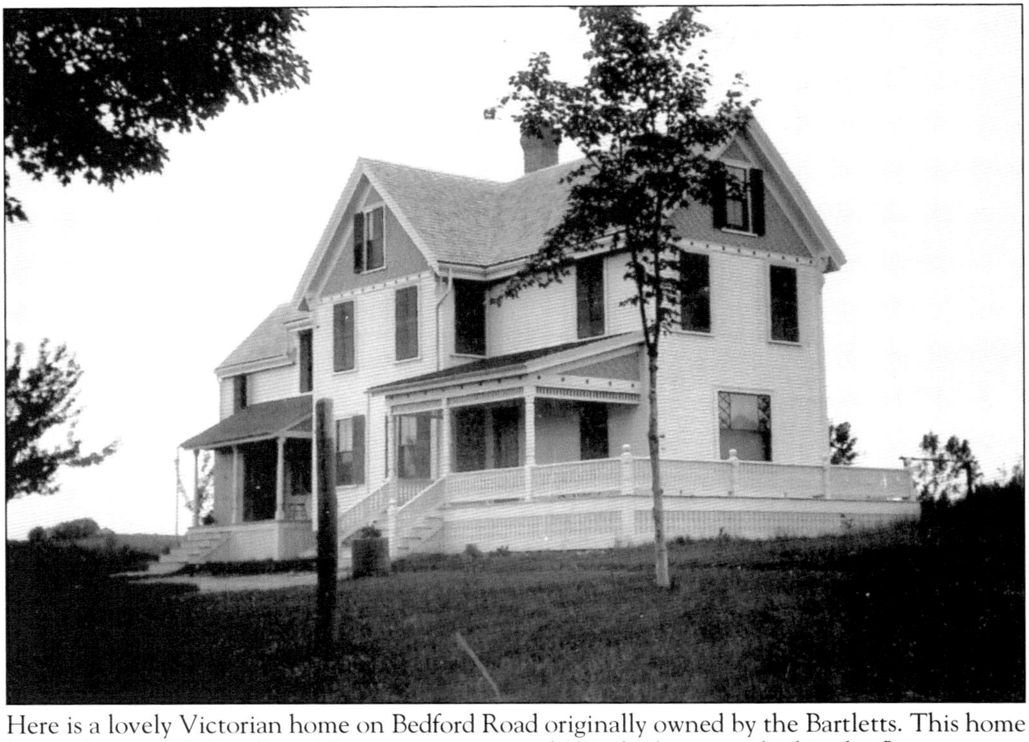

Here is a lovely Victorian home on Bedford Road originally owned by the Bartletts. This home lost its barn in 1913 to fire. A horse, two cows, and 150 chickens perished in the flames.

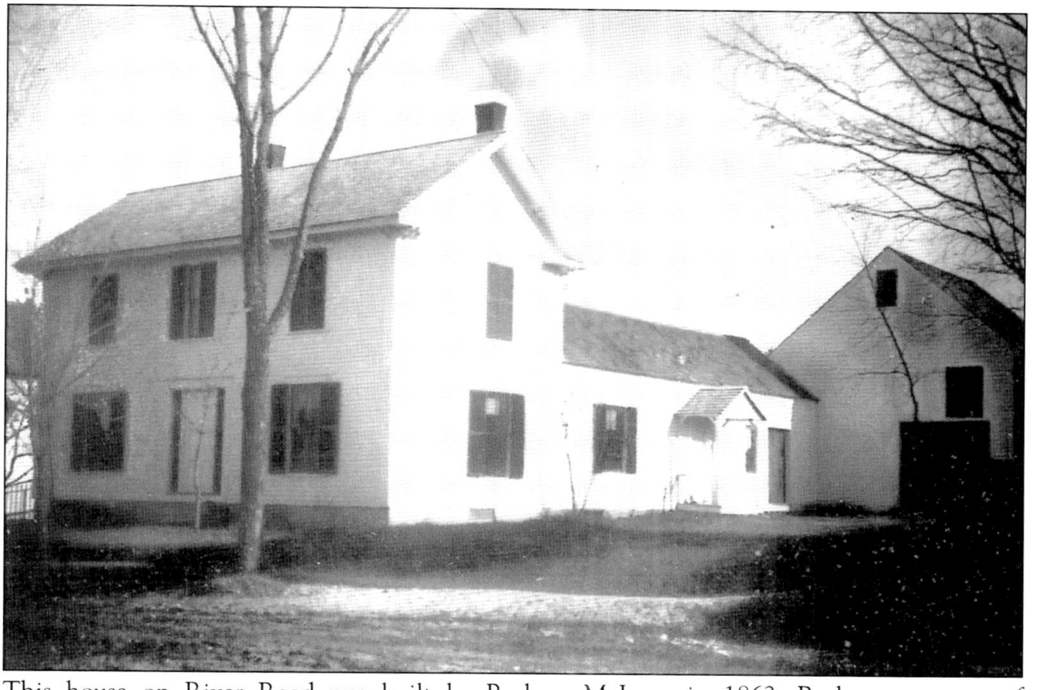

This house on River Road was built by Rodney McLane in 1862. Rodney was one of the McLane brothers who manufactured doors and windows in town. Later, the barn on the property held an antique and furniture refinishing shop.

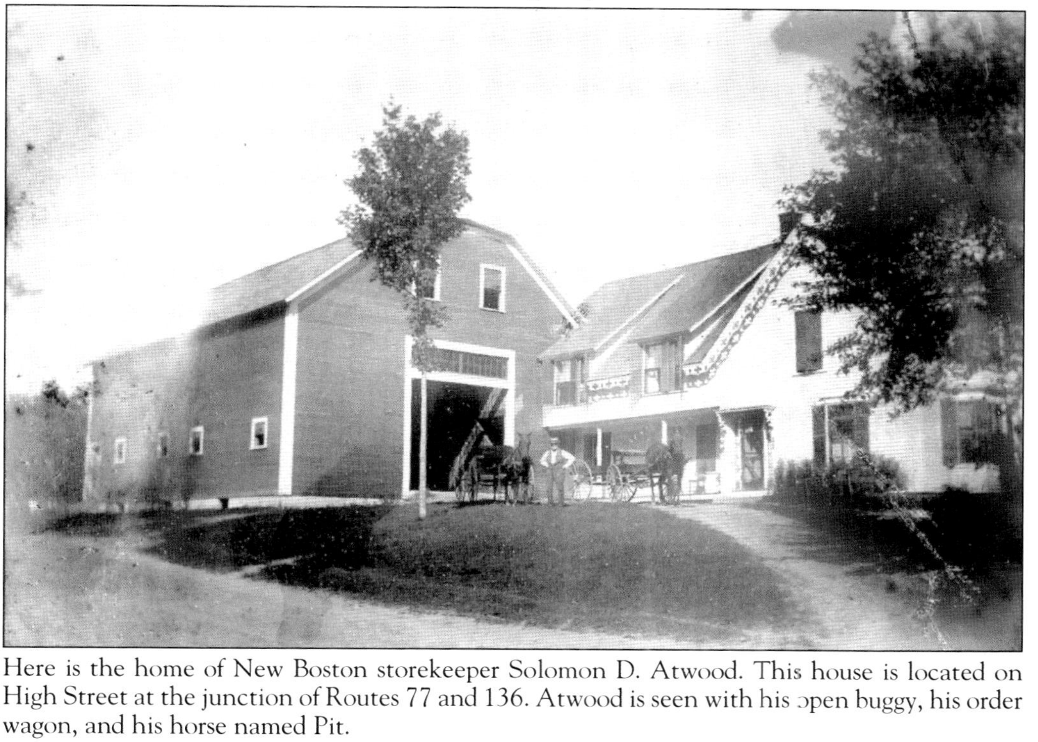

Here is the home of New Boston storekeeper Solomon D. Atwood. This house is located on High Street at the junction of Routes 77 and 136. Atwood is seen with his open buggy, his order wagon, and his horse named Pit.

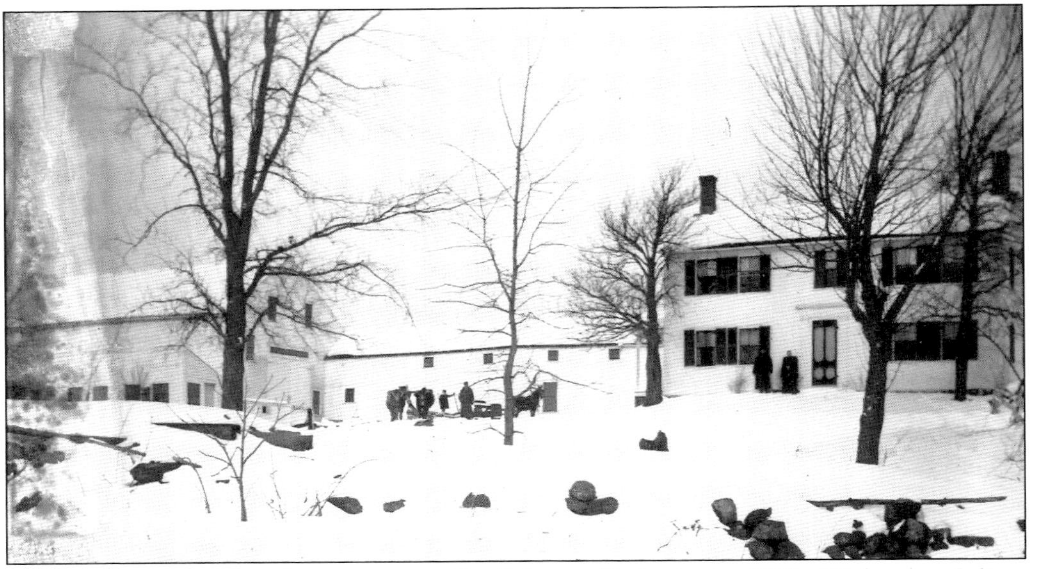

This house on Dougherty Lane was owned by Solomon Dodge in the 1800s. His brother, Julian, was a member of the second regiment of Berdan's Sharpshooters during the Civil War.

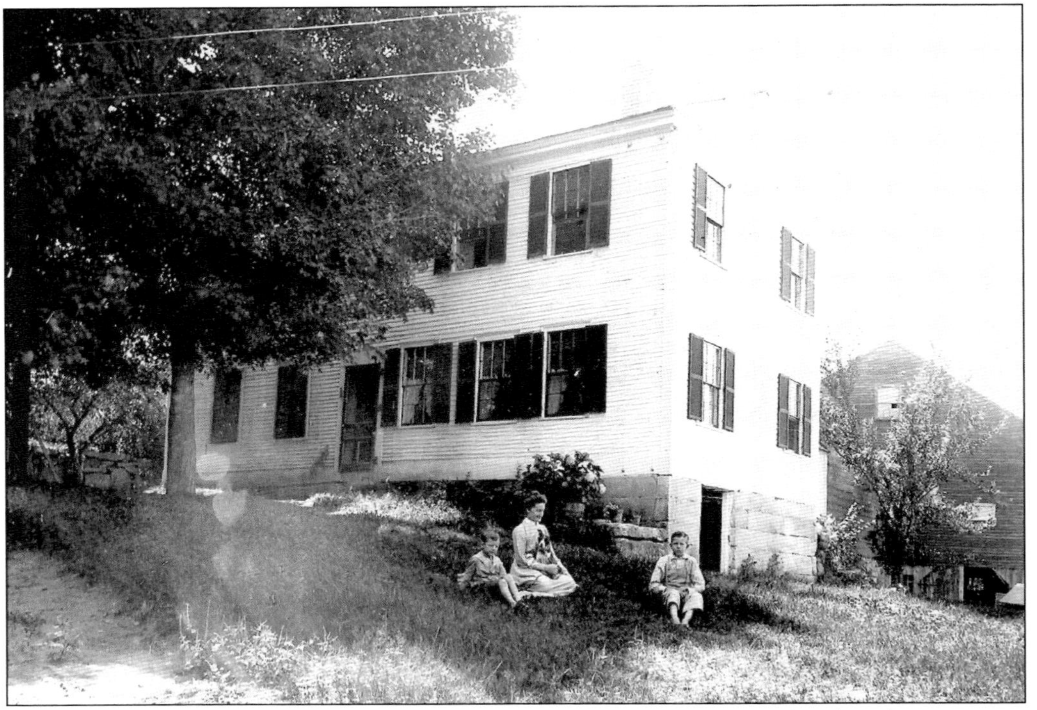

Here is a peaceful scene showing Sadie Saltmarsh with her children, Paul and Carl.

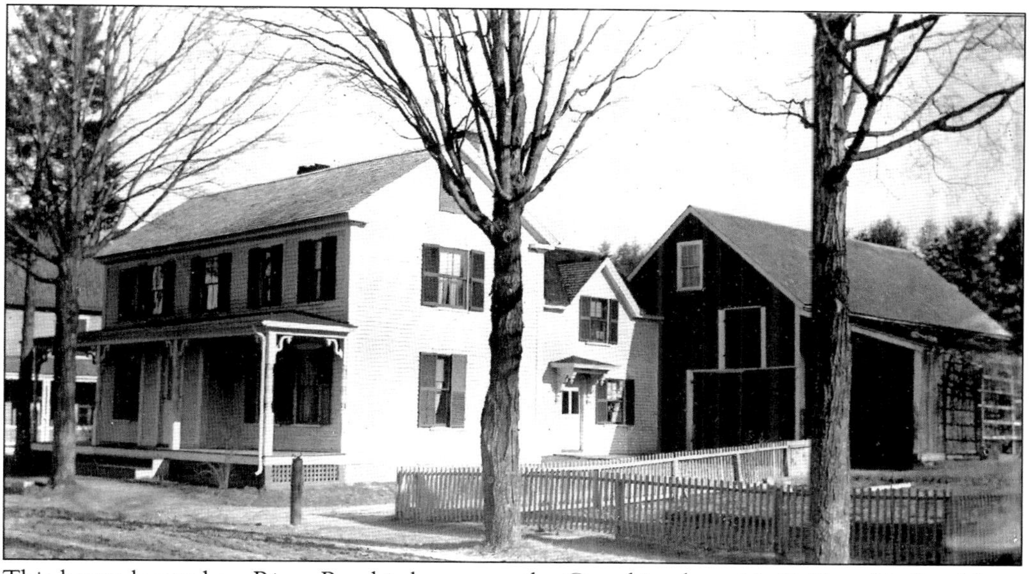

This house located on River Road is known as the Crombie place. N. C. Crombie lived here from 1856 until his death in 1880, after which his son and daughter-in-law occupied the home. This house was also once the home of Arthur Holt, a local undertaker.

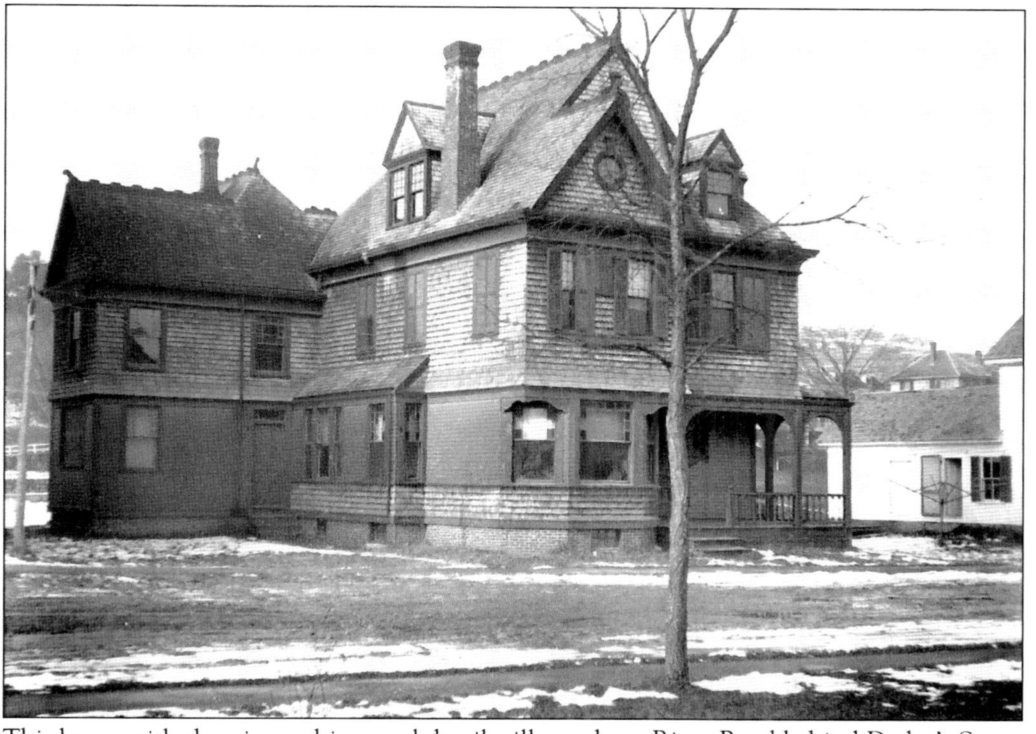

This house with the nice architectural detail still stands on River Road behind Dodge's Store. Charles Farley built this house in 1888 after the village fire. Farley had a workshop in the ell where he made violins from the wood of old furniture. After his wife, Julia, drowned in the river behind the house in 1893, Farley left town and went to work with a Boston violinmaker.

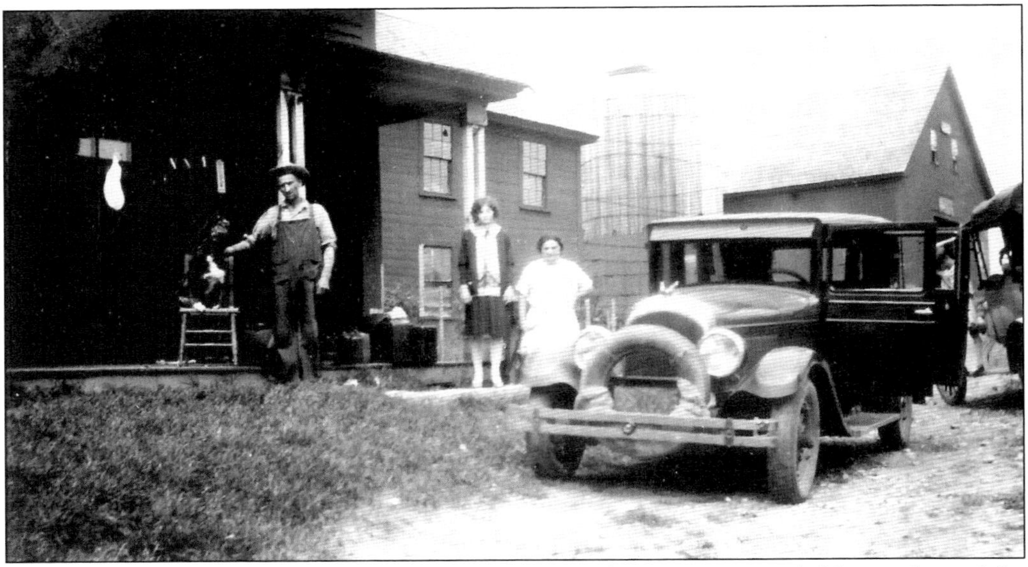

Here is the Gomes place on Misty Lane. The people in the picture are probably members of the Heath family, who once operated a farm here. In March 1949, the barn and silo burned down. All of the cattle and farm equipment were lost in the flames. (Donated by Y. Gomes.)

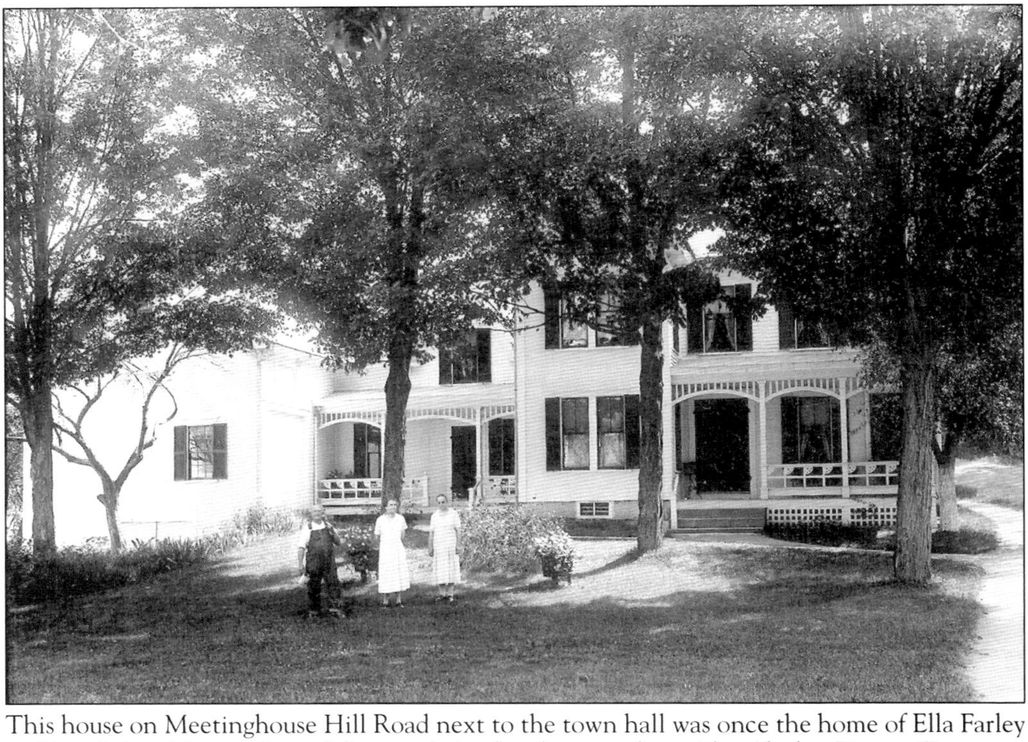

This house on Meetinghouse Hill Road next to the town hall was once the home of Ella Farley and her father, Henry. Two of the people in the photograph are identified as Dexter Green, on the left, and Josie Hadley, on the right.

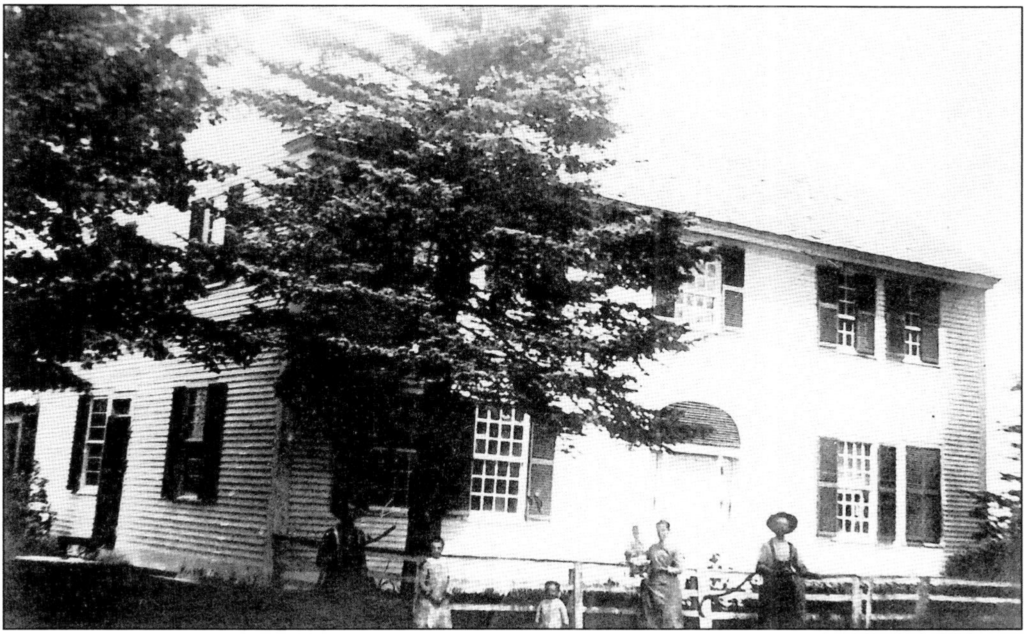

This home on Molly Stark Lane was destroyed by fire in September 1887. It was owned at the time by Julian Lease, who was a harness maker. New Boston's old hand tub, Constitution No. 2, was used to fight the fire. The house could not be saved, but two barns on the property were spared.

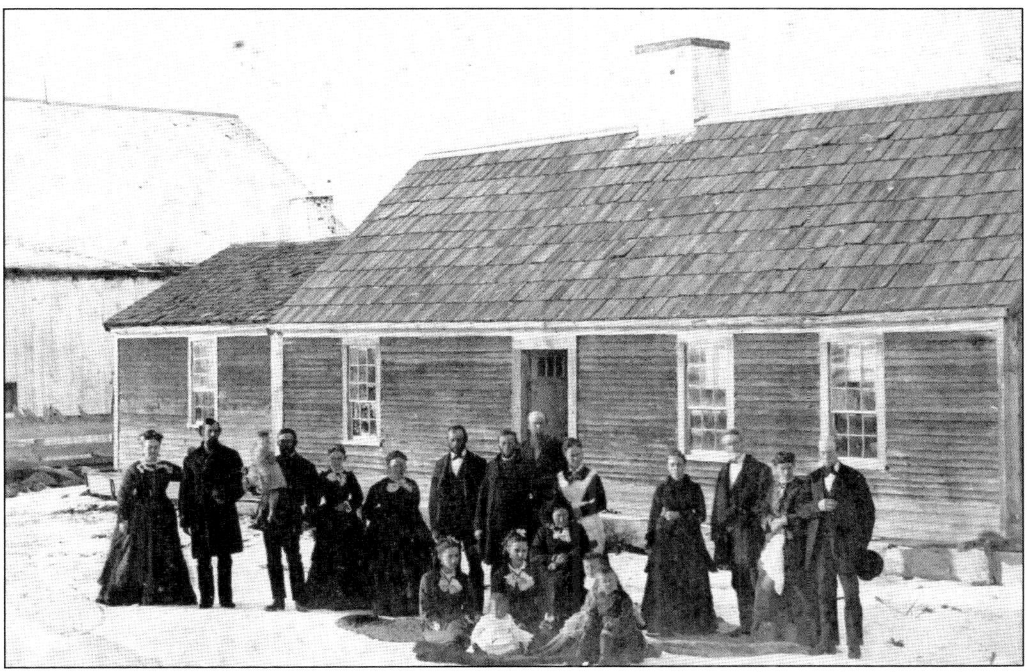

This old Allen Dodge farm on South Hill Road was taken down to make way for a larger house. Posing in front of the house is the extended Dodge family, including grandparents, aunts, uncles, and cousins.

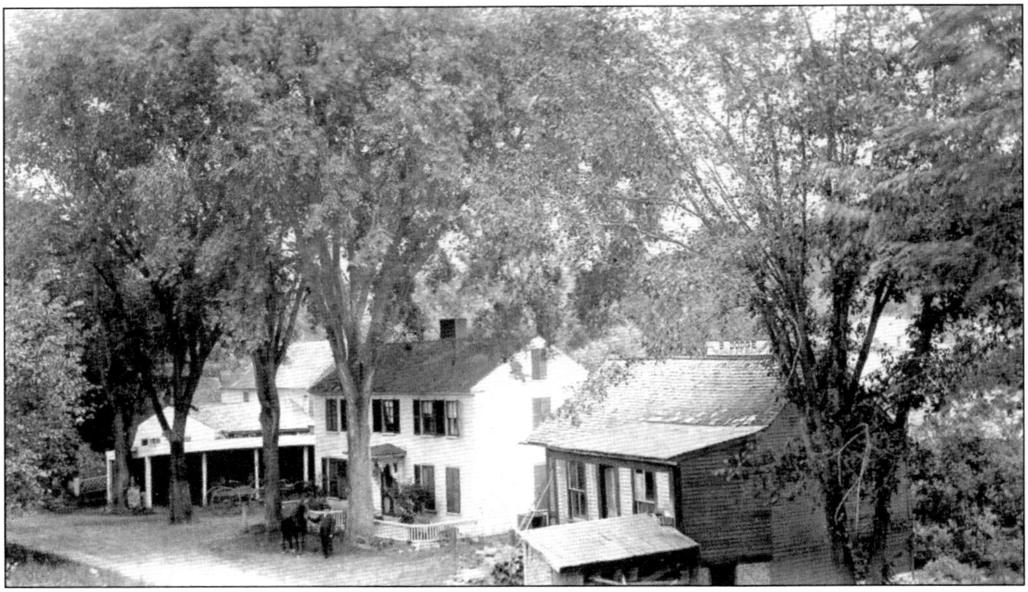

The home of Benjamin Dodge III is seen in this view, taken c. 1881. The house is located on Maple Street. Notice the sign atop the barn on the right. The Dodges were storekeepers in town for generations.

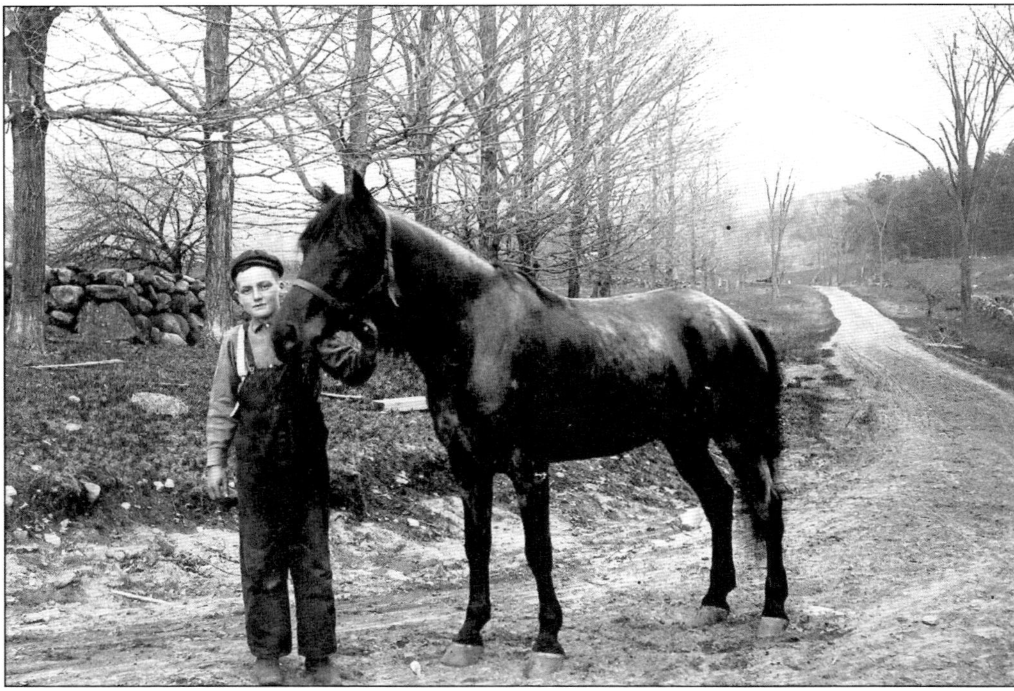

This photograph of Paul Reed with his horse depicts how New Boston looked during its earlier days. Few streets were paved until the late 20th century. Folks meandered through town on narrow dirt lanes like the one in the picture. A lot has changed since the settlers arrived here in 1733.

Two

The Molly Stark Cannon

All military accouterments were returned to the State except Molly Stark.
Those hardy souls who had preserved and protected her. . . . would not give her up.
—Clement Lyon, New Boston Artillery Company, 1963

Like New Boston itself, the history of the Molly Stark cannon, or "Old Molly," is rich, varied, and may never be known completely. In 1743, the cannon and a mate were built in Paris, ornately decorated with a shield and crown flanked by American Indians armed with bows and arrows. After traveling by ship across the Atlantic Ocean to protect the citizens of Quebec, the cannons were captured from the French soon thereafter by the British at the Battle of the Plains of Abraham in 1759. Both cannons again changed hands when they were surrendered to Gen. John Stark at Bennington in 1777.

The Molly Stark cannon (named affectionately after General Stark's wife) served in defense of the British siege at Detroit, Michigan, during the "second Revolutionary War," the War of 1812, and was actually recaptured by the British after the surrender of the city. As fate would have it, though, the Americans captured Old Molly from the British once again, this time at the Battle of Fort George during the same war.

Prior to his death in 1822, Gen. John Stark removed Old Molly from storage at the first arsenal built by the United States in Watervliet, New York. Old Molly was retired from active duty and presented to the New Boston Artillery Company by General Stark for the company's contributions to the success of the Battle of Bennington. This was an incredible honor bestowed upon New Boston. When the artillery company disbanded in 1852, everything except Old Molly was returned to the State of New Hampshire.

Not surprisingly, numerous neighboring towns attempted to claim Old Molly as their own after the dissolving of any New Boston legal authority in 1852. New Boston residents were forced to keep a secret guard over the cannon's location until the New Boston Artillery Company was legally formed anew as a volunteer organization in 1938, strictly tasked to maintain custody of, and properly care for, the cannon. Since then, Old Molly has become indelibly (and legally) written into New Boston's past, present, and future.

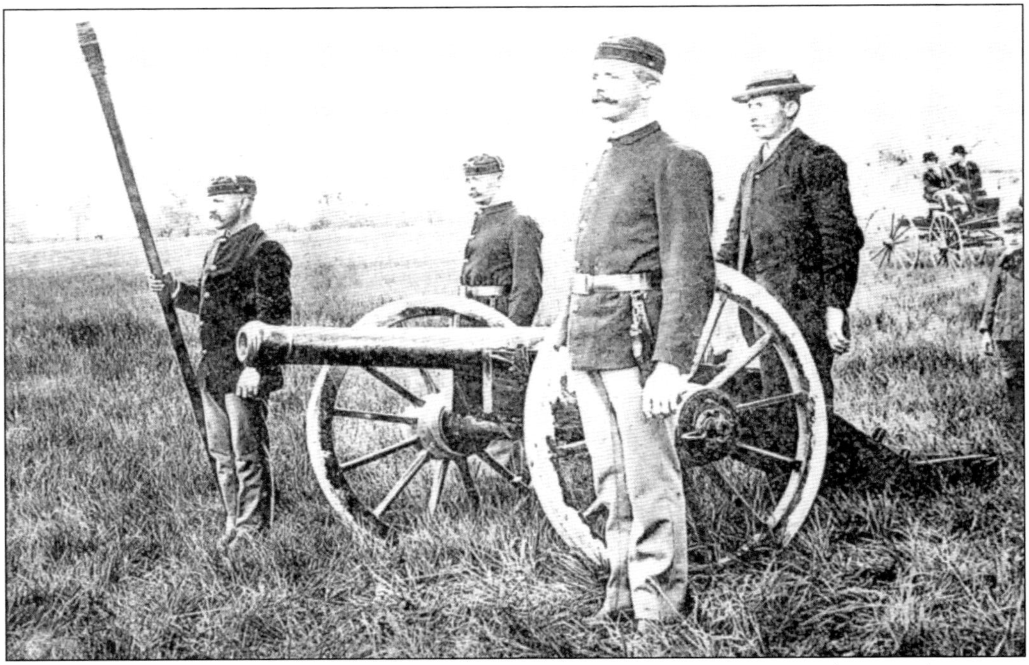

This image is from a postcard that was printed in Germany for S. D. Atwood, a storekeeper in New Boston. It depicts the Molly Stark cannon, a Revolutionary War four-pounder that was captured from the British by Gen. John Stark at the Battle of Bennington on August 16, 1777. The cannon was named after the general's wife, Molly.

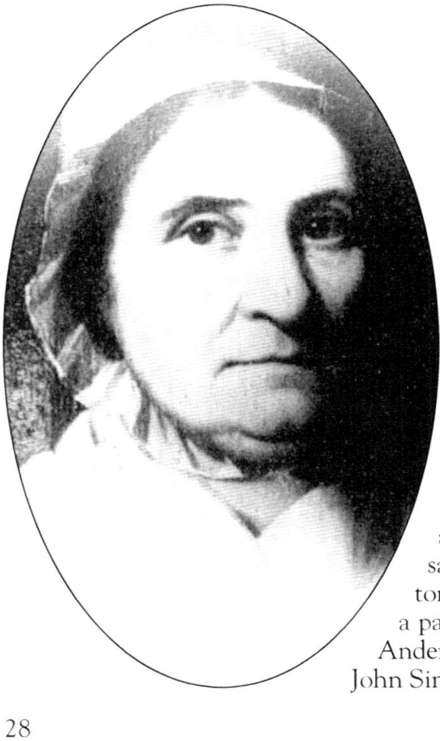

Here is a portrait of Elizabeth "Molly" Page Stark, after whom the cannon was named. When the general captured Old Molly and three other cannons at the Battle of Bennington, he is reputed to have said, "We have met the enemy and they are ours, or tonight Molly Stark sleeps a widow." This picture is from a pamphlet entitled "The Molly Stark Cannon," by Leon Anderson and came originally from a c. 1774 painting by John Singleton Copley.

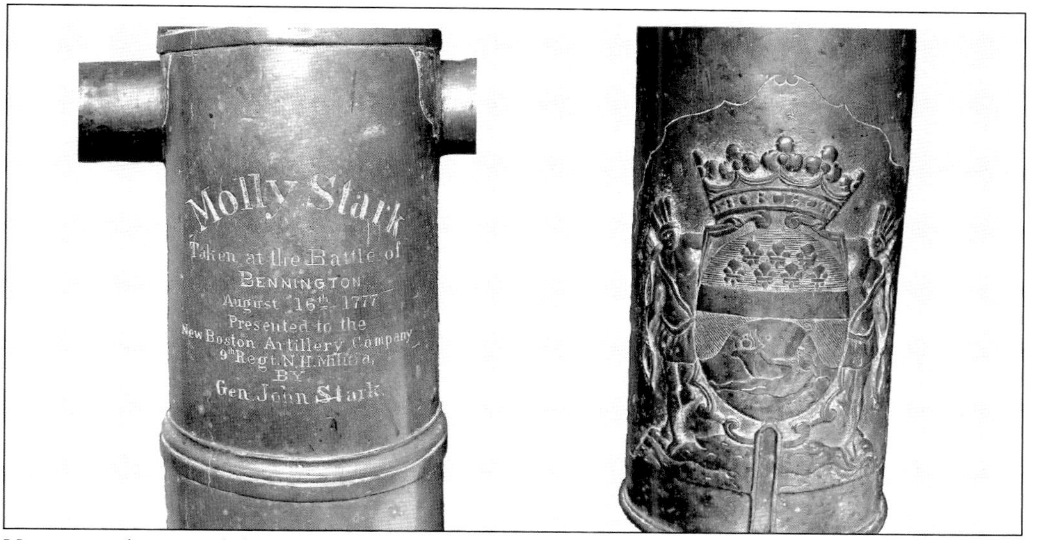

Here is a closeup of the ornate carving and the inscription on the cannon. The inscription reads, "Molly Stark Taken at the Battle of Bennington August 16th, 1777 Fresented to the New Boston Artillery Company 9th Regt. N.H. Militia By Gen. John Stark." Another inscription at the base reads, "Fait a Paris - 1743." (Photograph by J. Hansen.)

Here is a photograph of the cannon on the lawn in front of the town hall. Old Molly has been the proud possession of the town of New Boston for generations. The New Boston Artillery Company has had official custody of the cannon since 1938. Every male citizen of New Boston over the age of 18 is eligible to become a member of the company upon signing an oath of allegiance.

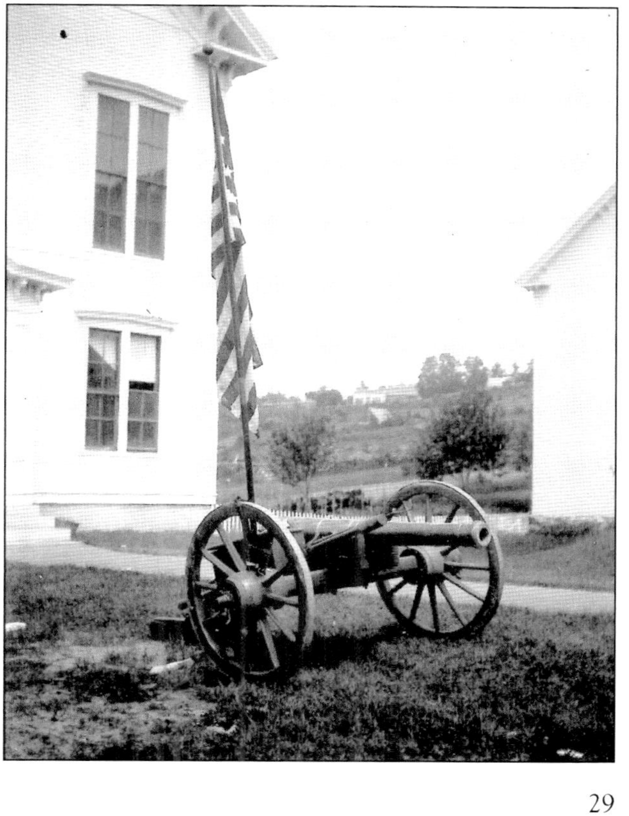

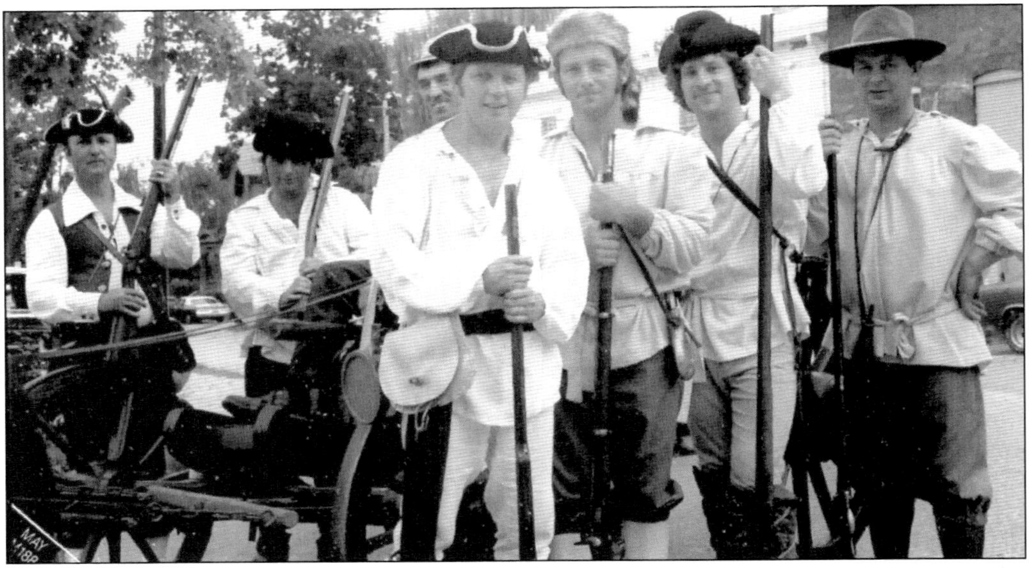

This photograph shows several members of the New Boston Artillery Company in 1977 at the 200th anniversary of Molly's capture in Bennington. Although an act of the New Hampshire legislature abandoned the old militia in 1851, it reorganized in 1938 to become the official guardians of the cannon. Pictured here are, from left to right, unidentified, Stephen Kennedy, unidentified, Wayne Daniels, Paul Wilson, Bob Belanger, and Jerry Kennedy.

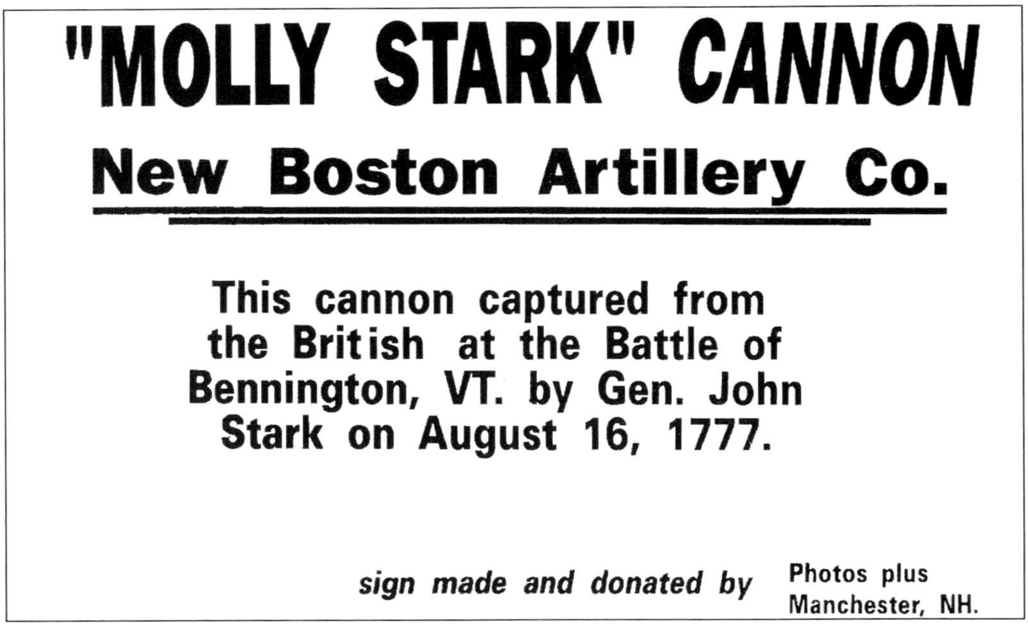

The New Boston Artillery Company uses this sign for its official events with the cannon. For many years, other cities and towns wanted to gain possession of Molly. It is reported that the cannon had to be hidden at various times to prevent unauthorized acquisition. As one story goes, Old Molly was once hidden at the bottom of a millpond. Storing the cannon and its carriage in two different locations made it difficult to steal, and that practice continues today. (Photograph by J. Hansen.)

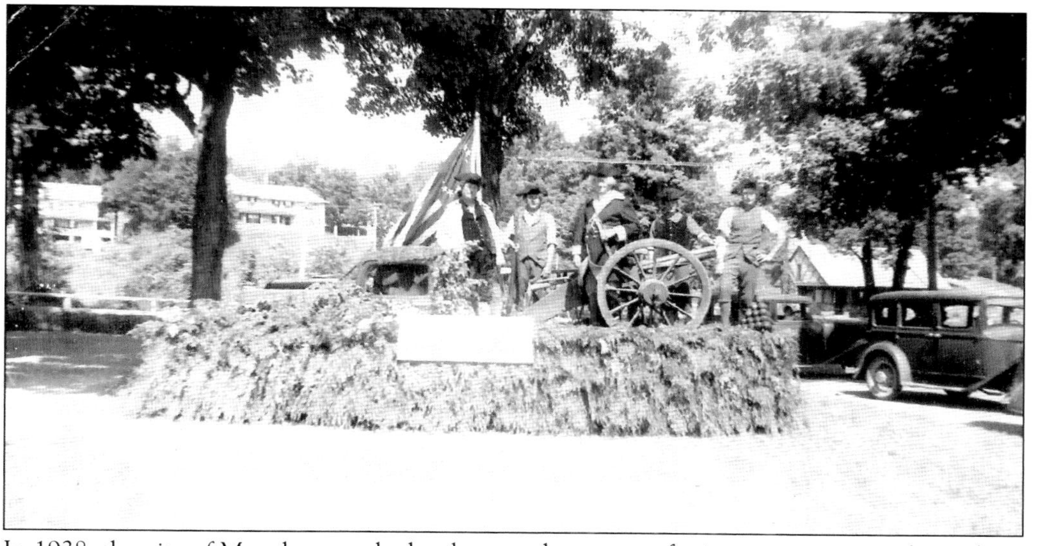

In 1938, the city of Manchester asked to borrow the cannon for its sesquicentennial parade in Concord. It was this request that moved the citizens of New Boston to reorganize the artillery company to become defenders of the cannon. This float was made for Molly's first public appearance in the parade on June 21, 1938. Capt. Arthur Holt, William Fiske, Ken Purrington, George Mansfield, and Bill Fox escorted it to the event.

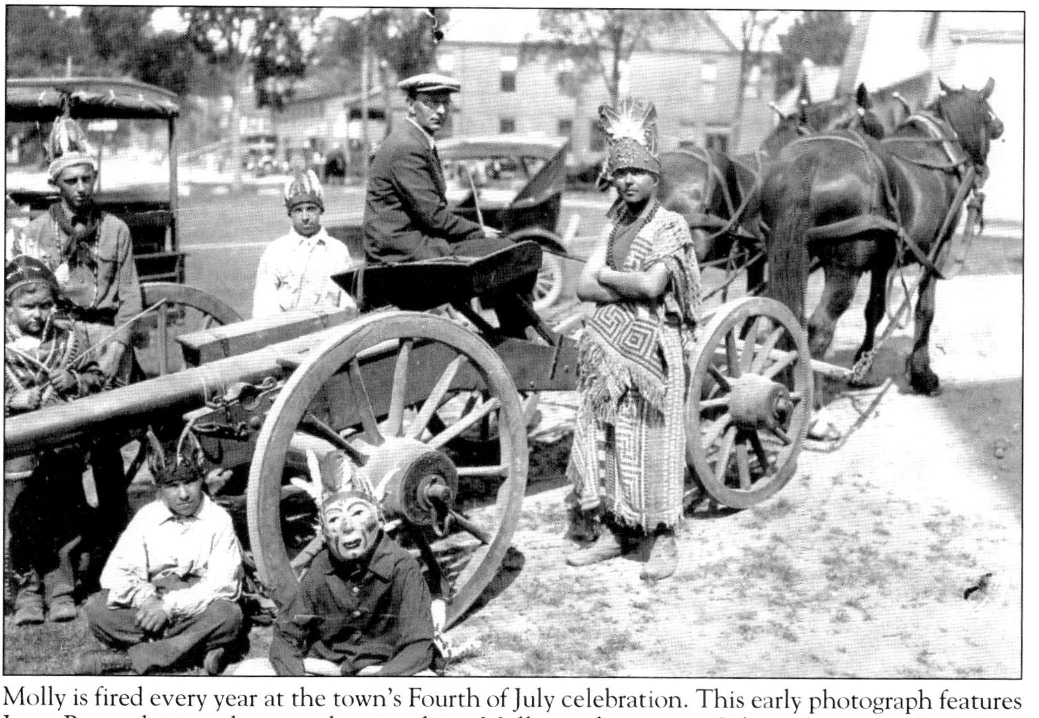

Molly is fired every year at the town's Fourth of July celebration. This early photograph features Jesse Byam driving the cart that is taking Molly to the event. Others shown to the left of the cannon are Marshall French, Harland Brown, and Robert Daniels. Shown to the right of the cannon are Ernest Daniels and Charles French (standing). The masked figure seated in the foreground is unidentified.

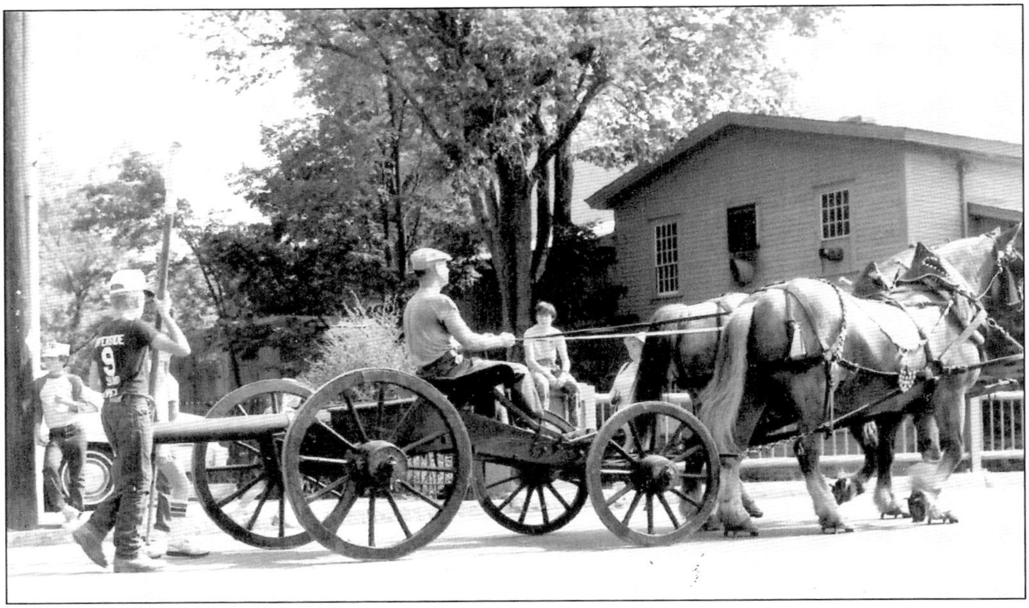

Little has changed except the costumes in this much more recent photograph, taken c. 1983. A pair of horses is transporting Molly to the playground where the annual three-gun salute will occur.

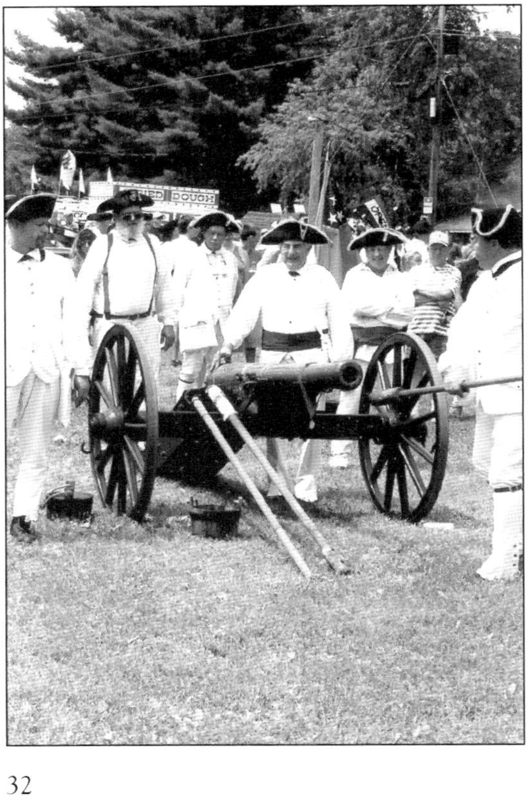

As part of the annual Fourth of July festivities, members of the New Boston Artillery Company dress in period costumes to fire the cannon. This photograph features Howard Leonard, with his hand on the cannon, and Dave Wilson, in the suspenders. (Courtesy of B. Mitroff.)

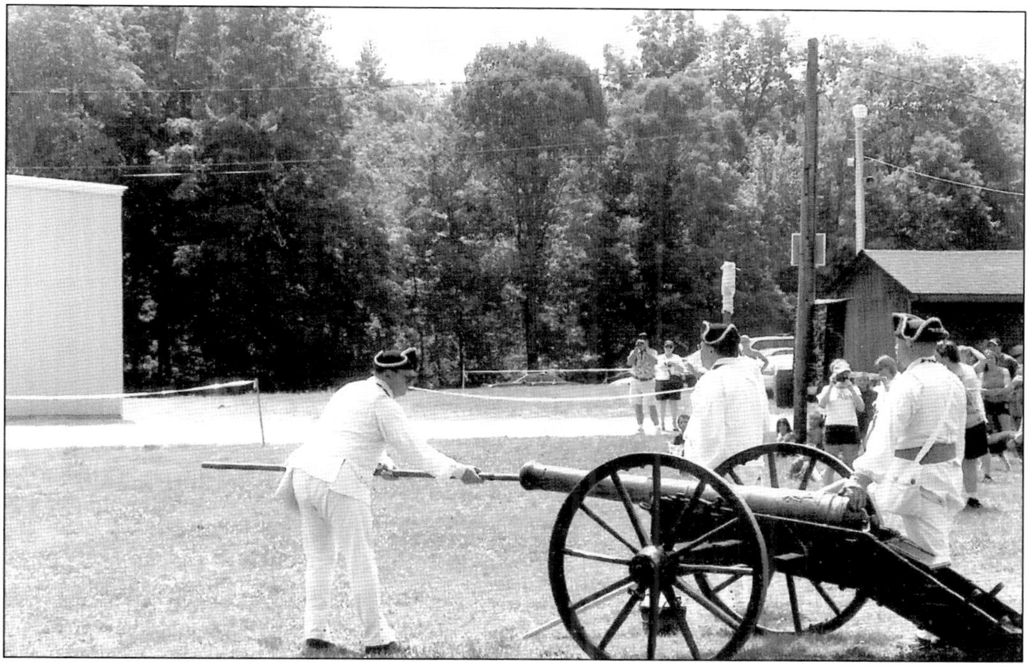

Members of the New Boston Artillery Company stuff the Molly Stark cannon with paper before a crowd of interested onlookers. The cannon will be fired safely while producing much noise and smoke. (Courtesy of P. Brendle.)

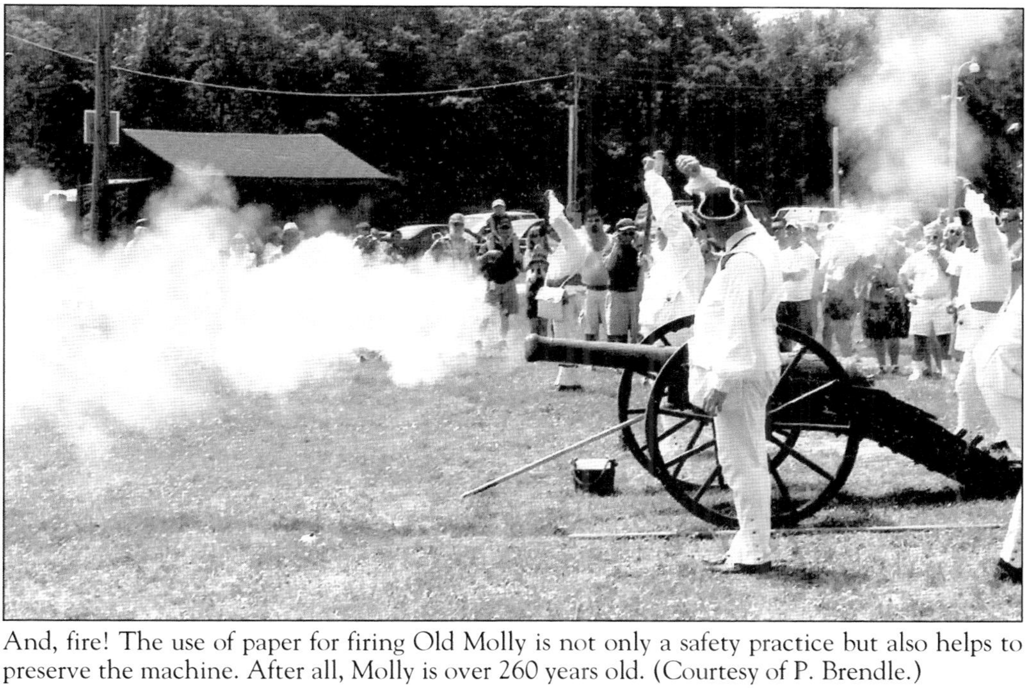

And, fire! The use of paper for firing Old Molly is not only a safety practice but also helps to preserve the machine. After all, Molly is over 260 years old. (Courtesy of P. Brendle.)

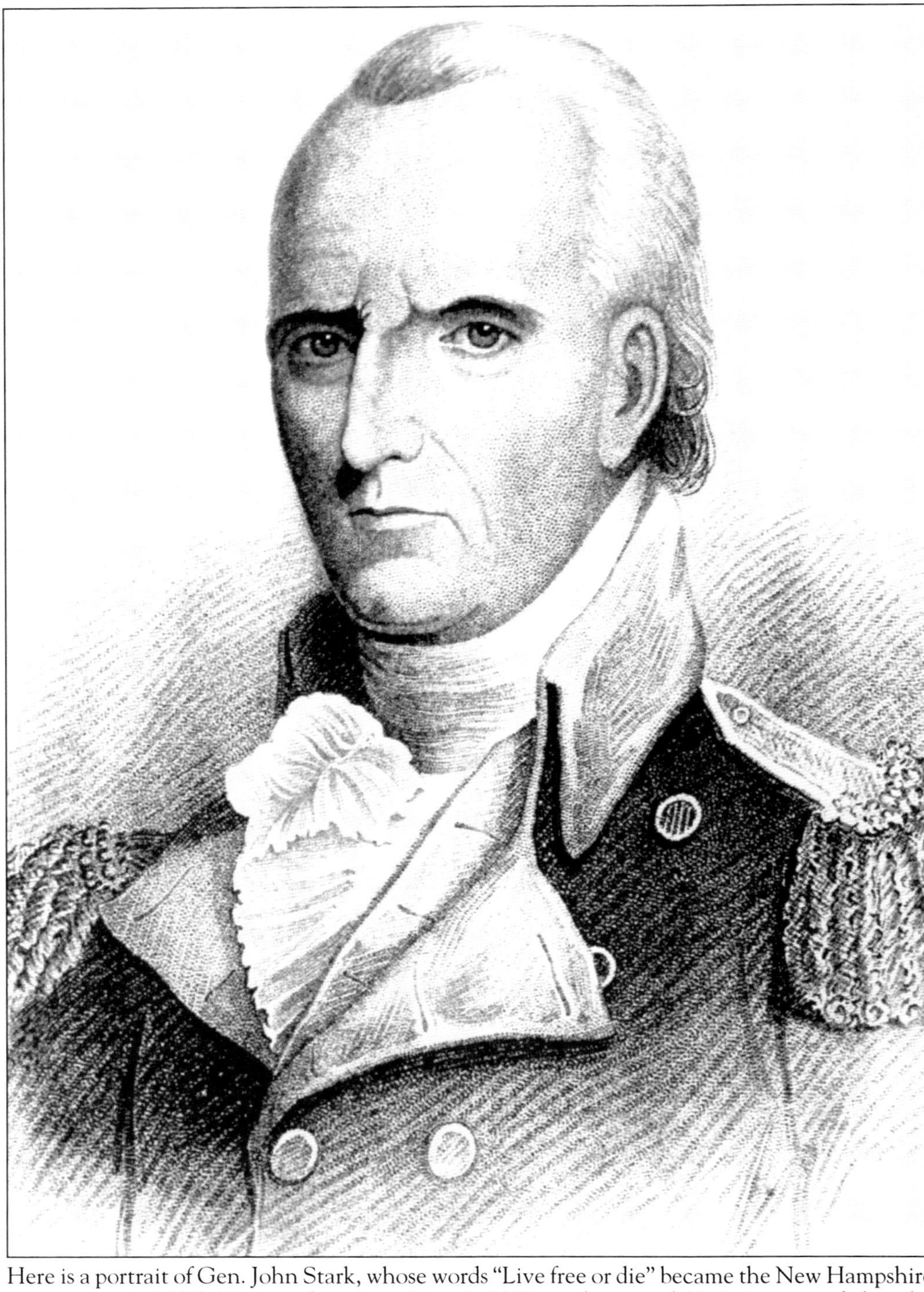

Here is a portrait of Gen. John Stark, whose words "Live free or die" became the New Hampshire state motto in 1956. He passed away on May 8, 1822, at the age of 94. It is reported that the Molly Stark cannon was fired as a tribute to the general on the day of his burial. (Courtesy of the New Boston Artillery Company.)

In 1982, a decanter commemorating the Molly Stark cannon was produced in a limited edition and sold in New Hampshire state liquor stores. Each of the 5,000 decanters manufactured were numbered, and decanter No. 1 is on display at the New Boston Historical Society. The decanter has become a collector's item.

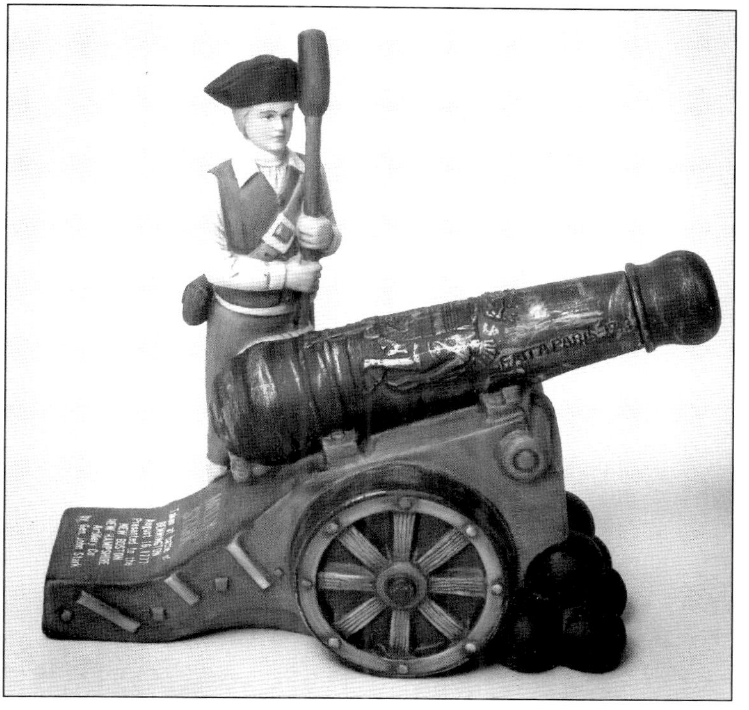

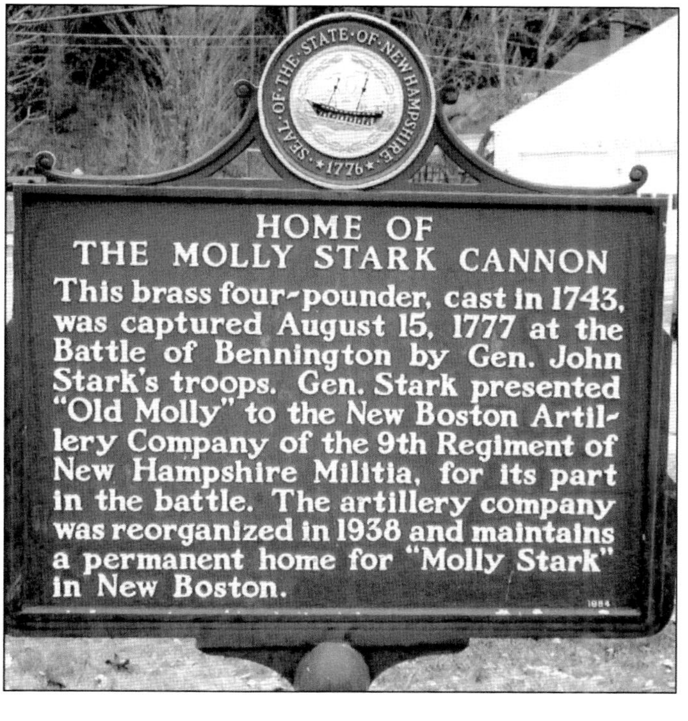

In 1984, the proud citizens of New Boston placed this historical marker on the common. It was sponsored by the New Boston Artillery Company and Rep. Roland Sallada. Gov. John Sununu fired Old Molly after the unveiling. (Photograph by J. Hansen.)

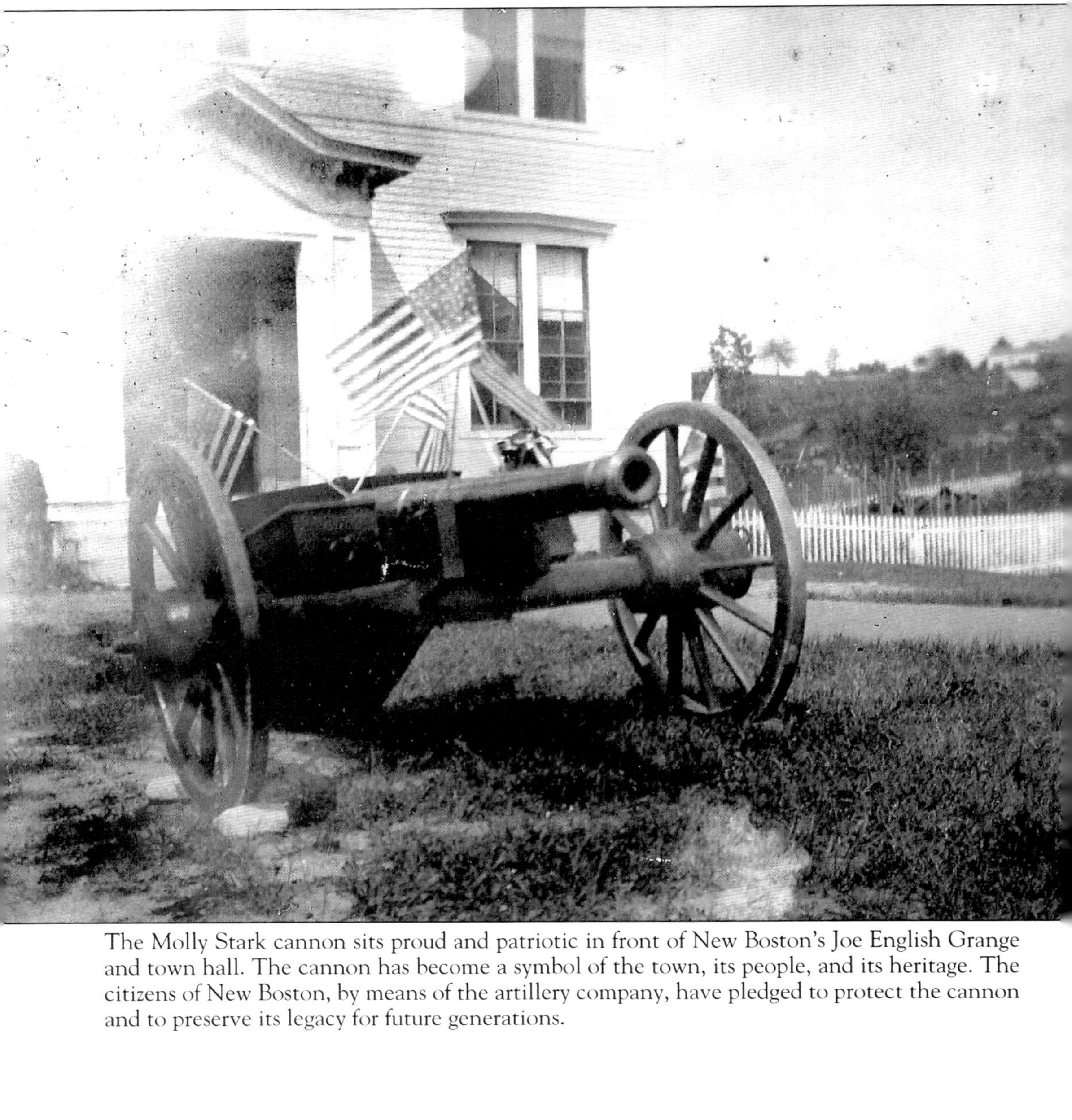

The Molly Stark cannon sits proud and patriotic in front of New Boston's Joe English Grange and town hall. The cannon has become a symbol of the town, its people, and its heritage. The citizens of New Boston, by means of the artillery company, have pledged to protect the cannon and to preserve its legacy for future generations.

Three

On the Farm

Home to the old barn, spreading wide,
The sunshine flickering on the floor,
As when in days now far away,
We tossed and tumbled in the hay.

—New Boston Old Folk's Day, 1903

For the earliest settlers of Lane's Town, pioneer life was characterized by constant hardships. Although fertile and promising, the land had to be first cleared of large trees and what must have seemed an endless crop of stones in every shape and size. Most of the trees were burned prior to sowing the fertile soil with rye or corn. Diets did not include milk until sufficient land was cleared for cows. The first farm animals were typically sheep, and they required precious log enclosures for protection from wolves.

The first settlers were farmers because their survival depended on self-sufficiency. Any manufactured or store goods had to be transferred by horseback (or dragged by horse) from older towns such as Exeter or Portsmouth. Besides, there was very little money in circulation at the time. However, as New Boston became more populated, established, and cleared, farming remained a part of daily life and became not simply a source of sustenance but also a means of commerce. In time, the scythe, the sickle, the hand rake, and the flail made room for the mower, the sower, the horse rake, the great harvester, and the steam thresher.

The most commercial, and famous, of all the New Boston farms was the Valley View Farm, established by J. R. Whipple in 1881 and operated until his death in 1912. After his creamery was built, the local farmers had a cash market for their farm products. At its peak, produce from the Whipple farm provided a monthly average of 2,000 quarts of cream, 6,000 quarts of milk, and approximately 4 tons of butter to three hotels in Boston owned by the J. R. Whipple Company—the Parker House, Young's Hotel, and the Hotel Touraine. These and other farm products were carried daily to the hotels by train, after it came to town in 1893. Ingeniously, the returning cars brought the hotel's waste food back for feeding the hogs and poultry, and the waste was also used as fertilizer material.

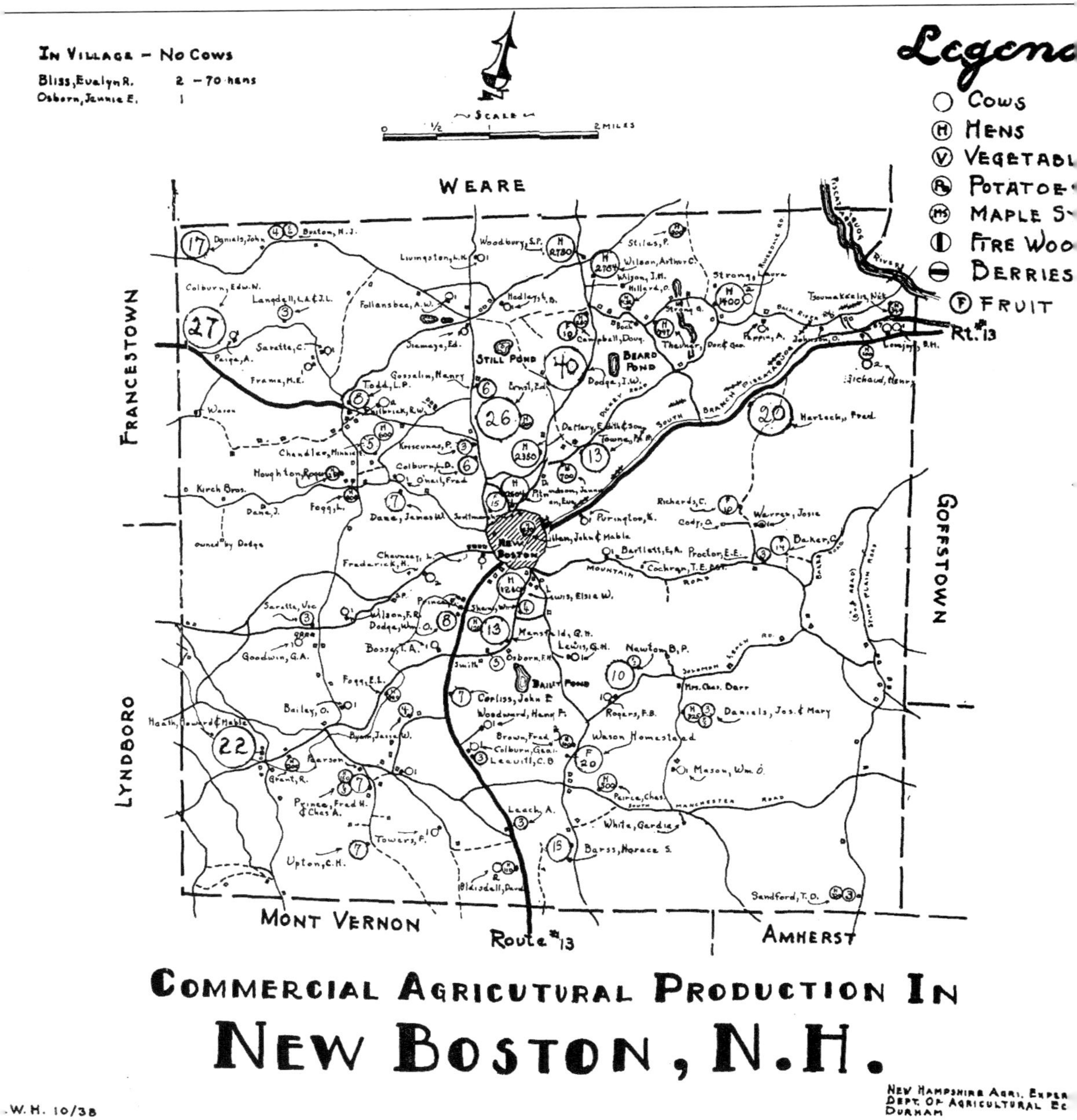

Like many New England towns, New Boston once had a thriving agriculture economy. This New Hampshire Department of Agriculture map from 1938 shows the locations of the town's farm operations and what they produced. Note that there were no cows living in the village, although a handful of hens resided there. (Donated by R. Todd.)

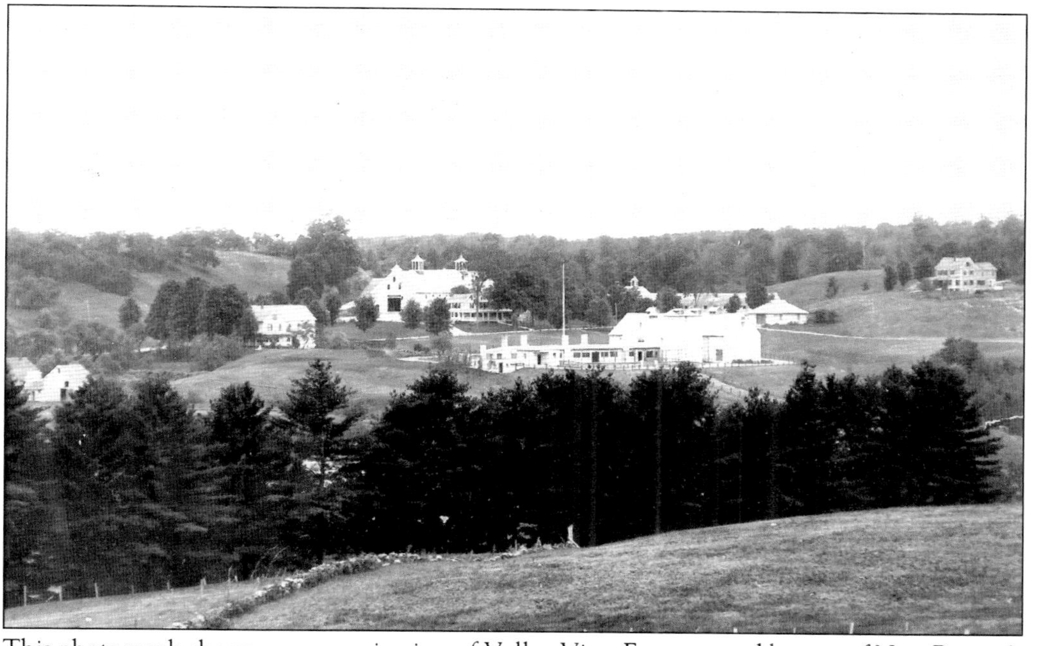

This photograph shows a panoramic view of Valley View Farm, owned by one of New Boston's wealthiest and most enterprising citizens, J. R. Whipple. In addition to Valley View, Whipple owned the New Boston Dairy and the Muzzey and Hutchinson Farms. Whipple's operation supplied farm products for his three Boston hotels—Young's Hotel, the Hotel Touraine, and the Parker House.

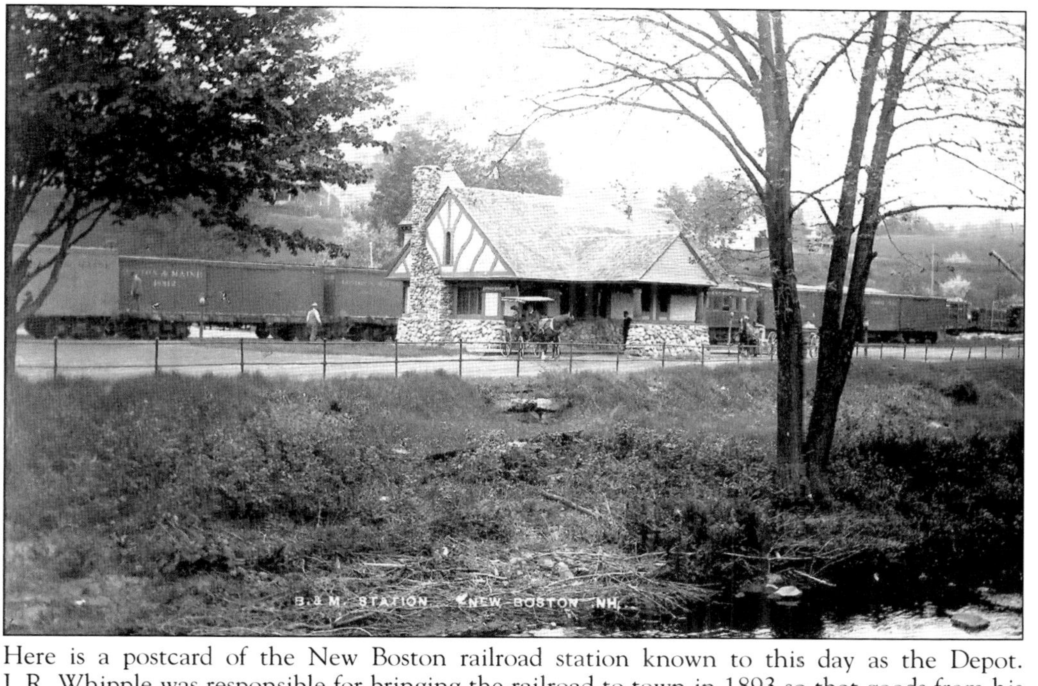

Here is a postcard of the New Boston railroad station known to this day as the Depot. J. R. Whipple was responsible for bringing the railroad to town in 1893 so that goods from his farms could be more easily shipped to his hotels in Boston.

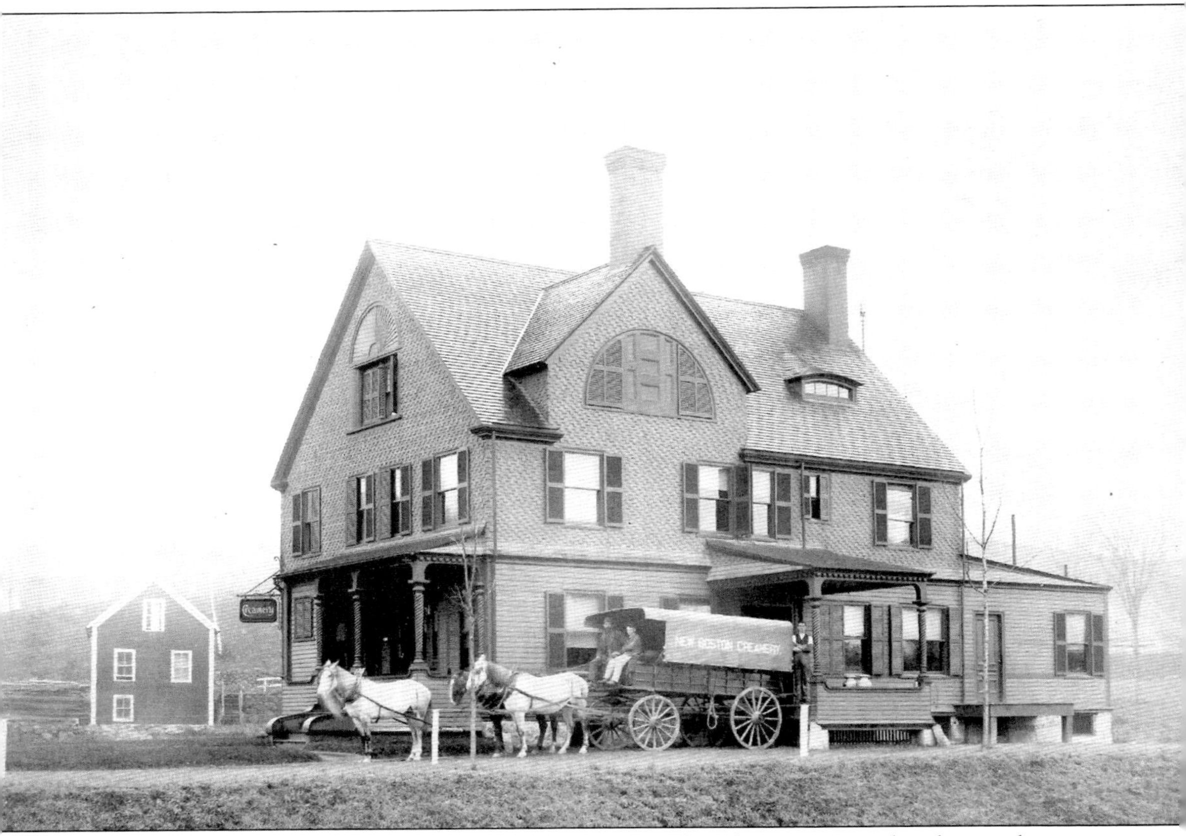

Here is the creamery, owned and operated by J. R. Whipple. To ensure cleanliness, the interior of the structure was built entirely of concrete, white glazed tile, and iron. In this photograph, a creamery worker is loading a horse-drawn wagon with goods for shipment to Boston.

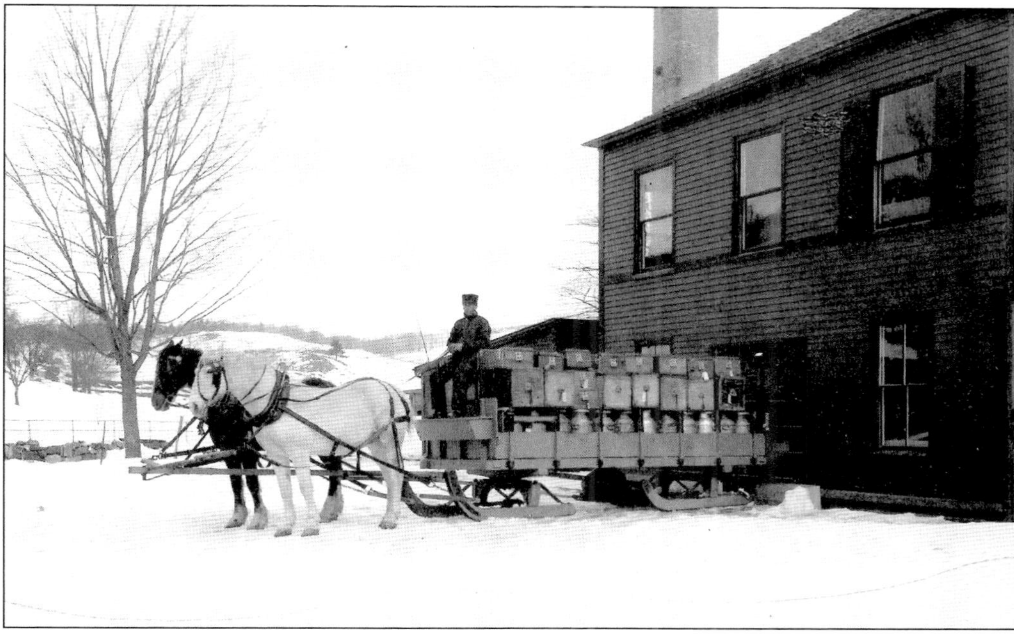

A wagon delivers milk to the creamery in this photograph. A local man known for his dedication to the creamery's operation was Frank Mitchell. He and his mule team began delivering milk to the creamery in 1890, soon after it opened. After 25 years, the miles that he had covered in his daily rounds could have taken him around the world five times.

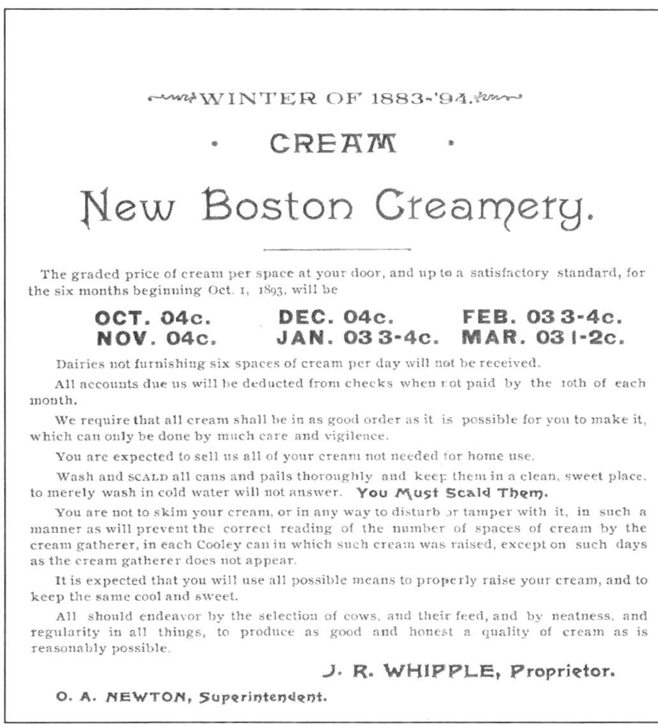

WINTER OF 1883-'94.

CREAM

New Boston Creamery.

The graded price of cream per space at your door, and up to a satisfactory standard, for the six months beginning Oct. 1, 1893, will be

OCT. 04c.	DEC. 04c.	FEB. 03 3-4c.
NOV. 04c.	JAN. 03 3-4c.	MAR. 03 1-2c.

Dairies not furnishing six spaces of cream per day will not be received.

All accounts due us will be deducted from checks when not paid by the 10th of each month.

We require that all cream shall be in as good order as it is possible for you to make it, which can only be done by much care and vigilence.

You are expected to sell us all of your cream not needed for home use.

Wash and SCALD all cans and pails thoroughly and keep them in a clean, sweet place. to merely wash in cold water will not answer. **You Must Scald Them.**

You are not to skim your cream, or in any way to disturb or tamper with it, in such a manner as will prevent the correct reading of the number of spaces of cream by the cream gatherer, in each Cooley can in which such cream was raised, except on such days as the cream gatherer does not appear.

It is expected that you will use all possible means to properly raise your cream, and to keep the same cool and sweet.

All should endeavor by the selection of cows, and their feed, and by neatness, and regularity in all things, to produce as good and honest a quality of cream as is reasonably possible.

J. R. WHIPPLE, Proprietor.

O. A. NEWTON, Superintendent.

In spite of its size, consisting of 350 head of cattle, Valley View was unable to meet all of the needs of the hotels, and superior-quality milk was sought from other local farms. To ensure good quality, these rules for the dairies were published along with price information. This one is from the winter of 1883–1884.

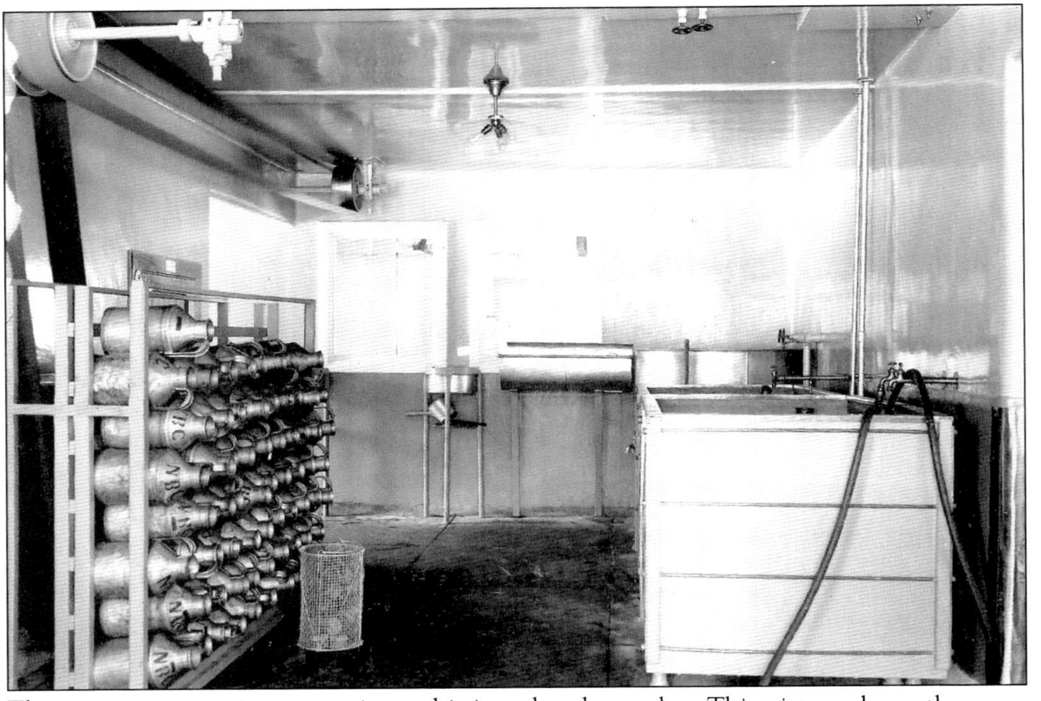

The creamery operation was quite sophisticated and complex. This picture shows the room where the raw milk was deposited into vats for processing.

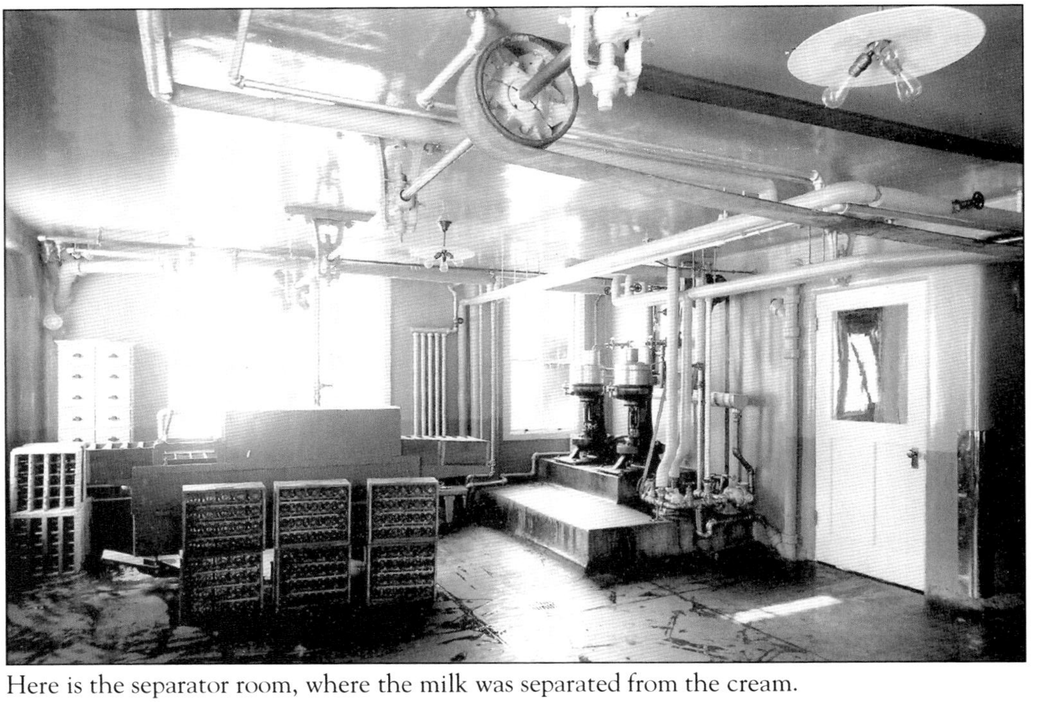

Here is the separator room, where the milk was separated from the cream.

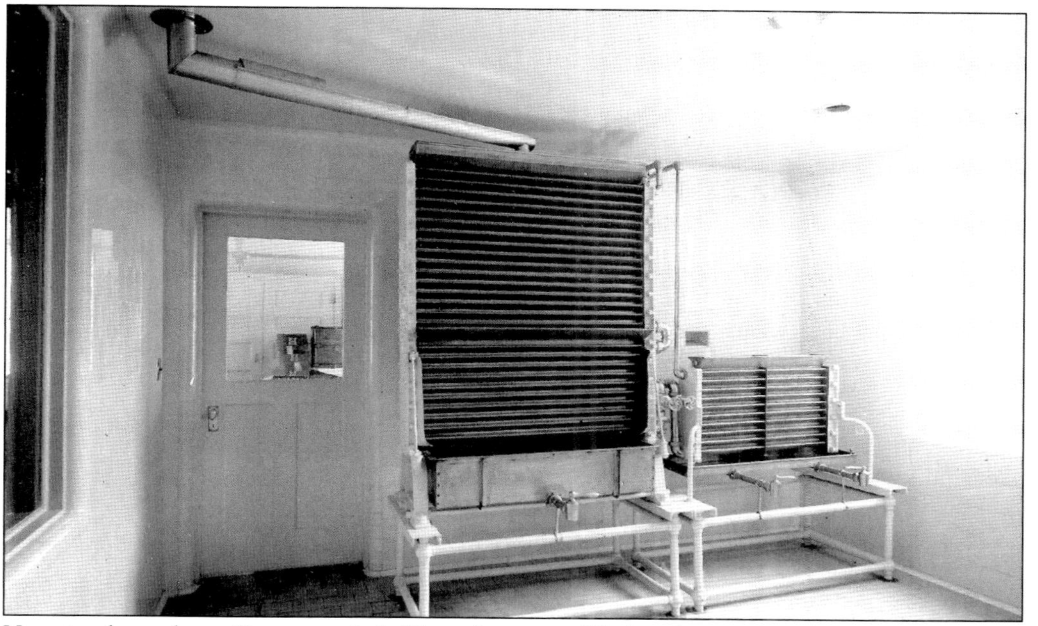

Here is where the milk was cooled. The tubes were filled with a cooling brine solution. The warm milk ran down over the outside of the tubes and was collected at the bottom.

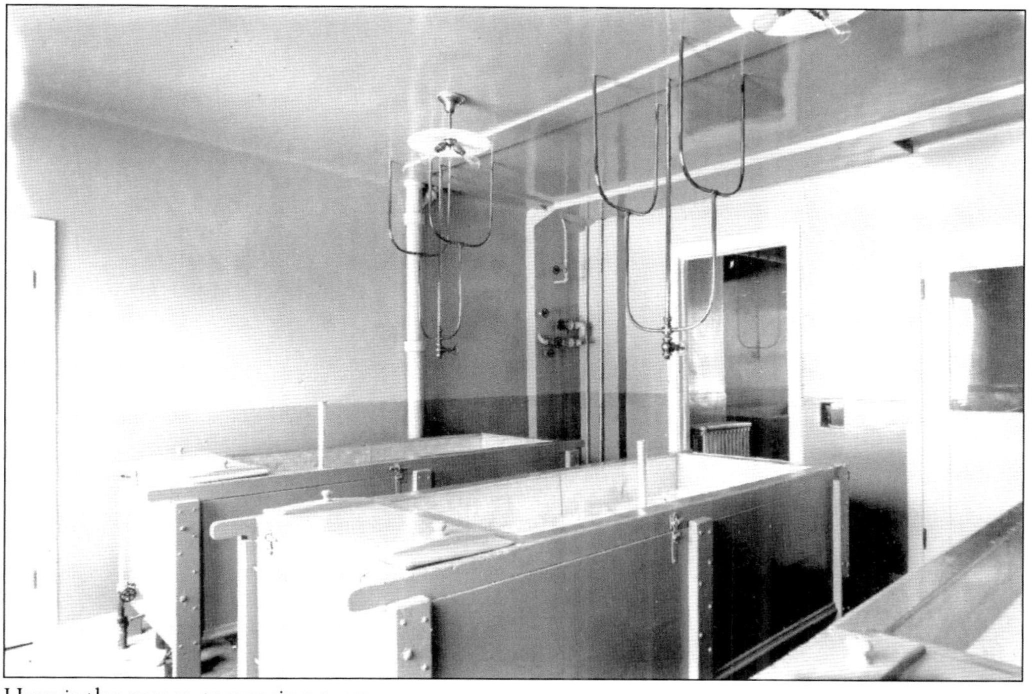

Here is the cream-tempering room.

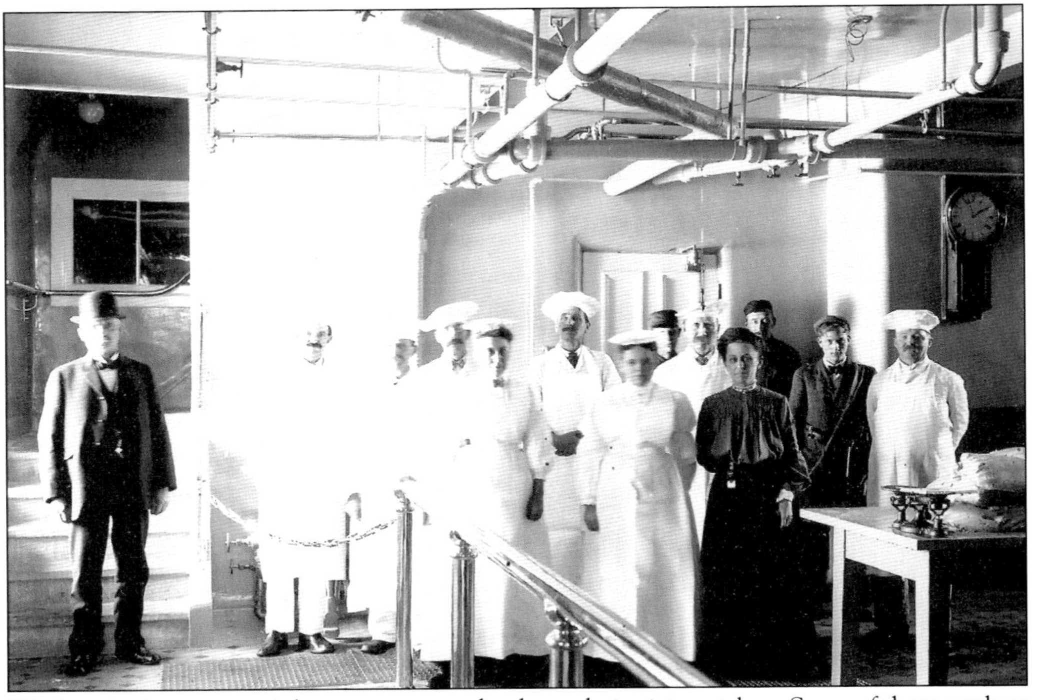

Workers in the creamery's butter room stand to have their picture taken. Some of these workers are Will Heath (6th from the left), Dennis Peasley (9th from the left), Ray Newton (12th from the left), and Ed Rose (13th from the left).

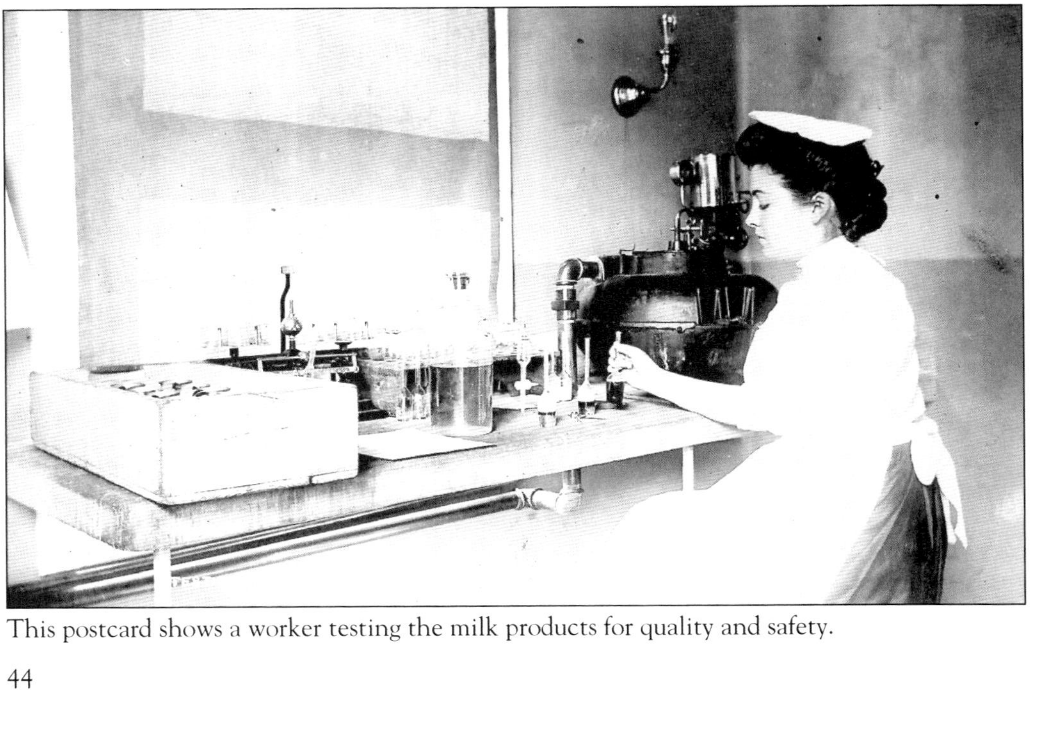

This postcard shows a worker testing the milk products for quality and safety.

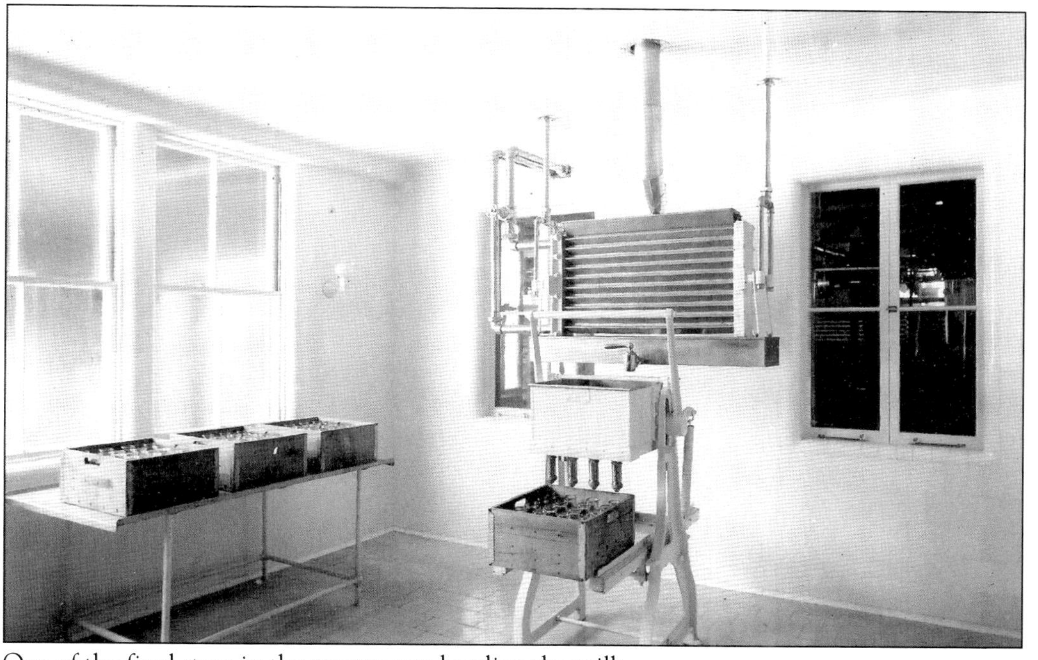

One of the final steps in the process was bottling the milk.

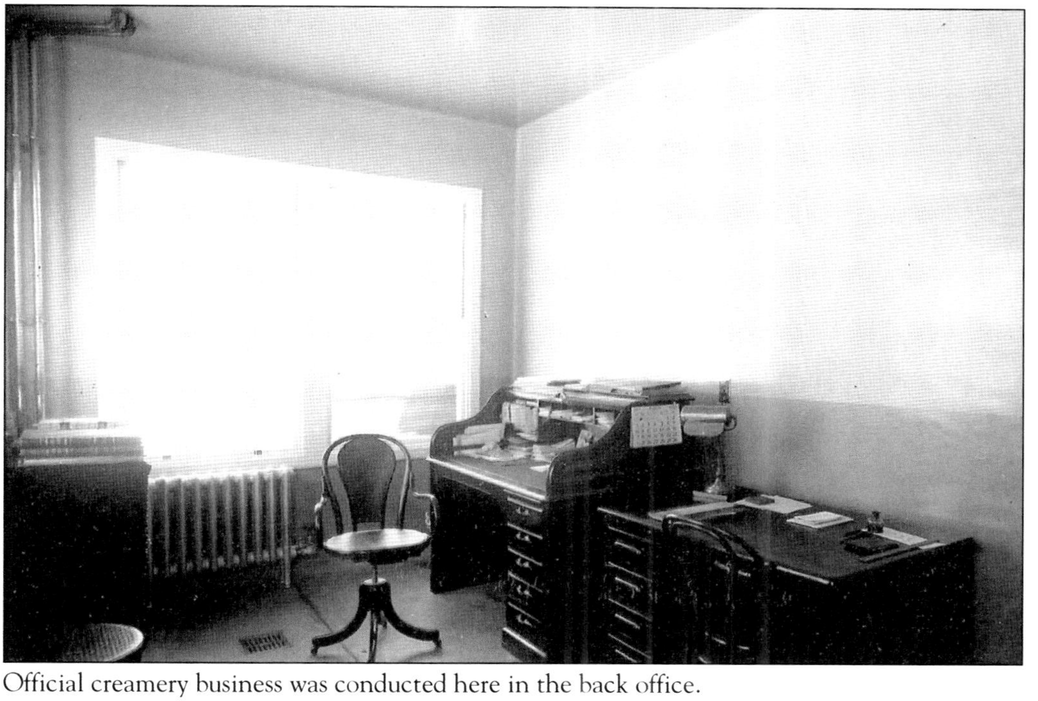

Official creamery business was conducted here in the back office.

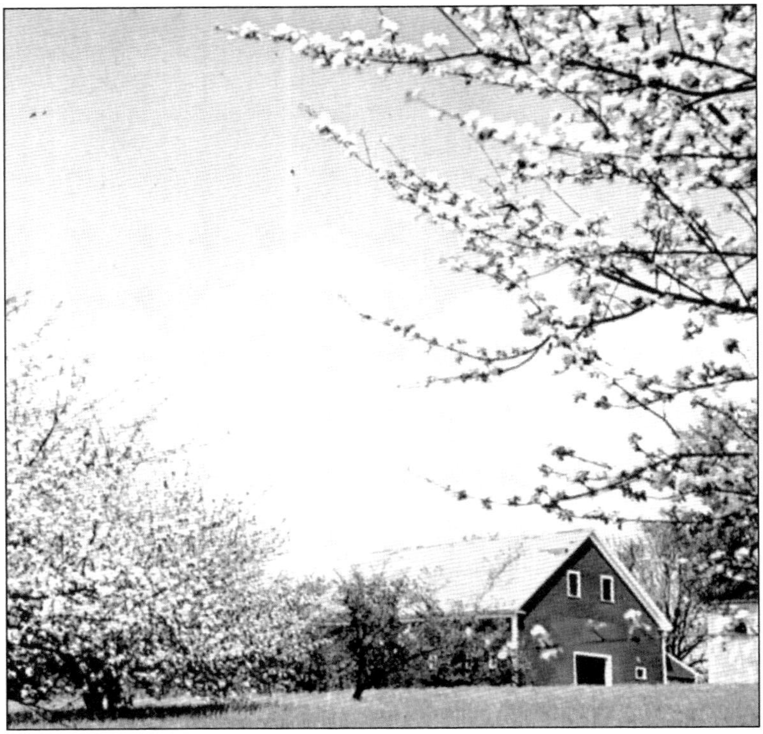

Dairy farming was not the only agricultural activity carried out in New Boston. The area was, and still is, known for its orchards. The Mapadot Orchard, named for family members Ma, Pa, and daughter Dot Cann, has been a fixture here since 1938. Fred "Pa" Cann hired Future Farmers of America boys to plant the apple trees. Charlie, Bill, and Bob Colburn and Howard Towne, among others, were paid 35¢ a hole for this work. (Courtesy of C. Davis.)

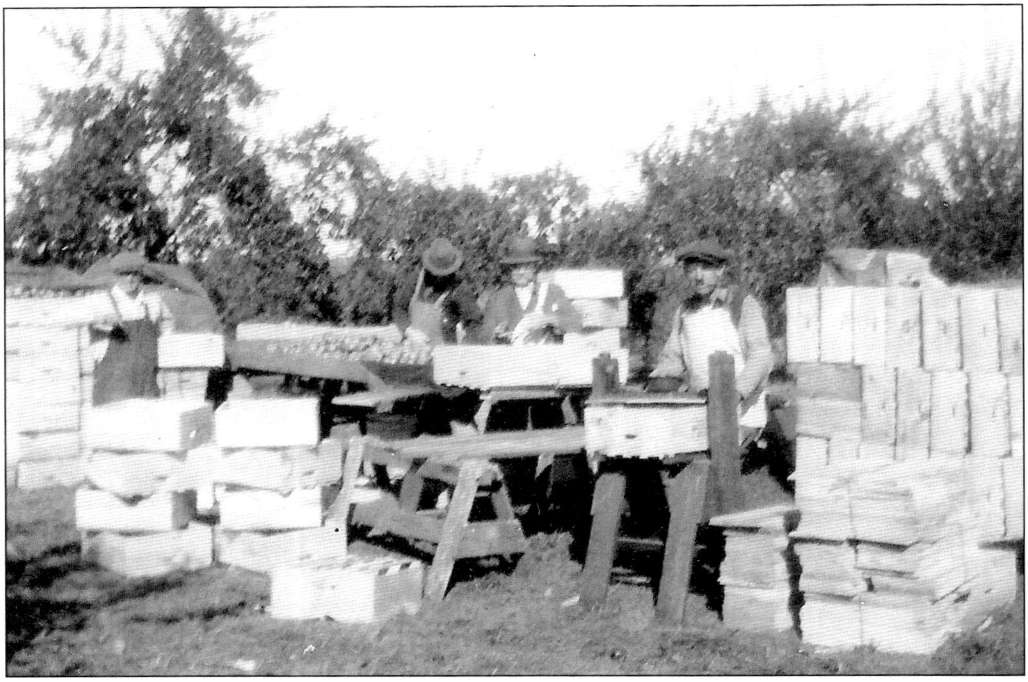

Here is a group of workers sorting apples at Mapadot when it was known as Pitman's Orchard. This photograph was taken in 1929. The Mapadot Orchard still exists, although it is no longer owned by the Canns. Customers can pick their own apples here on crisp fall days.

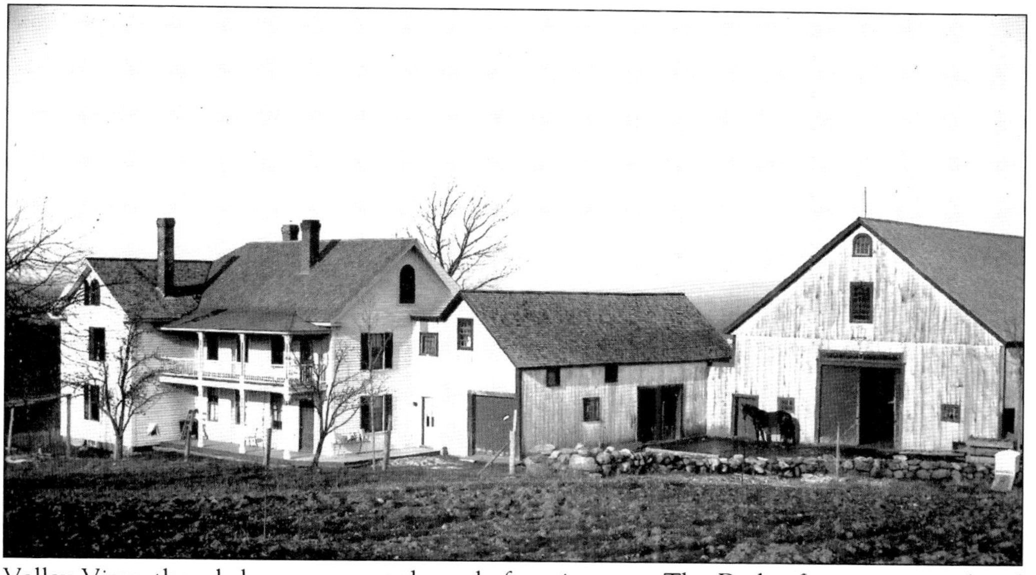

Valley View, though large, was not the only farm in town. The Dodge farm was owned and operated by the Dodge family for generations. It ran its dairy operation until 2002, when the doors were closed on the last remaining dairy farm in town.

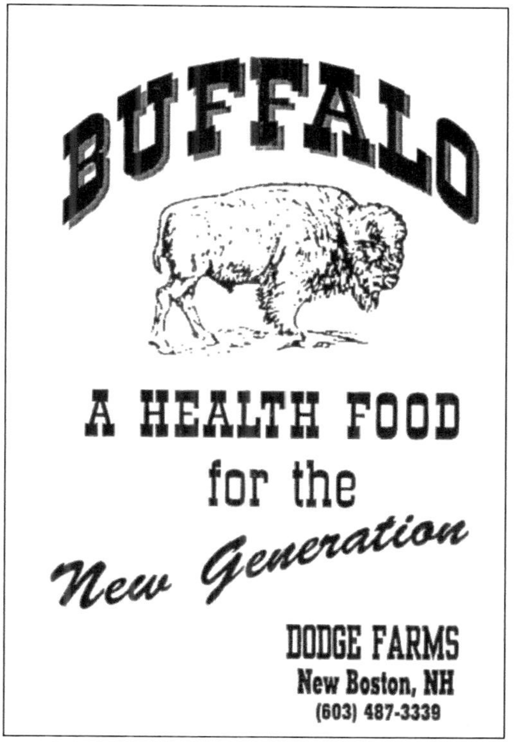

One of the more interesting Dodge farm products was buffalo meat. These wooly creatures drew sightseers to the family farm when Jimmy Dodge bought them in the early 1990s. This flyer promotes buffalo meat as a healthy alternative to beef and provides cooking instructions as well.

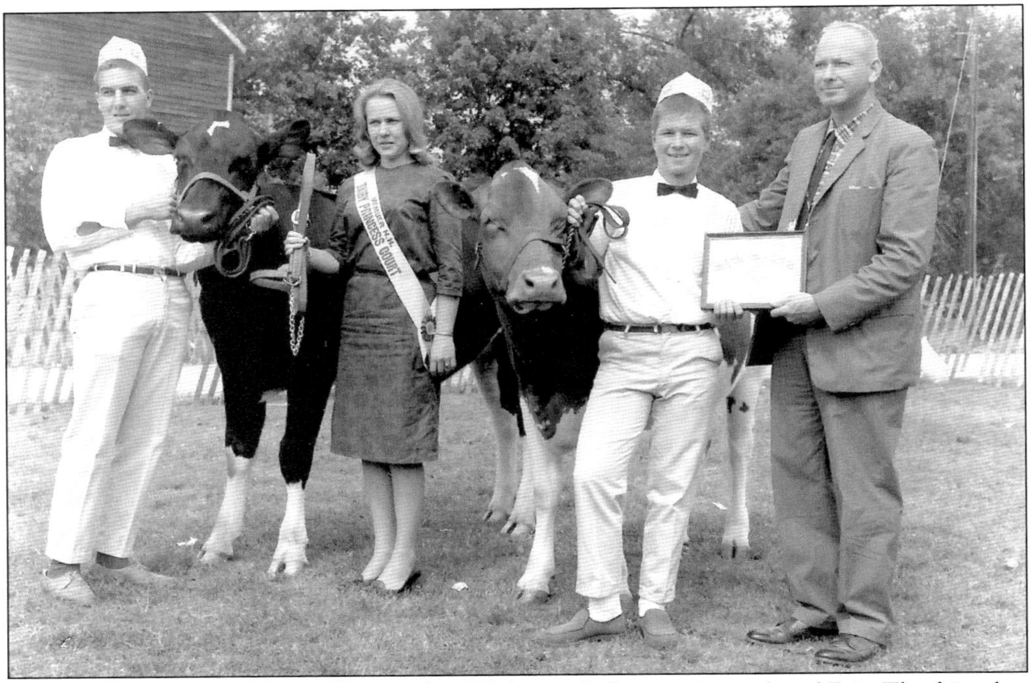

New Boston has always played host to the Hillsborough County Agricultural Fair. The fair takes place every September at the 4-H fairgrounds off Route 13. In these two photographs, proud winners of the livestock contests show off their awards. Although little farming takes place in town these days, in 2002, an enterprising grower named Charlie Houghton produced the world's largest pumpkin, weighing 1,337.6 pounds. (Courtesy of B. Dodge and the Hillsborough County 4-H Foundation.)

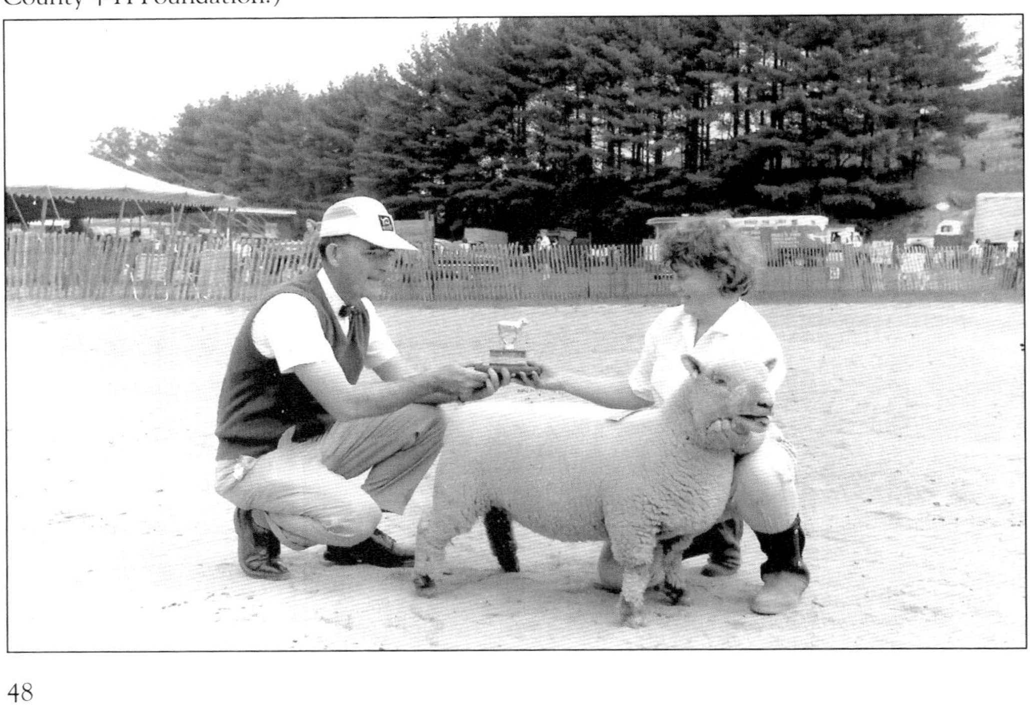

Four

In the Classroom

For one thing New Boston deserves praise; and that is, that she has taught her children to spell their mother tongue, which not all highly-educated persons are able to do.
—J. A. Goodhue, New Boston resident, 1863

The pioneering spirit of the first settlers did not rest at clearing the land and creating homesteads; it also sought to provide schooling for their children even before New Boston was incorporated in 1763. At that time, there was no formal location or building for school. Instead, individual residents either employed teachers on their own or sent their children to established towns from which they emigrated, such as Londonderry, where schools already existed.

By 1769, records indicate that New Boston had built a small building adjacent to the meetinghouse that was used for schooling and quickly became known as the Session House. However, not all of the town children could travel daily to the Session House. So, in 1773, 24 pounds were raised for the selectmen to divide it as they saw fit. A teacher was employed and traveled to five areas, or districts, of the town, and taught for a few months in each district. By 1792, five residents were selected as school overseers; the group was a precursor to the present-day elected school board.

Increasing in both population and town organization, New Boston peaked at 18 separate school districts in 1856. After this, consolidation and centralizing of the schools was the trend, and by 1898, only nine schools were supported by the town for a total of approximately 300 students. It appears that not all of the remaining schools were established to the same scholarly standards. As noted in an 1899 town report, in some of the districts "a great deal of roughness and tardiness occurred." In 1935, only the Village School remained, where it continued to educate through high school until 1965, after which high school students were educated in neighboring Goffstown.

Today's lone school is named New Boston Central School and enrolls approximately 500 students. In keeping with New Boston's long tradition of quality education, it was recognized as the New Hampshire Elementary School Representative of Excellence in 2003. Unlike generations of the past, however, few (if any) students of the present will reminisce about long walks through shady woods or hard benches in old schoolhouses.

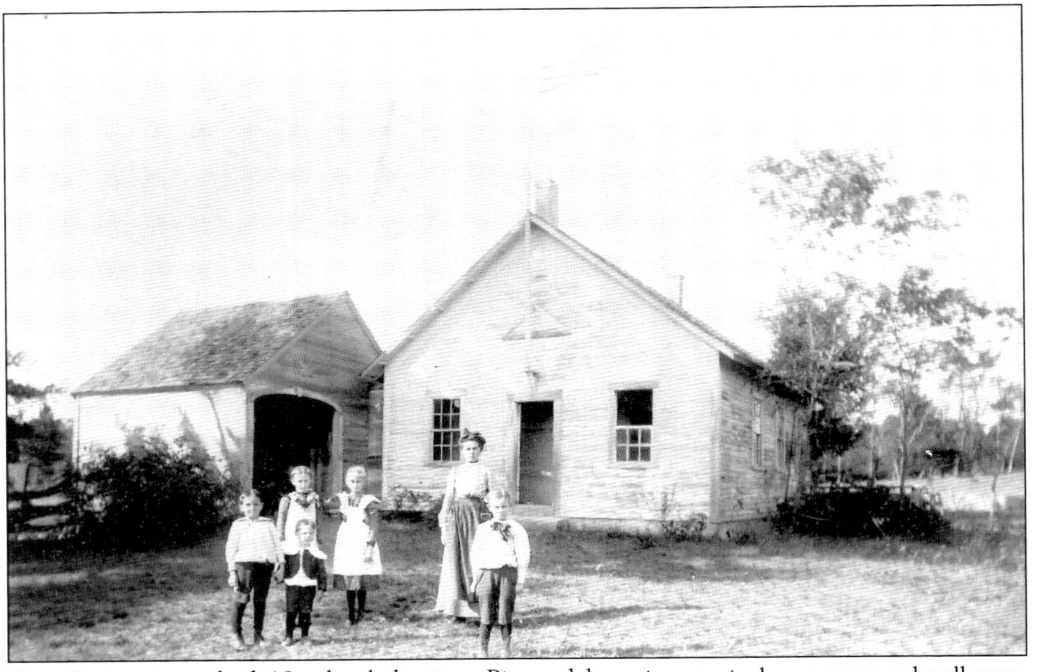

New Boston once had 18 school districts. Pictured here is a typical one-room schoolhouse. Schoolhouse No. 1 was on the map of 1863 in the town history. It was located on the missile base side of Chestnut Hill Road opposite the old Barnard places. Records show that in 1800 the school received $3.24 of the school budget, and in 1861, only three boys and one girl were in attendance. Schoolhouse No. 1 closed when New Boston's school district united with Amherst's.

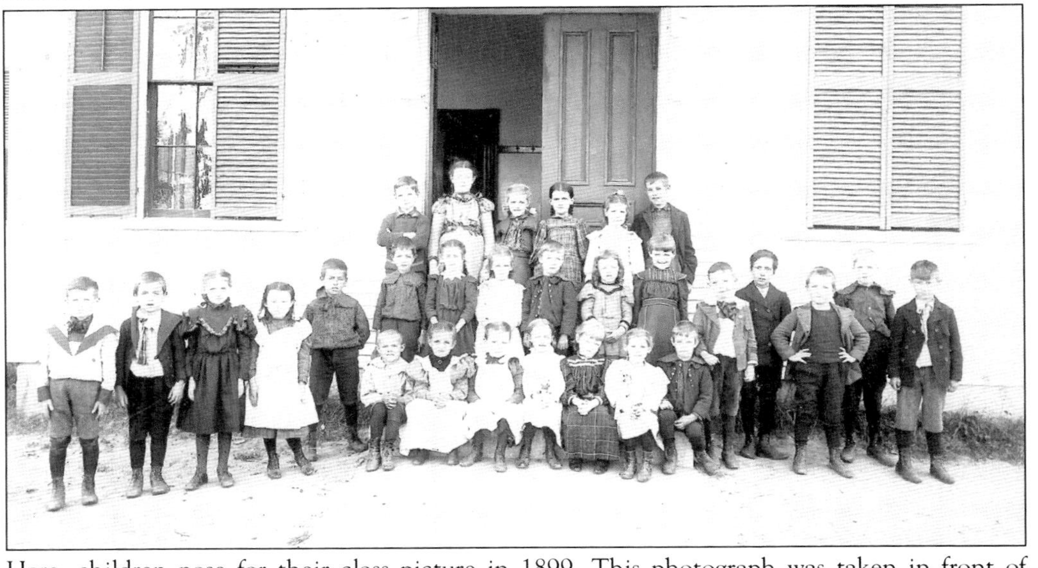

Here, children pose for their class picture in 1899. This photograph was taken in front of the Village School, which eventually housed all grades. In earlier years, children would have attended Schoolhouse No. 2, on Bedford Road, or Schoolhouse No. 3, located on the missile base. It was near Schoolhouse No. 3 that Sevilla Jones was shot by her rejected suitor, who then shot himself. This school later became known as the Sevilla Jones School.

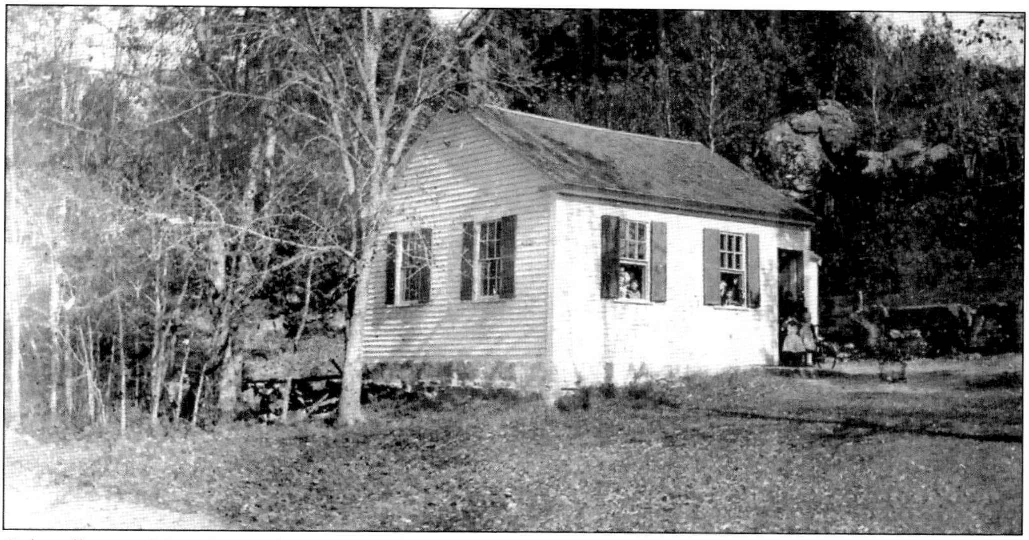

Schoolhouse No. 4 was known as Capt. Lamson's School, Mrs. Roger's house, and the Joe English District. In the 1880s, the Merrill, Kelso, Herrick, and Wason family children attended school here. Hattie Todd and later Nettie Marden taught in Schoolhouse No. 4 for several terms. In 1881, the mothers of the district purchased a U.S. map for the school. This was also the first school to have a flag.

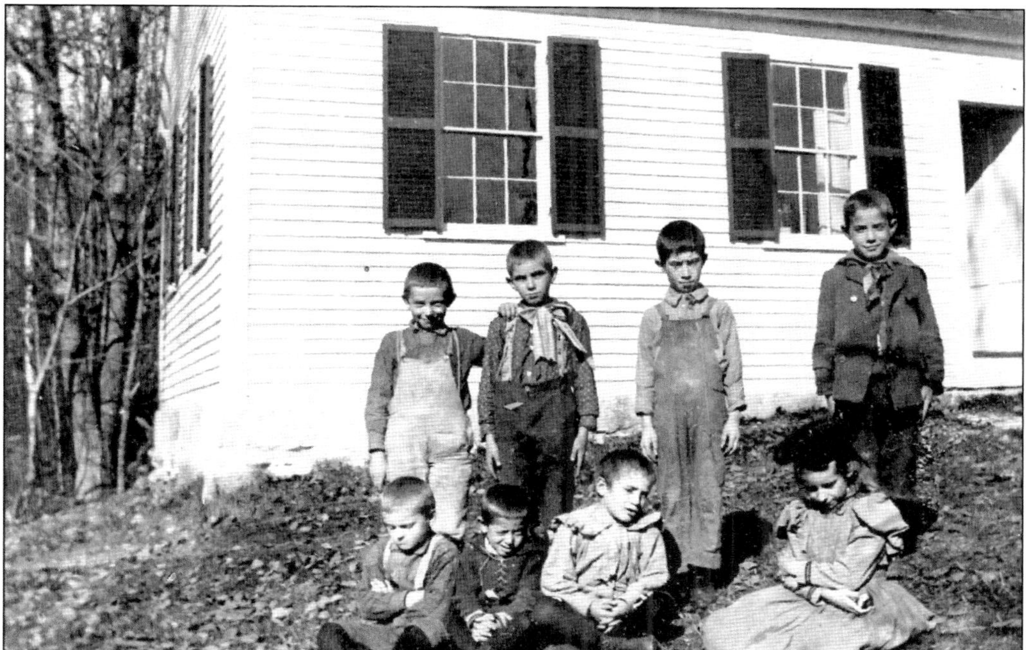

Here, children pose outside Schoolhouse No. 4. It is difficult to determine when all of the schoolhouses were built. Most available information tells us when schools were rebuilt to replace the originals. We know that in 1804 it was voted that each district was to build its own school. These schools ranged in size, for they housed as few as 3 students or as many as 46. (Courtesy of N. Poole.)

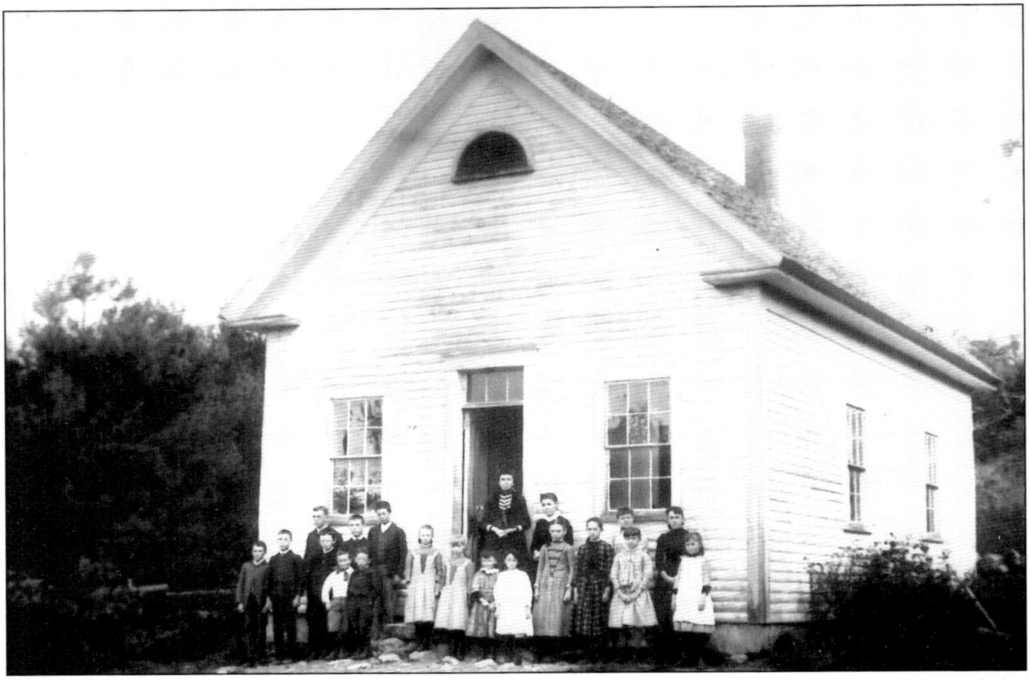

This photograph of Schoolhouse No. 5, the South Hill School, was taken sometime around the turn of the century. The Leavitt, Byam, and Tower family children attended this school. The school was built on October 15, 1804. The building committee was to furnish a gallon of rum for its construction, and the total cost was $257.25. The school closed in 1930.

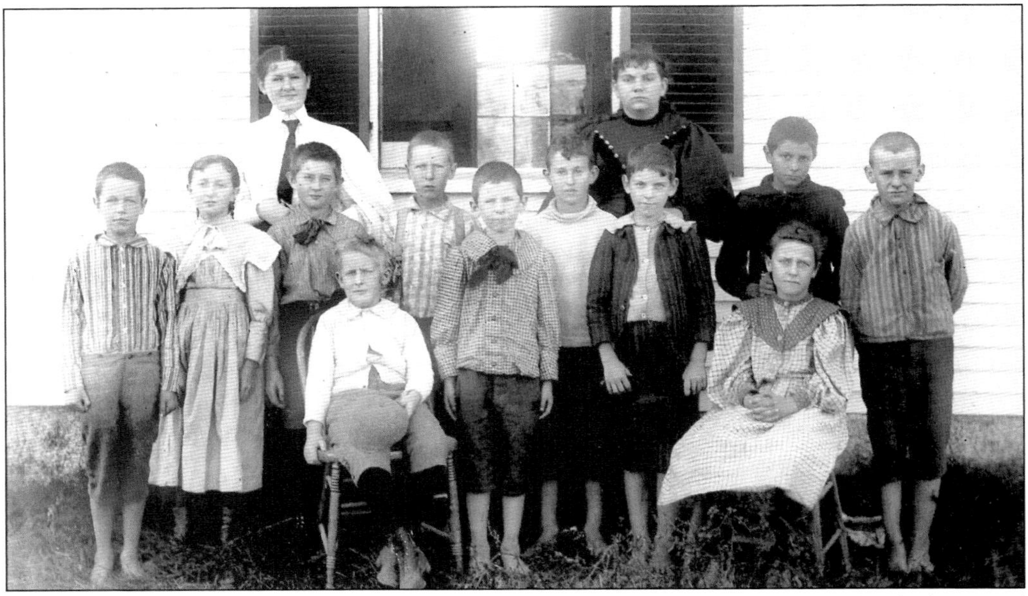

Here is a 1901 group shot from one of the town's 18 school districts. The light clothing and bare feet imply that this picture was taken during the summer session. These students may have attended Schoolhouse No. 6, on Lyndeboro Road, or perhaps Schoolhouse No. 7, on Cochran Hill Road. The latter was rebuilt in 1861 for a cost of $212.

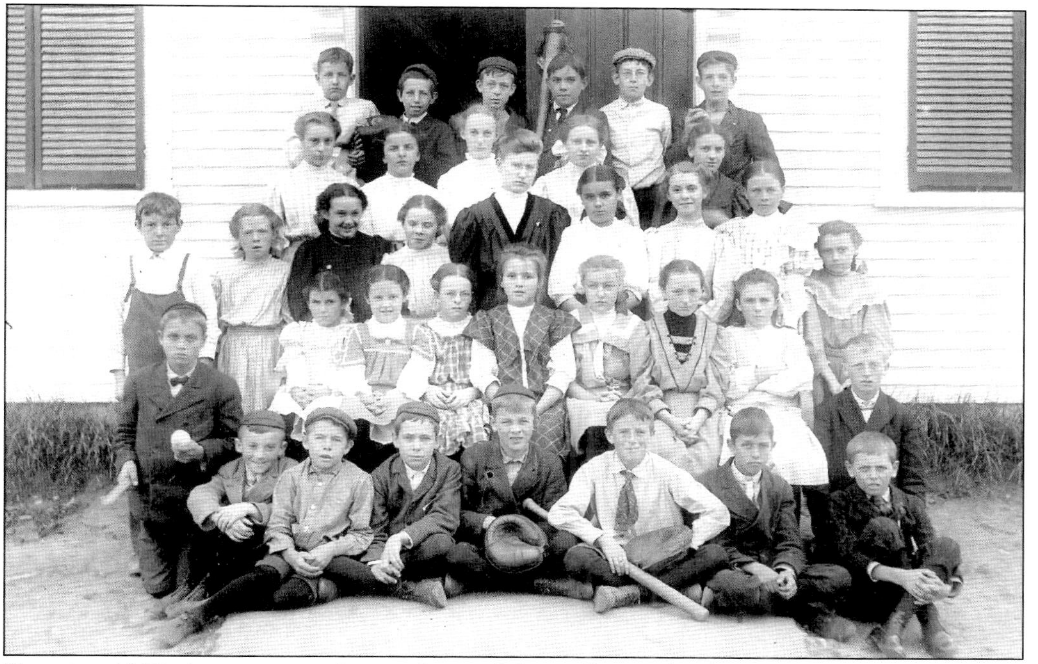

Here is a 1908 class picture taken in front of the Village School. The teacher in the middle of the shot is Miss Woodman. Many of these children are ready for recess, as evidenced by the balls, bats, and gloves they are holding. The original school on this site was known as Schoolhouse No. 8. It was built in 1857 and burned in the fire of 1887.

This 1910 class picture shows one of the town's smaller classes, with only seven students. Another of New Boston's schools was Schoolhouse No. 9, known as the Wilson Hill School. This school was rebuilt in 1872 for a cost of $625. Schoolhouse No. 10, the Howe Bridge School, burned in 1869 and was rebuilt in 1871. It closed in 1888, when the district united with Parker Station.

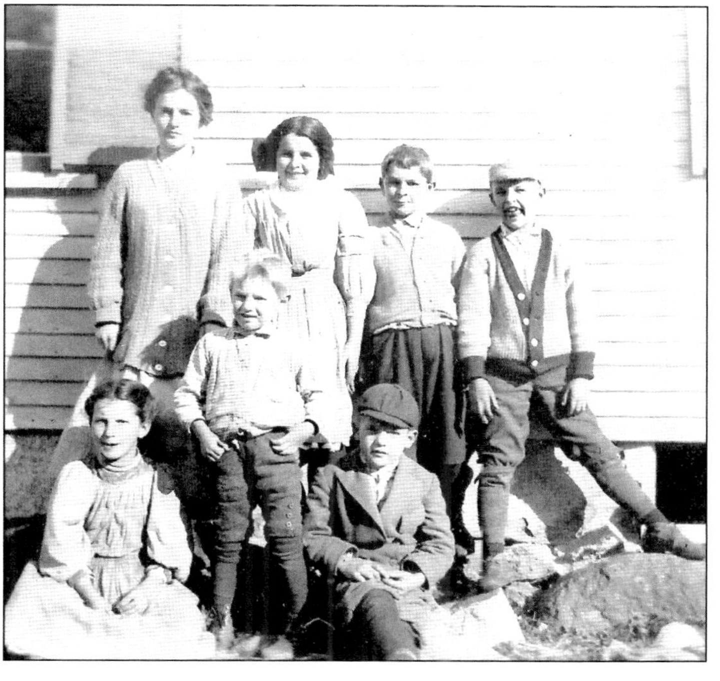

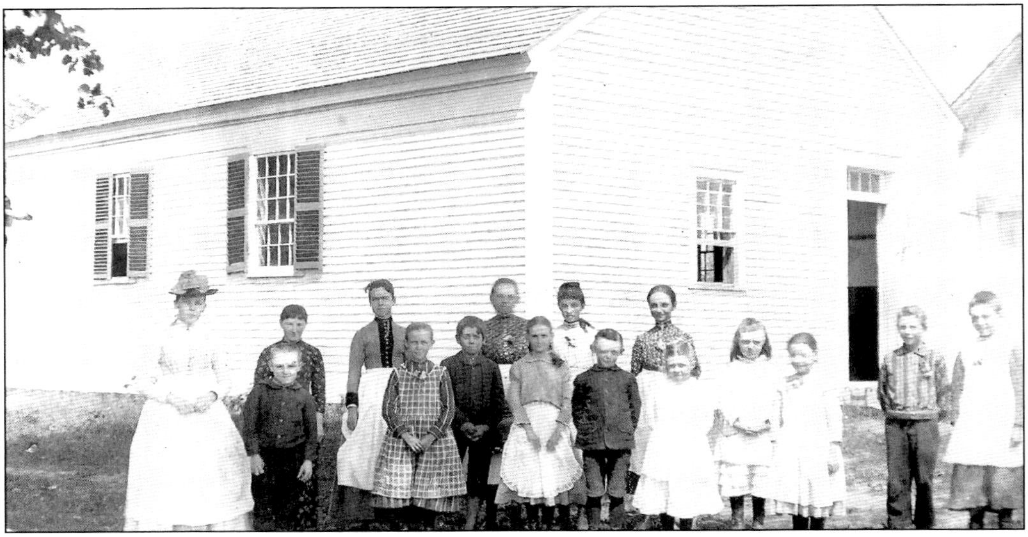

Schoolhouse No. 11 was located on Francestown Road. In 1851, there were three students attending when Philantha Whipple taught here. In 1864, there was no money for the fall term, and a private school was opened under the charge of Lydia McNeil, whose wages were paid by the parents, "the good effects of which were seen through the year." In the late 1800s, this school became known as "Annie's School" for its teacher, Annie Atwood, seen here on the left.

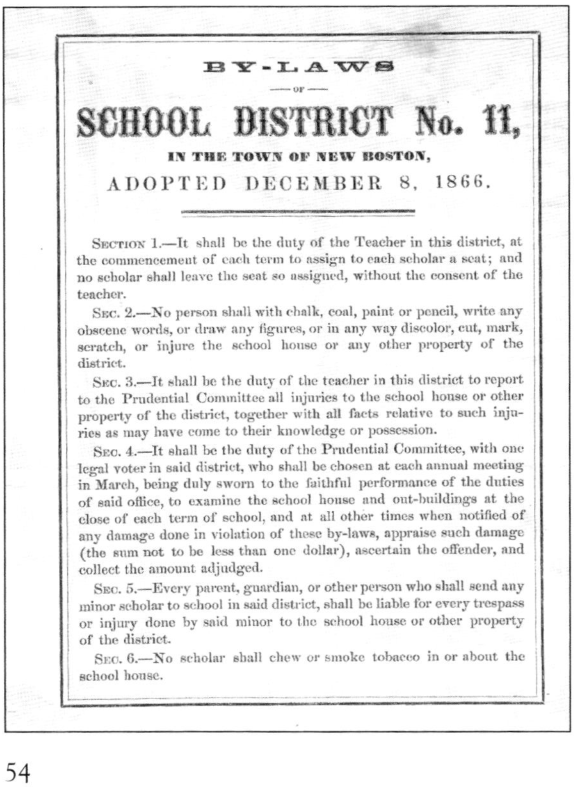

BY-LAWS

—OF—

SCHOOL DISTRICT No. 11,

IN THE TOWN OF NEW BOSTON,

ADOPTED DECEMBER 8, 1866.

SECTION 1.—It shall be the duty of the Teacher in this district, at the commencement of each term to assign to each scholar a seat; and no scholar shall leave the seat so assigned, without the consent of the teacher.

SEC. 2.—No person shall with chalk, coal, paint or pencil, write any obscene words, or draw any figures, or in any way discolor, cut, mark, scratch, or injure the school house or any other property of the district.

SEC. 3.—It shall be the duty of the teacher in this district to report to the Prudential Committee all injuries to the school house or other property of the district, together with all facts relative to such injuries as may have come to their knowledge or possession.

SEC. 4.—It shall be the duty of the Prudential Committee, with one legal voter in said district, who shall be chosen at each annual meeting in March, being duly sworn to the faithful performance of the duties of said office, to examine the school house and out-buildings at the close of each term of school, and at all other times when notified of any damage done in violation of these by-laws, appraise such damage (the sum not to be less than one dollar), ascertain the offender, and collect the amount adjudged.

SEC. 5.—Every parent, guardian, or other person who shall send any minor scholar to school in said district, shall be liable for every trespass or injury done by said minor to the school house or other property of the district.

SEC. 6.—No scholar shall chew or smoke tobacco in or about the school house.

Here is a copy of the school bylaws for School District No. 11, adopted on December 8, 1866. The rules have not changed much since then. Notice that "no scholar shall chew or smoke tobacco in or about the school house."

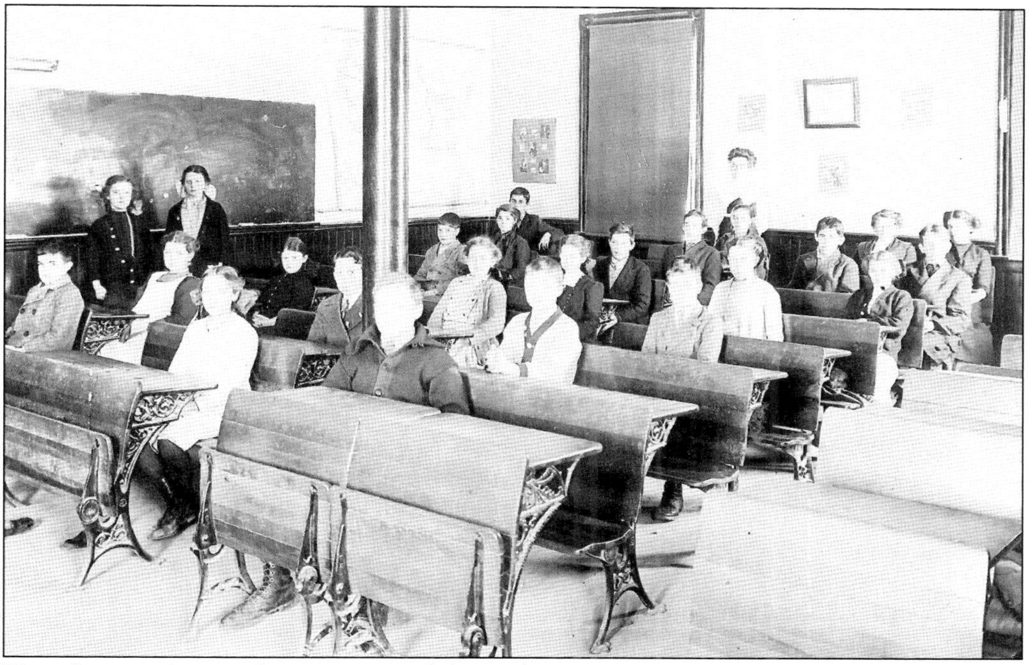

This photograph was taken *c.* 1913 and shows the interior of a Village School classroom. The students were apparently prepared to have their photograph taken, as they are seen here in their Sunday best. Another school, Schoolhouse No. 12, was located on Clark Hill Road. Two sisters taught here—Julian and Clara Dodge.

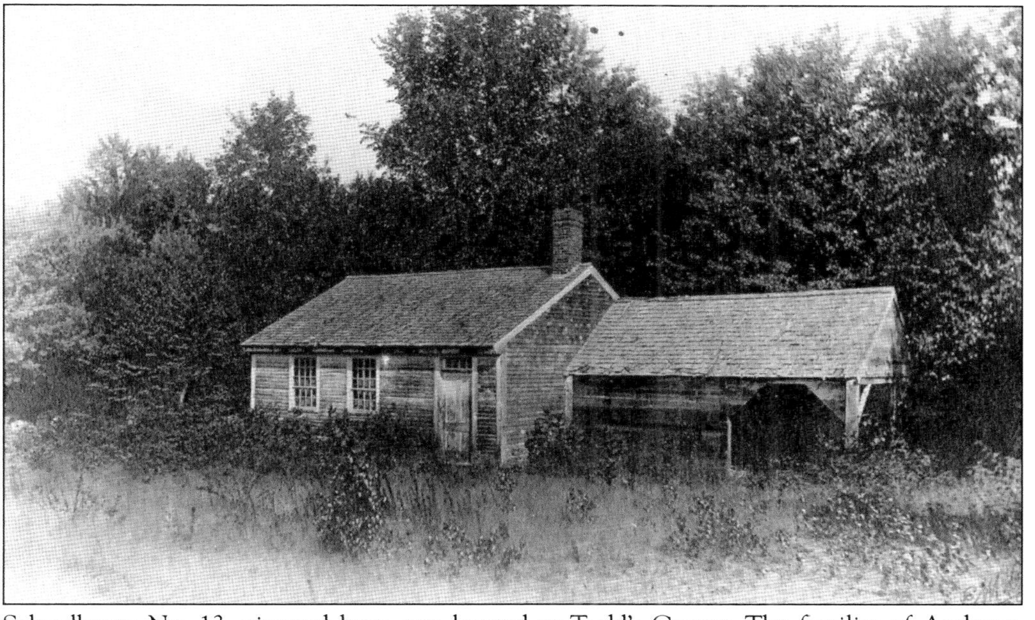

Schoolhouse No. 13, pictured here, was located at Todd's Corner. The families of Andrews, Langdell, Morgan, Bennett, and Todd sent their children to this school. School District No. 13 was always a large one, and when Philantha Whipple taught here in 1854, there were 28 students. Over $70 of the school allotment was used here, compared to $20 received by most schools.

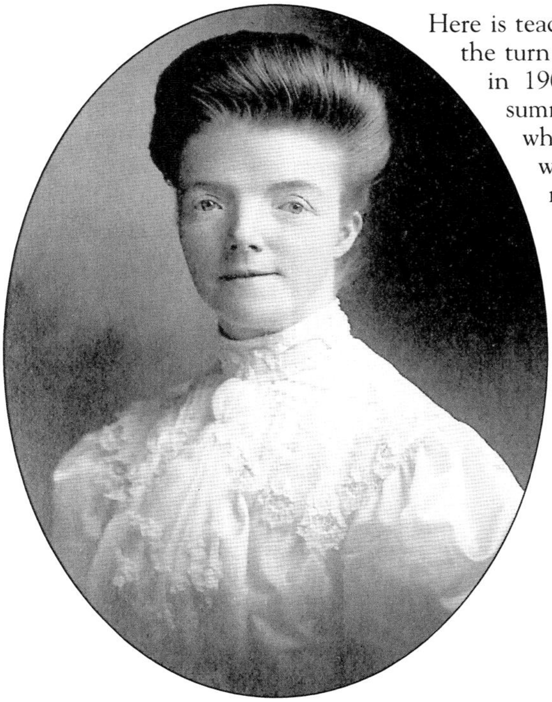

Here is teacher Mildred C. Warren in typical attire at the turn of the century. She taught in New Boston in 1907. The schools consisted of winter and summer sessions to accommodate the districts when a shortage of teachers existed. Teachers would often move from school to school as needed, perhaps to Schoolhouse No. 14, on Bunker Hill Road, or to Schoolhouse No. 15, on Saunders Hill Road.

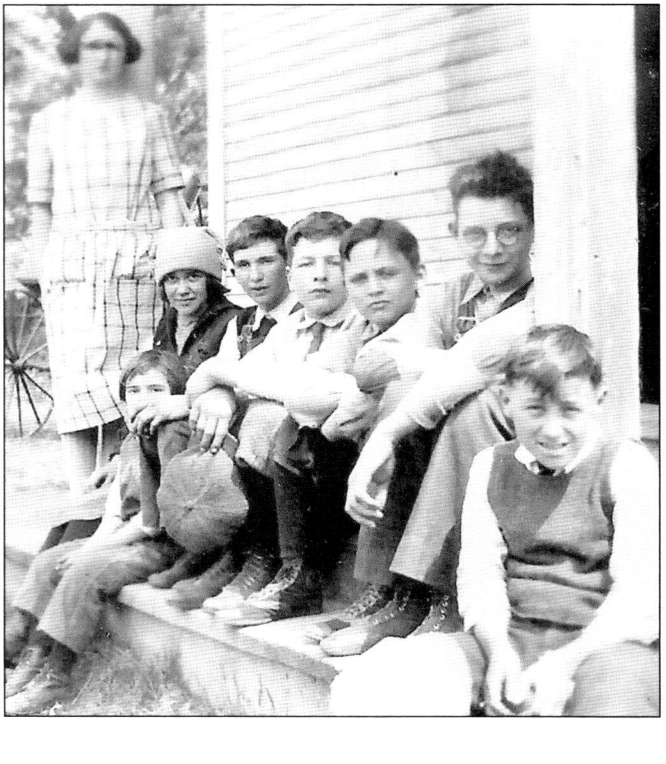

Schoolhouse No. 16 was located on Lull Road and was another of the town's larger school districts. This picture was taken *c*. 1921, when Marion Leavitt taught Calvin Robinson, Agnes Stevens, Eben Robinson, Arthur Provencher, Arthur Barnard, Harry Barnard, and Bill Lizzotte. Schoolhouse No. 17 was on Riverdale Road. By 1854, this district had united with the Weare school system. Schoolhouse No. 18 was known as the Village School and was located in the center of town.

This is a picture of the first high school building, which was built prior to 1887. This school was located in the center of town where the fire station now stands. At around the time of this photograph, the one-room schools were closing and students were attending the Village School, as the trend was toward centralization.

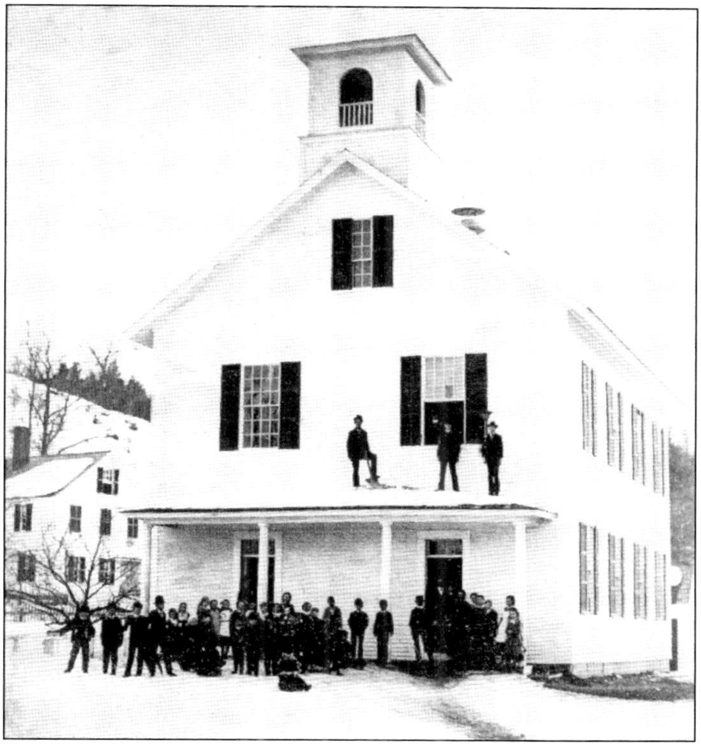

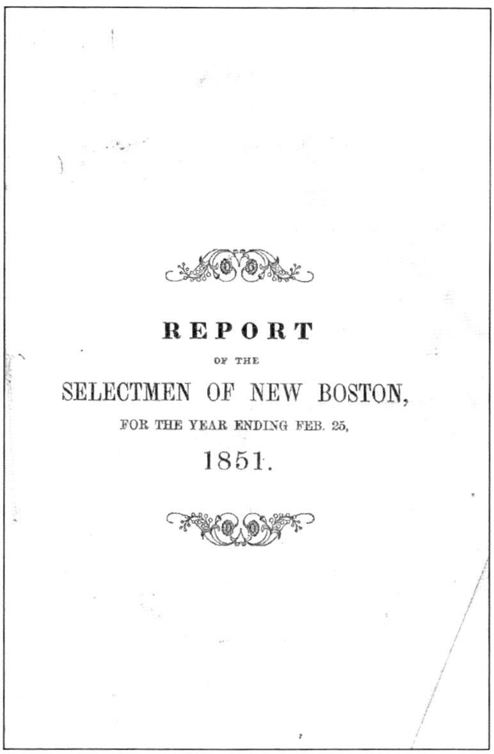

REPORT

OF THE

SELECTMEN OF NEW BOSTON,

FOR THE YEAR ENDING FEB. 25,

1851.

In this selectmen's report from 1851, the "Report of the Superintending School Committee" reads, "Fellow citizens, in presenting this report to you, your committee are happy to say that in their opinion, the schools in this town were never in a more prosperous condition than at present, though much remains to be accomplished to make them what they should be."

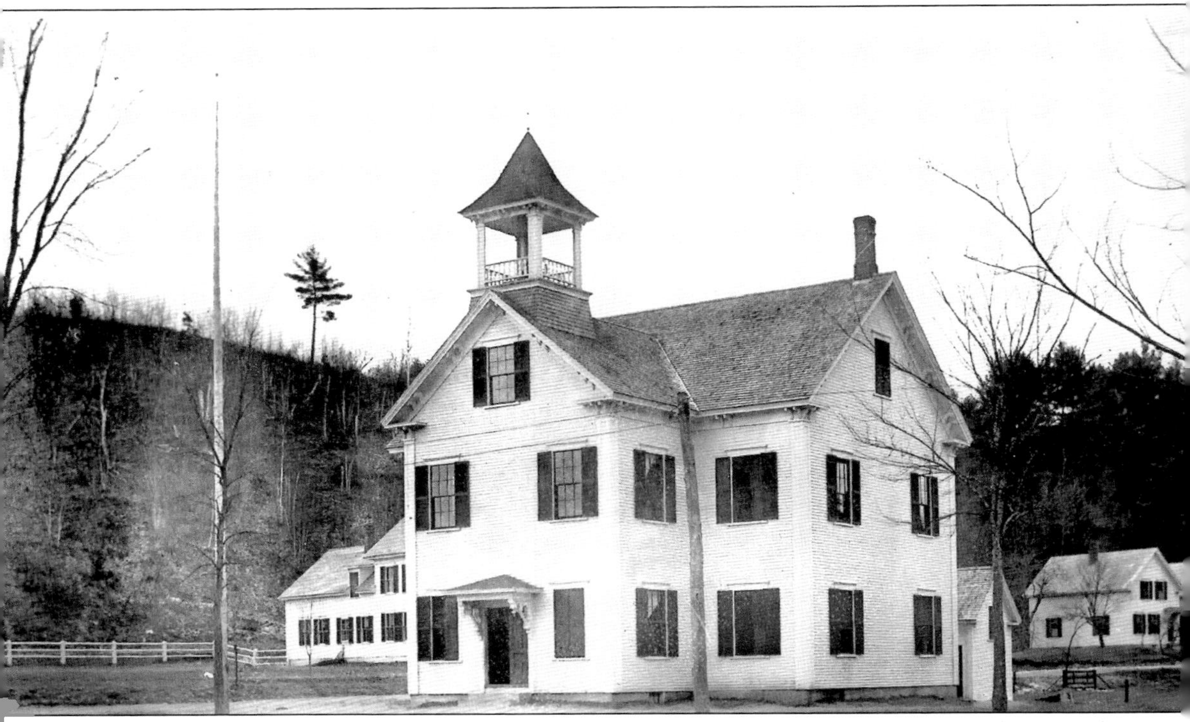

The school pictured here replaced the original high school, which was destroyed by fire. This building was constructed in 1892 on the site of its predecessor. The school report after the first year reads, "We believe the High School has been a real benefit to the town and hope it may become the general custom for the more advanced scholars from all parts of this town to attend this school." Grades one to six were housed downstairs in two rooms, grades seven and eight occupied one small room upstairs, and the high school occupied the remainder of the upper floor. This building was demolished in the early 1970s.

Julia Goodman was a member of New Boston's first high school graduating class in 1896. Goodman lived on River Road in the Kanzer house and later moved to the Will Dodge farm. Some of the grandchildren of the first graduating class still reside in New Boston and also graduated from New Boston High.

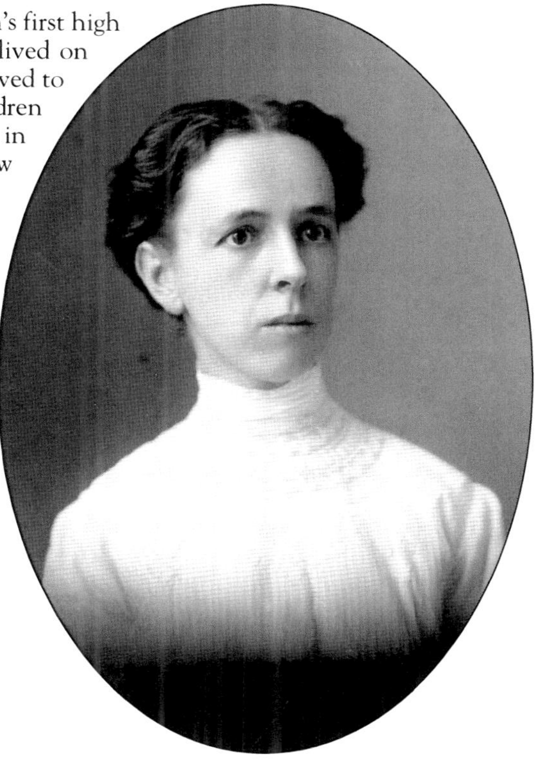

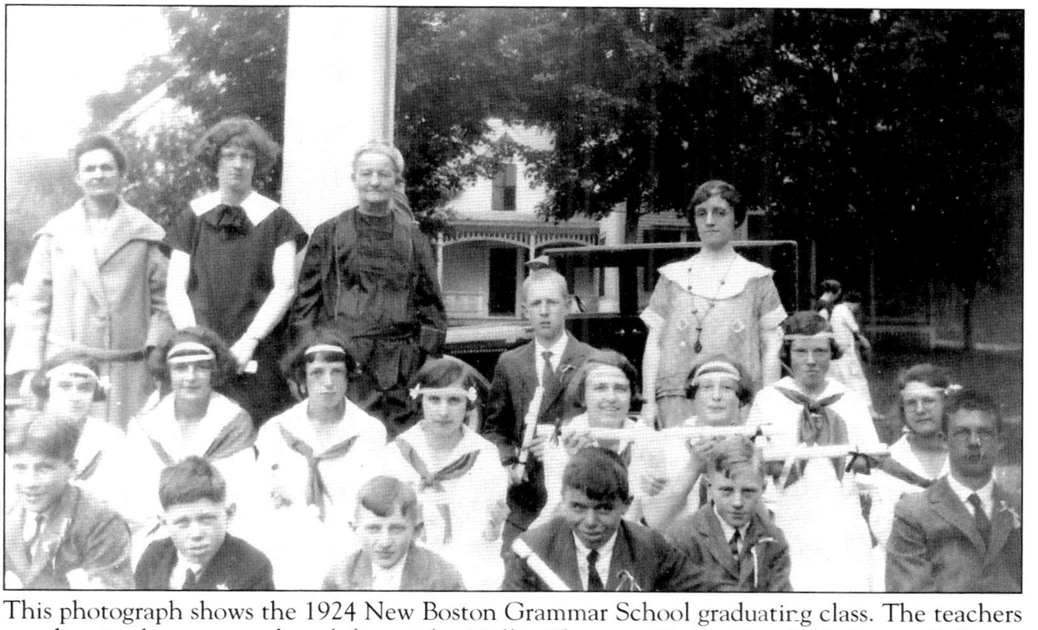

This photograph shows the 1924 New Boston Grammar School graduating class. The teachers standing in the rear are, from left to right, Nellie Chancey, Grace Mansfield, Jennie Colburn, and Mrs. Saunders.

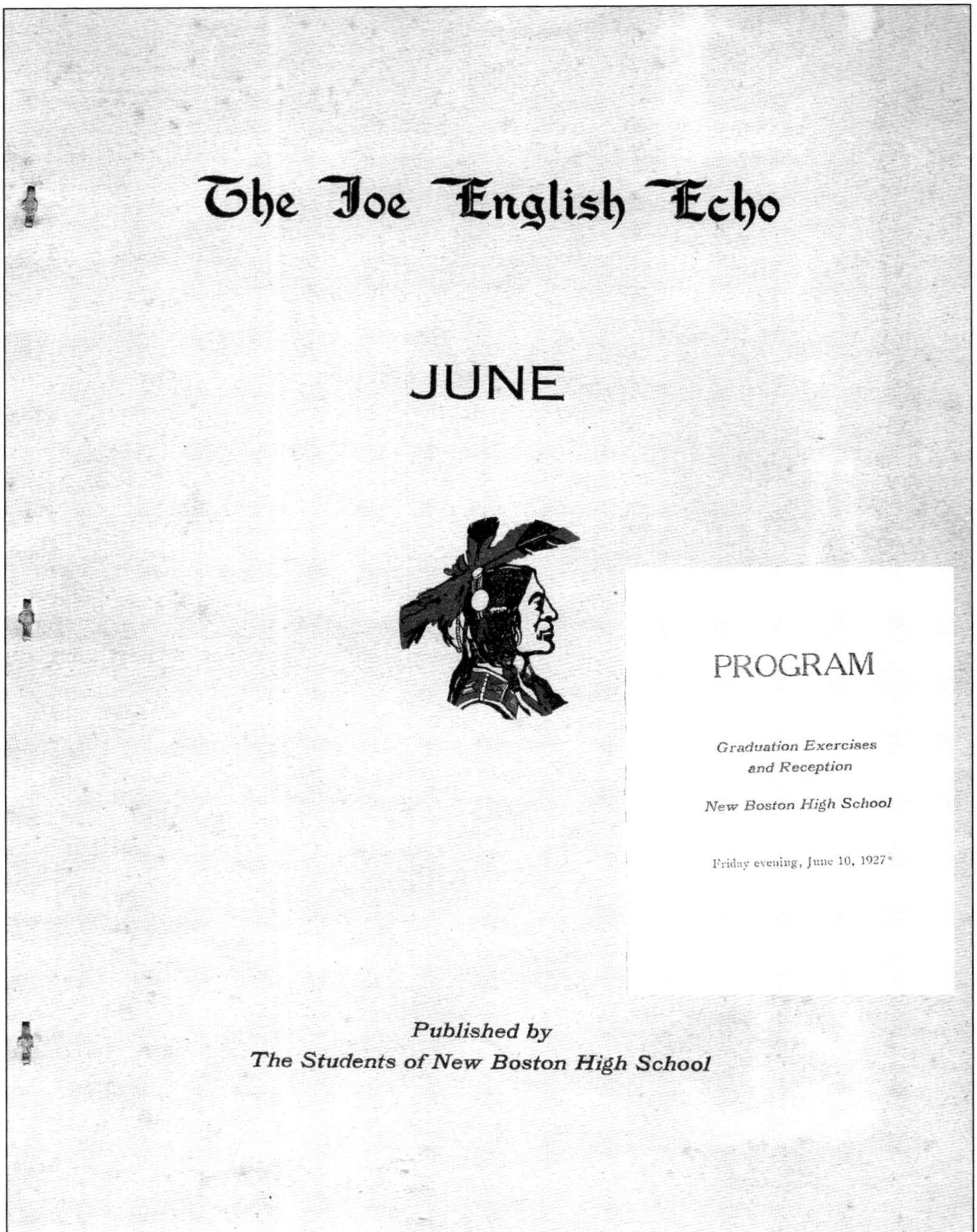

Here is the first issue of the high school yearbook, the *Joe English Echo,* published in 1927. Its name was decided by popular vote of the students, Joe English being a famous Native American of these parts. The name continued to be used for the yearbook for the duration of New Boston High School's existence. The inset shows a graduation program from the same year.

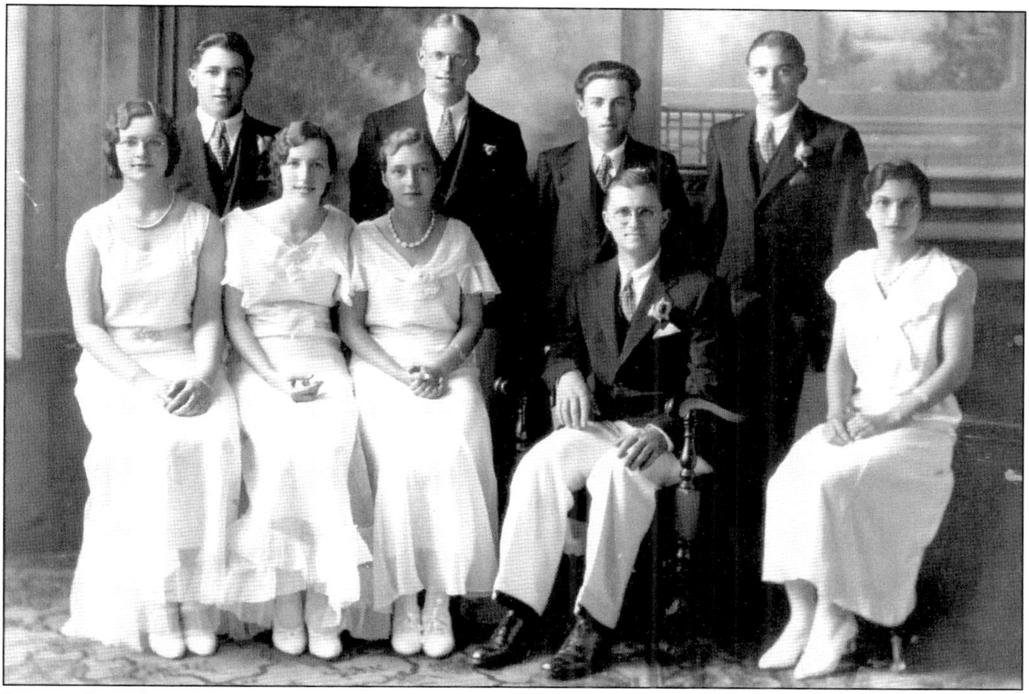

Pictured is the New Boston High School class of 1932. Seen here are, from left to right, the following: (front row) Evalyn Kirsch, Frances Skofield, Viola Leavitt, Ernest Nadeau (the principal), and Blanche Daniels; (back row) Victor Daniels, Paul Mansfield, George Daniels, and Henry Osborne.

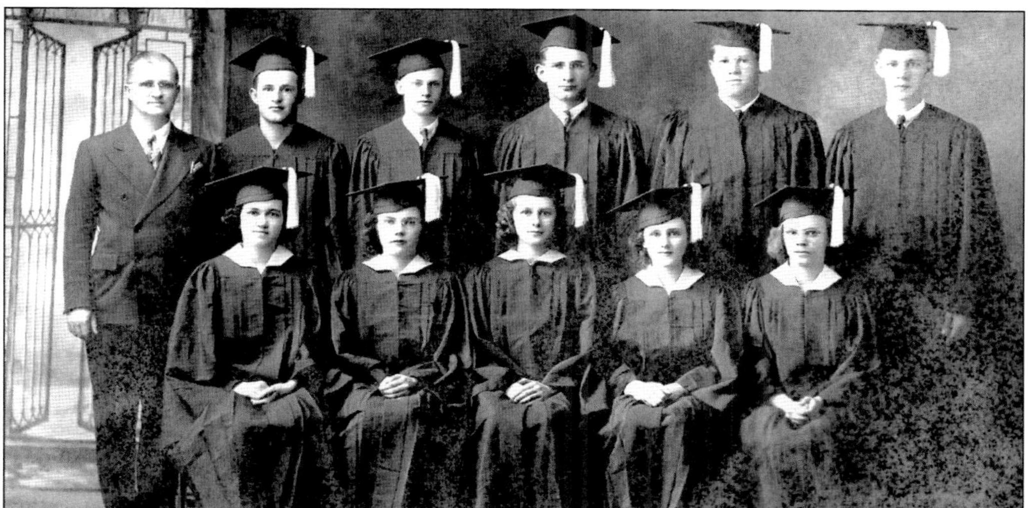

This attractive group of capped and gowned students represents the class of 1941. Pictured are, from left to right, the following: (front row) Bernice Gagnon, Muriel Bailey Elliott, Marjorie Savoy Bose, Marion Boulter French, and Phyllis Bose LaBossiere; (back row) Ernest Nadeau (the headmaster), Louis Christian, Clement Lyon Jr., John Corliss, Martin Colburn, and Charles Emerson. Of this group, Clem Lyon, Gilly Emerson, and Marjorie Savoy Bose attended the 1998 class reunion. (Courtesy of C. Lyon Jr.)

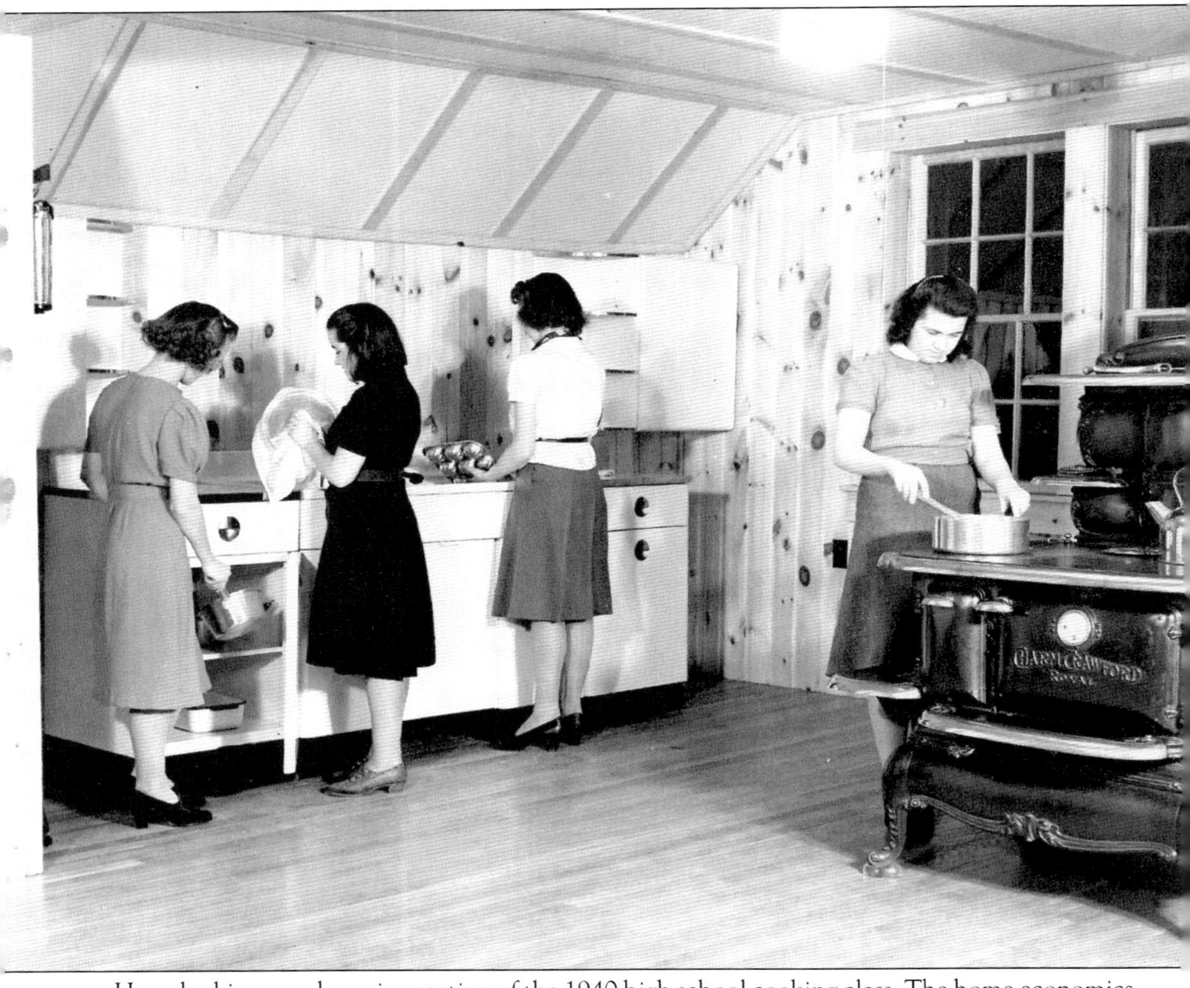

Here, looking very busy, is a section of the 1940 high school cooking class. The home economics rooms were located on the top floor of the Village School in what was formerly attic space. The boys in the agriculture course did the renovations. The students pictured are, from left to right, Phyllis Bose, Dorothy Gagnon, Barbara Saltmarsh, and Bernice Gagnon.

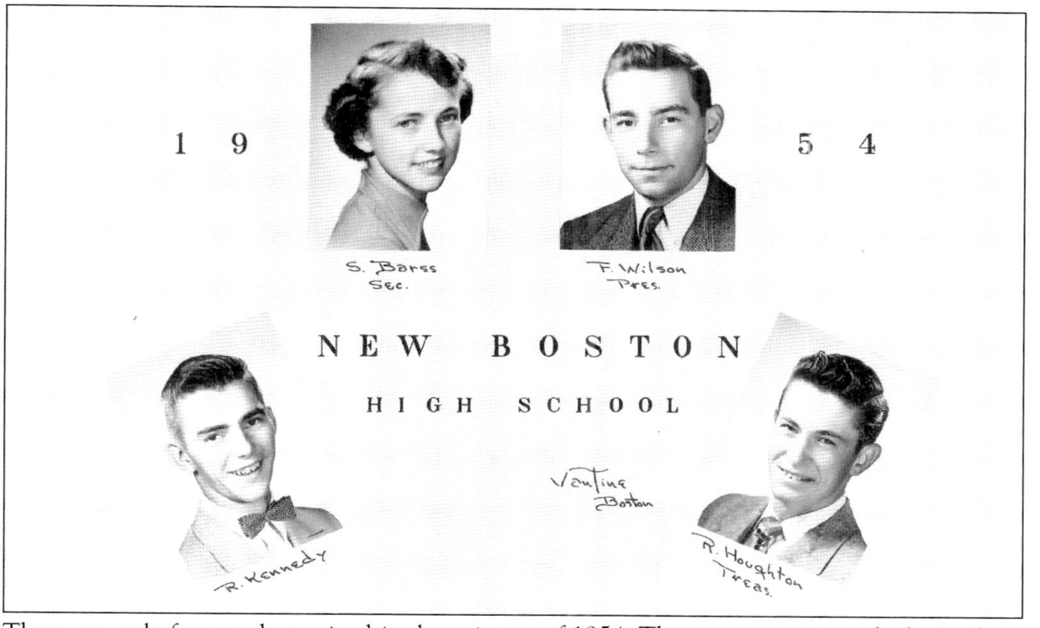

There are only four graduates in this class picture of 1954. They are, appearing clockwise from the lower left, R. Kennedy, S. Barss, F. Wilson, and R. Houghton. Because classes were so small, the high school was able to house six grades in its second-floor classrooms.

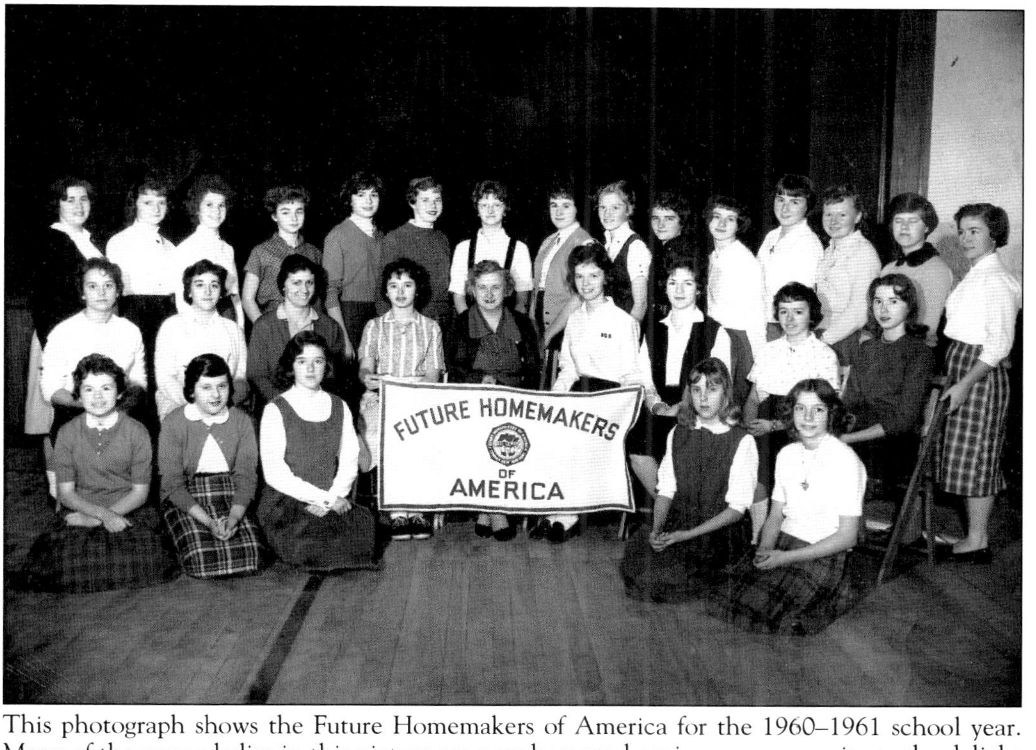

This photograph shows the Future Homemakers of America for the 1960–1961 school year. Many of the young ladies in this picture are now homemakers in our community to the delight of the gentlemen they married.

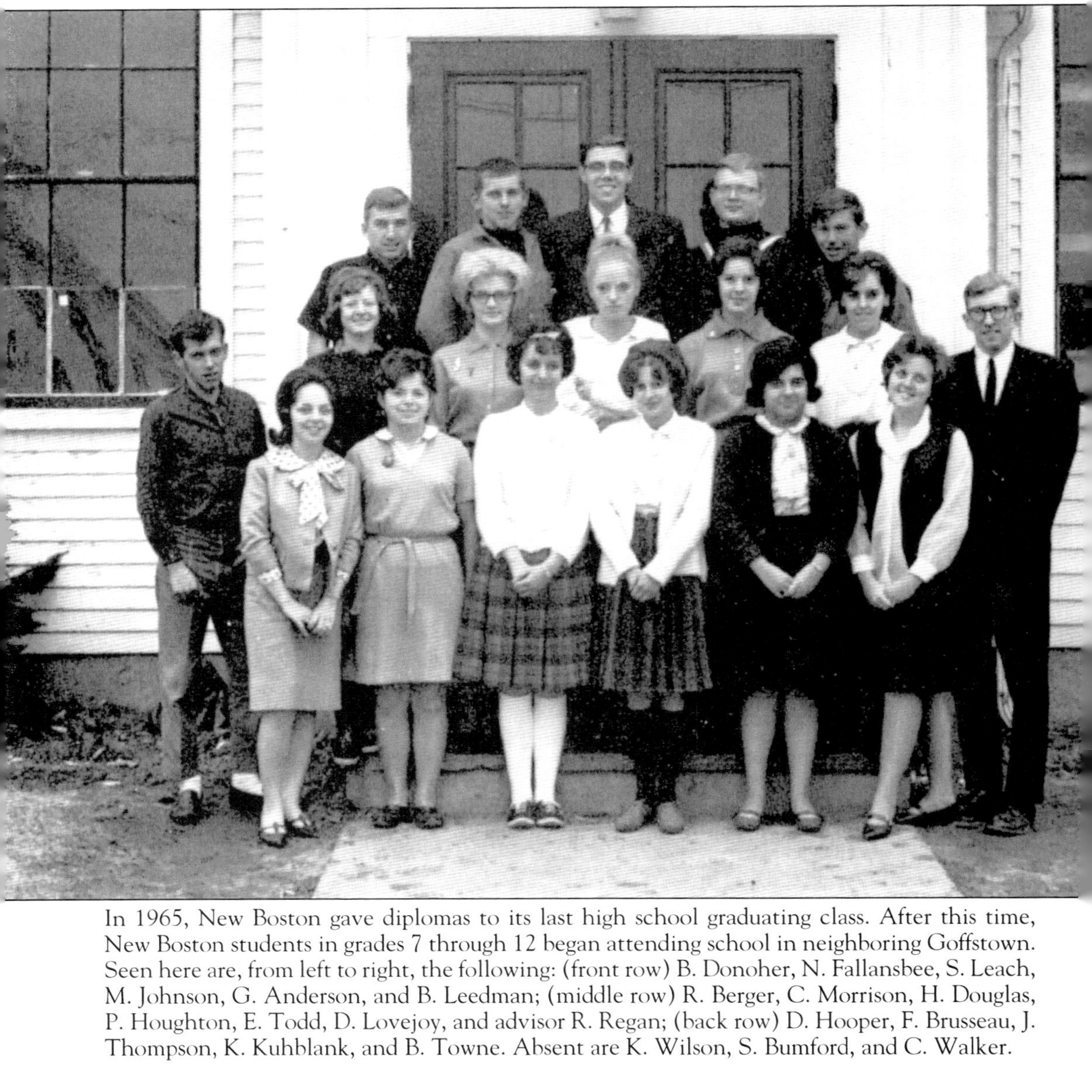

In 1965, New Boston gave diplomas to its last high school graduating class. After this time, New Boston students in grades 7 through 12 began attending school in neighboring Goffstown. Seen here are, from left to right, the following: (front row) B. Donoher, N. Fallansbee, S. Leach, M. Johnson, G. Anderson, and B. Leedman; (middle row) R. Berger, C. Morrison, H. Douglas, P. Houghton, E. Todd, D. Lovejoy, and advisor R. Regan; (back row) D. Hooper, F. Brusseau, J. Thompson, K. Kuhblank, and B. Towne. Absent are K. Wilson, S. Bumford, and C. Walker.

Five

At Work

Look, and see at our feet, New Boston village. . . .
The farm wagons rattle along to mill,
The pedestrians briskly climb the hill,
And the autos whirl up clouds of dust
With a constant air of, "Get there we must";
While along the river's winding way
The iron horse, twice, every day.

—New Boston Old Folk's Day, 1906

The earliest business in New Boston may have been a tavern, but without the Piscataquog River and its "winding way," true industry and perhaps New Boston itself would not have been established so soon before the Revolutionary War. The upper, middle, and lower branches of the Piscataquog were harnessed to truly establish industry in the form of sawmills, gristmills, textile mills, and even a paper mill. And it is no coincidence that perhaps the first store in New Boston, established c. 1755, consisted of a small stock of dry goods stored in a house close to Walker's mill.

The need for the early mills was simple; tables and chairs were generally unavailable until sawmills were able to produce board lumber. In addition to the mills, early industry consisted of tanneries, taverns, and additional dry goods stores that were established away from the upper or lower villages, such as at Todd's Corner. And sometimes industries converged, as when a bark mill supplied a tannery with bark to tan leather, and then the same bark was used by the town for ground cover in order to soften the travel by horse and carriage.

By the time the railroad came whistling in, on June 23, 1893, New Boston was home to factories that produced such items as chairs and knobs, doors, firearms, boxes, axes, piano cases, matches, and toy carriages. Ironically, it was an accidental fire from one of these factories (a barrel head factory) that spread to become the devastating village fire of 1887, burning to the ground nearly 40 buildings. Visitors from far-away cities traveled by rail to New Boston and became country summer boarders in many residents' comfortable and large country homes, such as the Baker house still standing on Baker Lane.

Electric lights on the village streets of New Boston were available before 1895, as an electricity-generating plant was built in the vacant piano case factory building, utilizing the Piscataquog River once again for the betterment of the town. Interestingly, there does not remain much industry in New Boston, despite its long history as a hardworking town that produced so many varied goods.

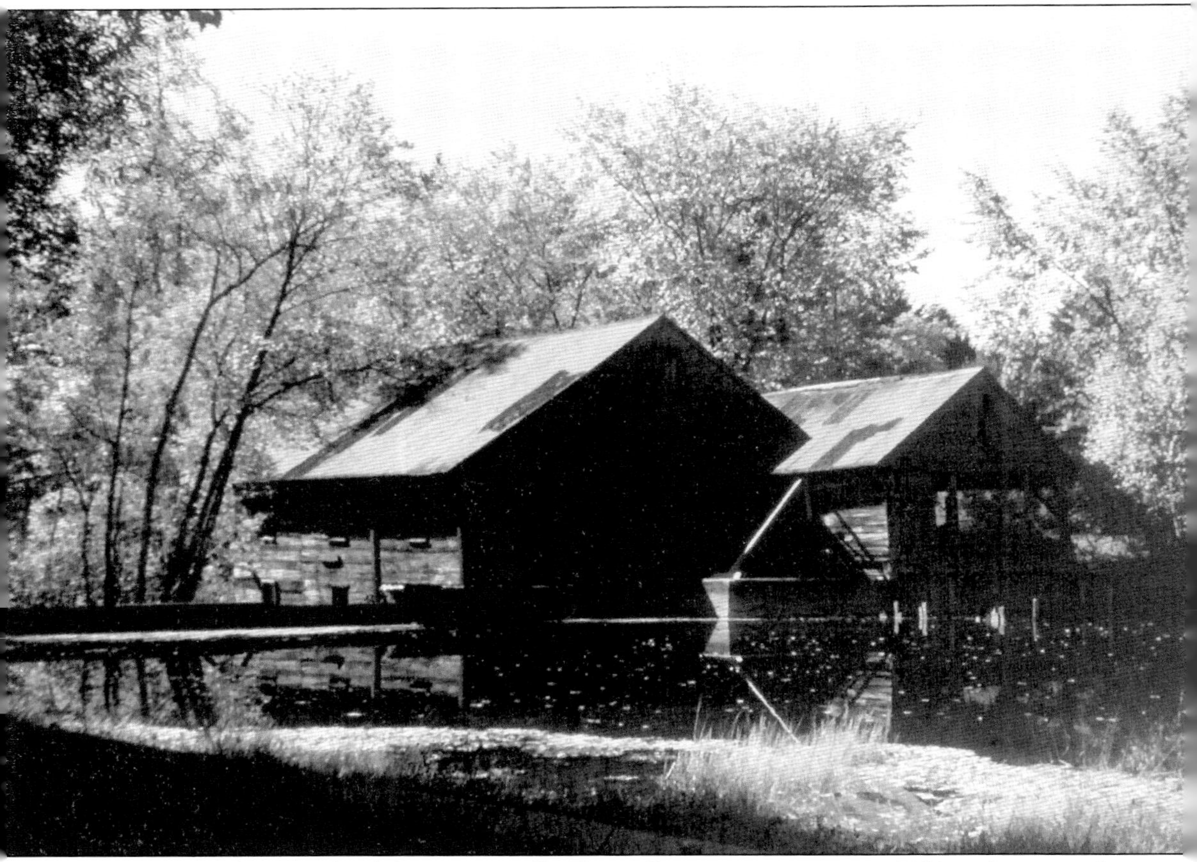

Here is a photograph of the Gregg mill. This mill was in operation in 1872 and remained in the Gregg family until 1893, when Daniel Gregg died and the mill was purchased by B. J. Lang. The Lang family summered in New Boston until 1937, when the farm was sold once again. This picture was taken by Dr. Albert Snay in 1949.

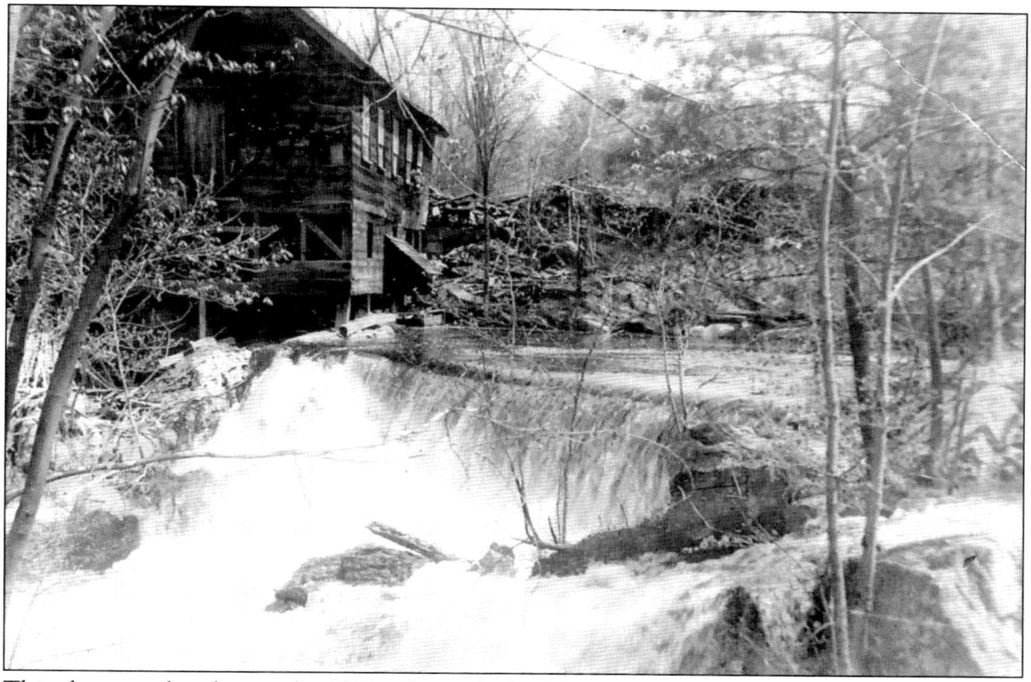

This photograph, taken in the 1930s, shows the building known at the time as the Hadley-Upton mill. According to records, this mill was built in 1751 and was New Boston's second sawmill. The original owner, Andrew Walker, became unpopular with the settlers, as he preferred to sell his goods to outsiders, from whom he could make more profit. This mill continued to saw lumber until c. 1950.

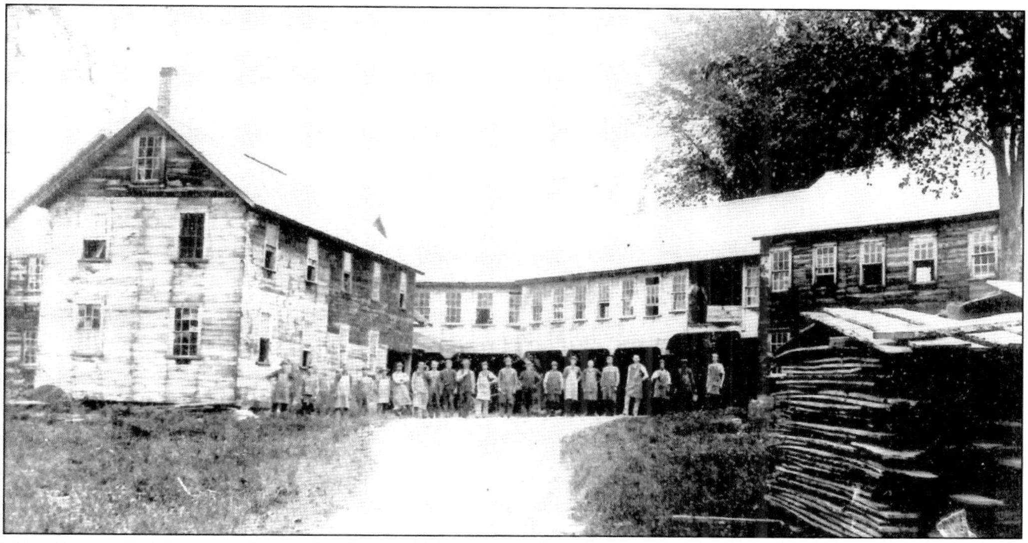

The Butterfield sawmill was built in 1799 along the Piscataquog River just over the line from North Lyndeborough. In this 1891 photograph, then owner David Butterfield can be seen standing by the hoist in the upper window. At some point, Butterfield experienced financial difficulties, and the mill was sold at auction. It had several more owners before it was torn down around the turn of the century.

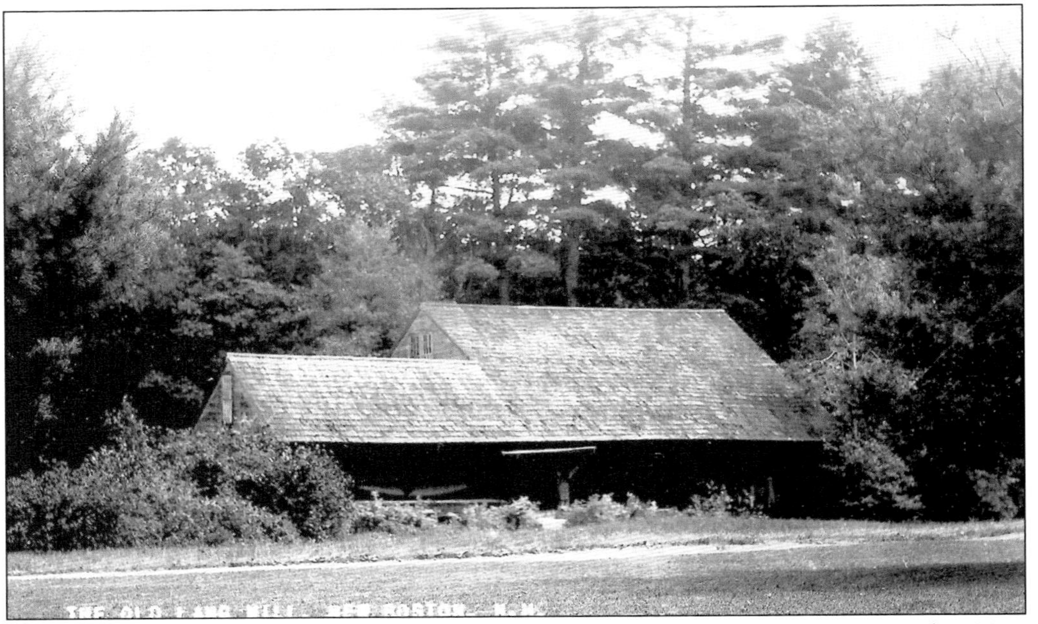

Here is a postcard of the old Lang mill, as it was known then. Waterpower was used in New Boston mills until the mid-1860s, when steam came into use. Millers had to coordinate their operations so that every mill on the river would have enough water to power the wheels.

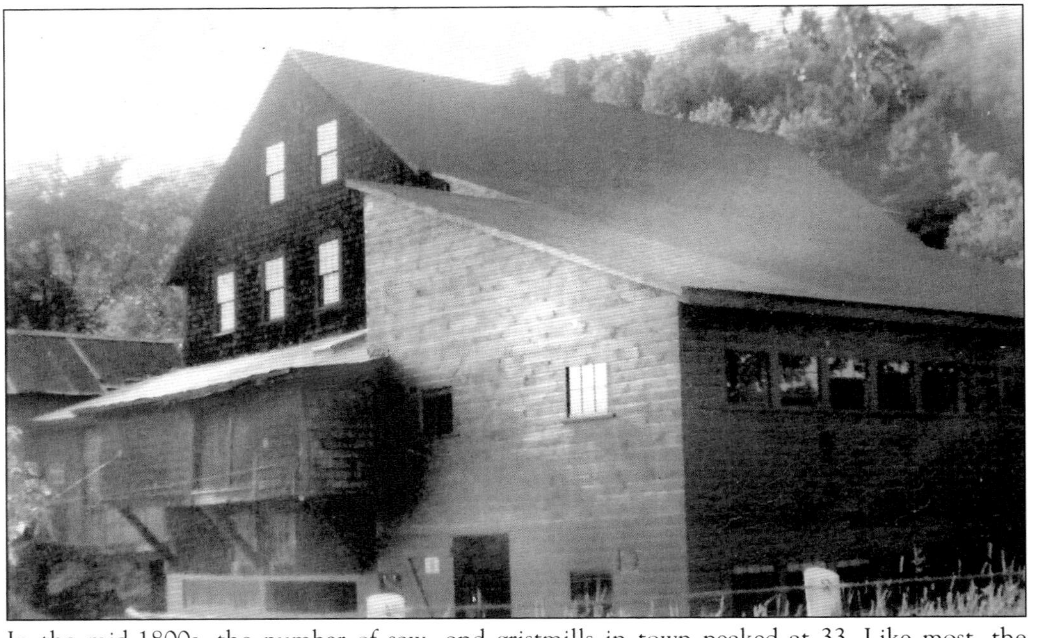

In the mid-1800s, the number of saw- and gristmills in town peaked at 33. Like most, the Sutherland mill had many lives. Originally a sawmill, it later became a box factory operated by Walter Kirsch. Kirsch manufactured here until the early 1950s, and the building was demolished in 1975. Only two mills remain in town in more or less their original state: the Gregg mill and the Hadley mill.

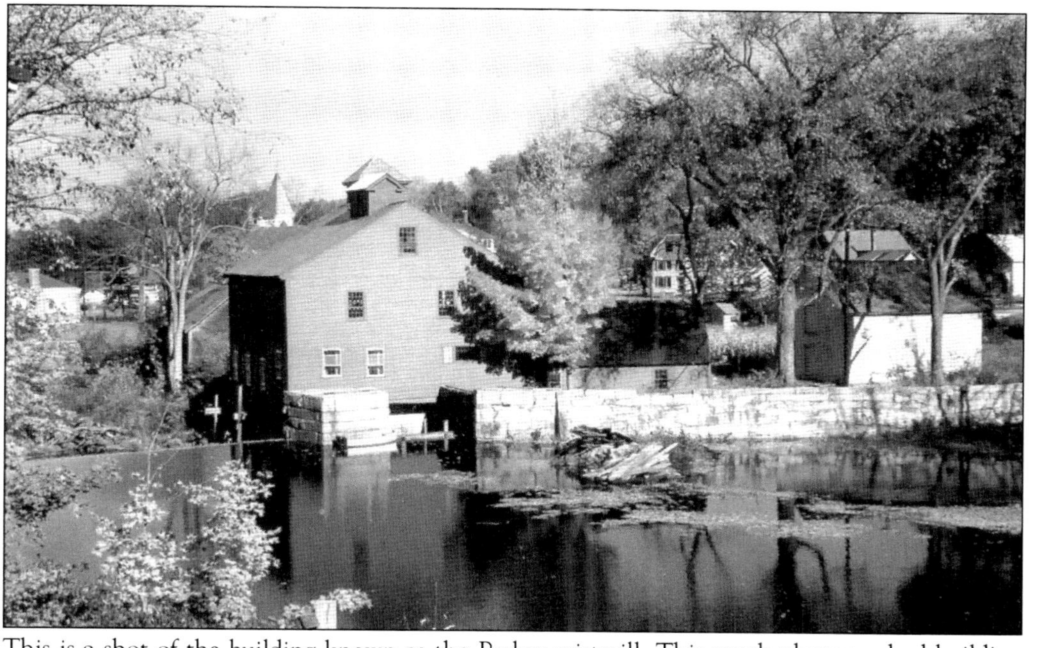

This is a shot of the building known as the Parker gristmill. This much photographed building is currently a private residence. It has appeared on calendars and on the cover of *New Hampshire Seasons* magazine and has even been the subject of a jigsaw picture puzzle. (Courtesy of R. Parker.)

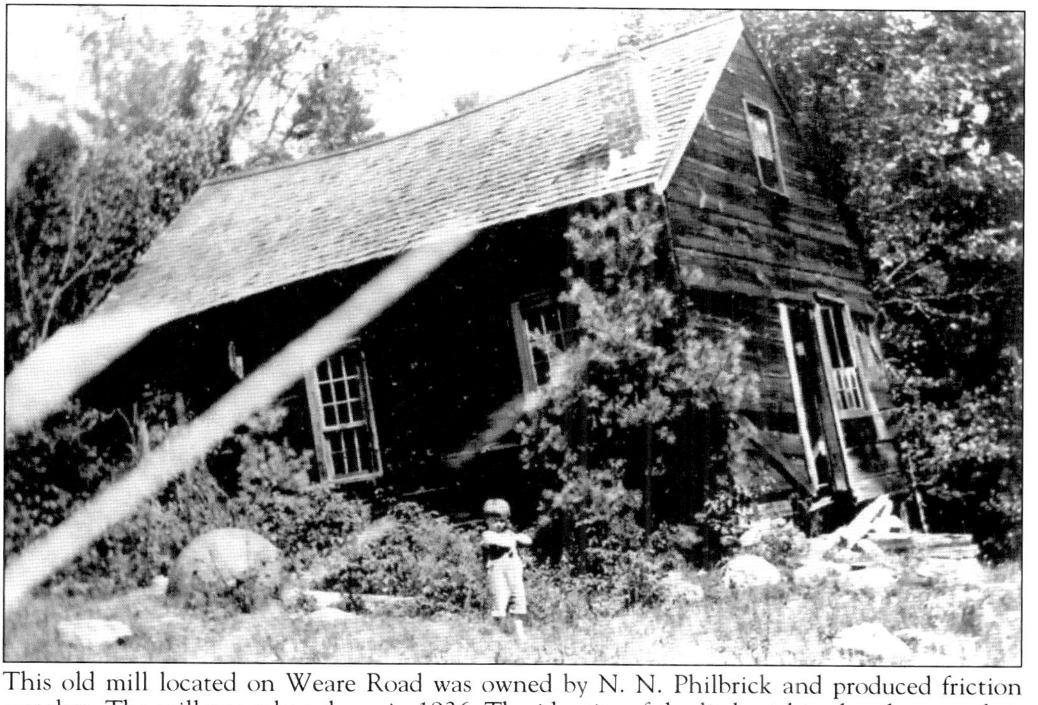

This old mill located on Weare Road was owned by N. N. Philbrick and produced friction matches. The mill was taken down in 1936. The identity of the little girl in the photograph is unknown. (Donated by M. Woodbury.)

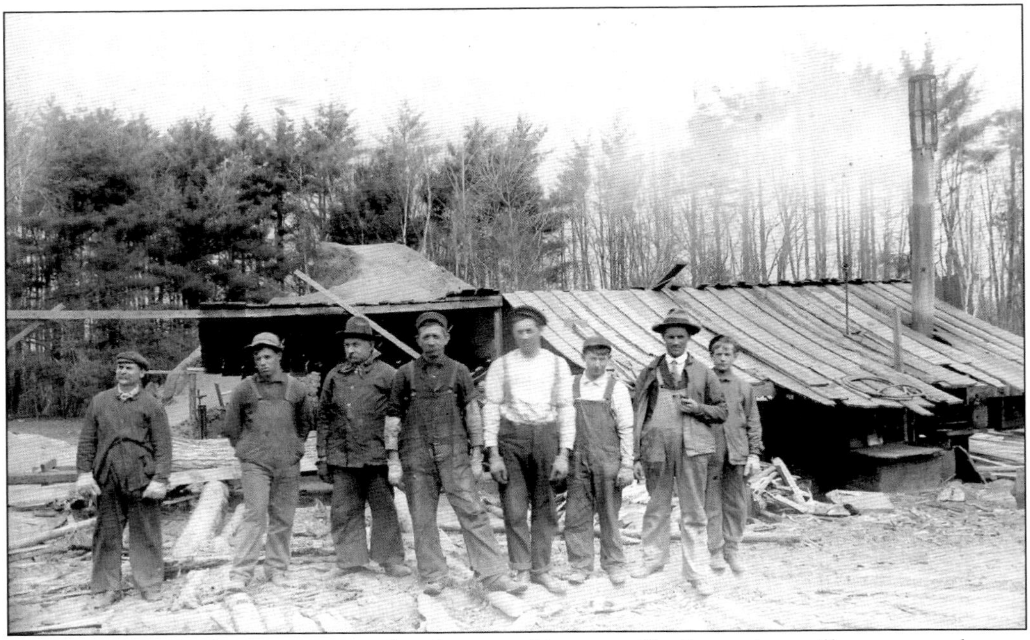

This photograph shows an example of a portable sawmill. Once the mills were no longer dependent on waterpower, it became more economical to move the mill to the lumber than vice versa. This mill was operated by steam, which can be seen pouring from the chimney on the right. Seen here are, from left to right, owner Fred F. Chancey, sawyer Herbert Christy, three unidentified men, Ralph Chancey, an unidentified man, and Lionel Chancey. (Courtesy of F. Chancey.)

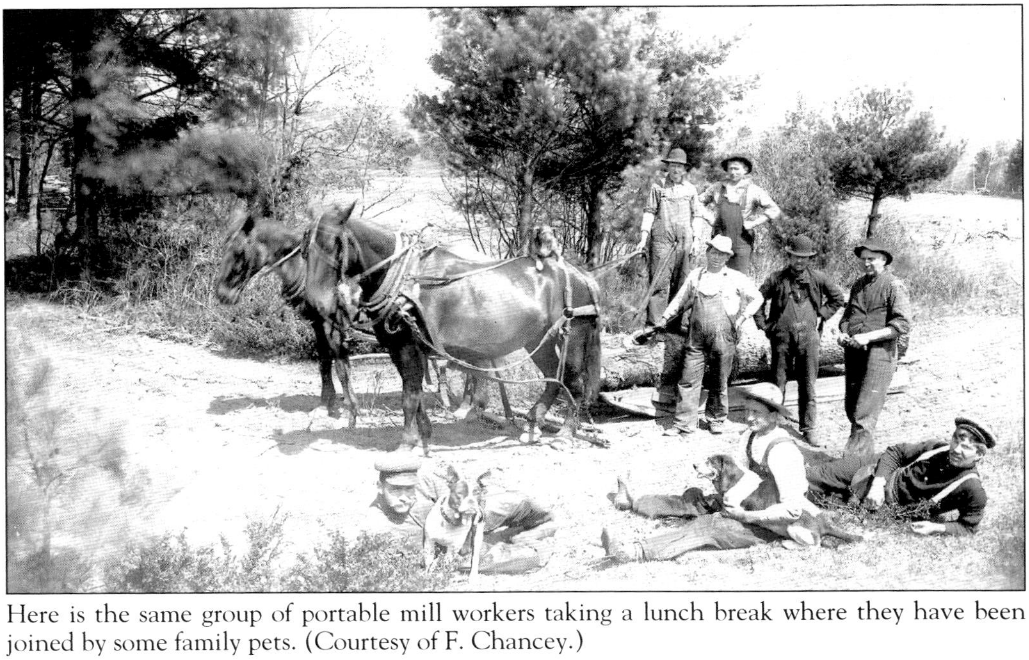

Here is the same group of portable mill workers taking a lunch break where they have been joined by some family pets. (Courtesy of F. Chancey.)

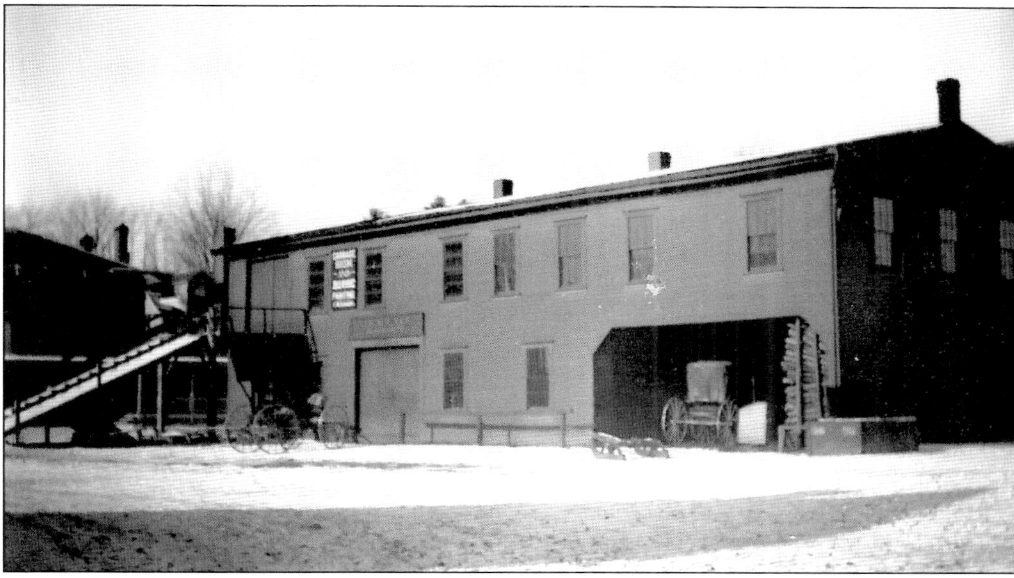

This building had many uses over the years. Originally a blacksmith shop, it contained a carriage paint shop on the second floor. The carriages were transported to the facility via the ramp, which can be seen on the left. In the 1940s, this building was converted to a necktie factory. The photograph below shows a display of the goods made there. At the rear of this building was the site of Wason's cooper shop, which sparked the great fire of 1887 that wiped out most of New Boston's center.

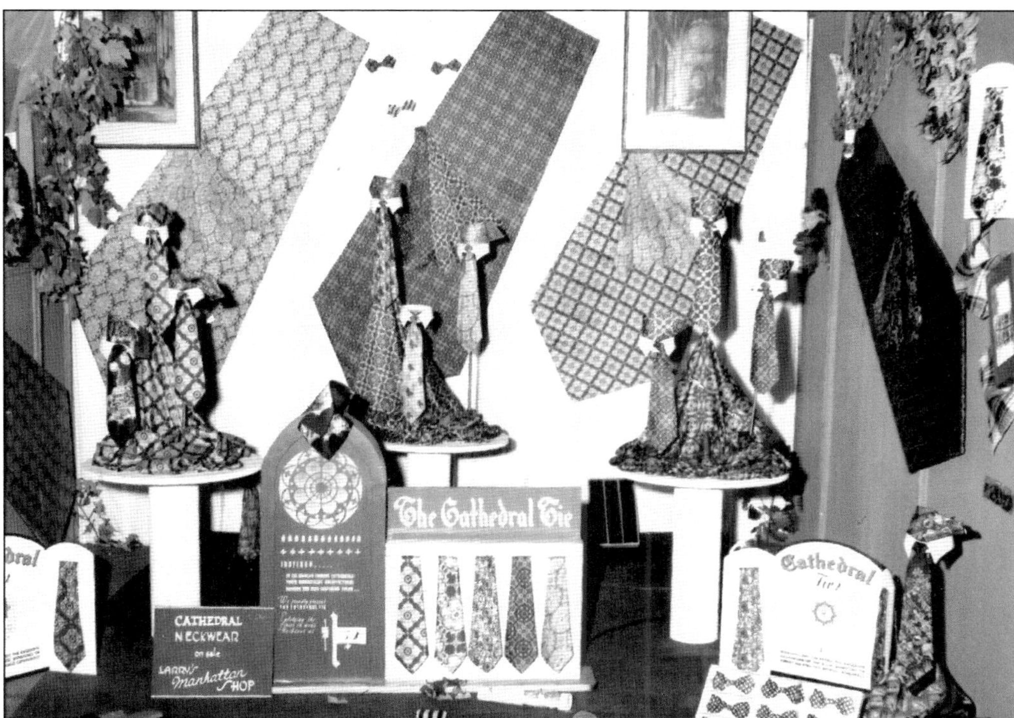

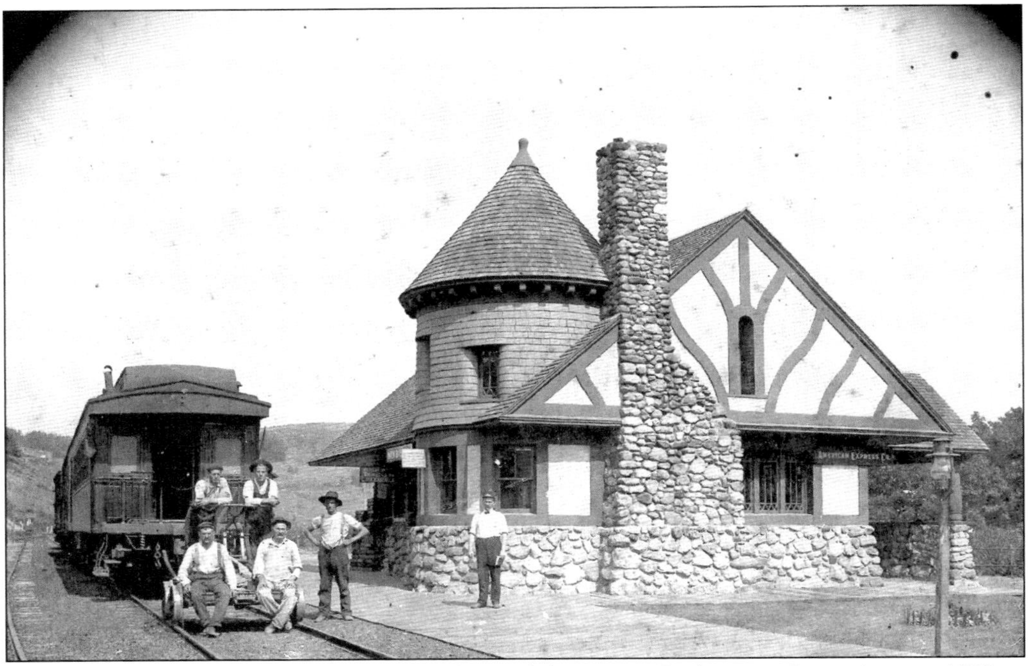

Here are some railroad workers resting in front of the Depot. Rail service began here in 1893 to much rejoicing by the townsfolk. Service was available between Parker's Station and the Depot in New Boston center, with one stop about halfway at Gregg's mill. Passenger service ended in 1931.

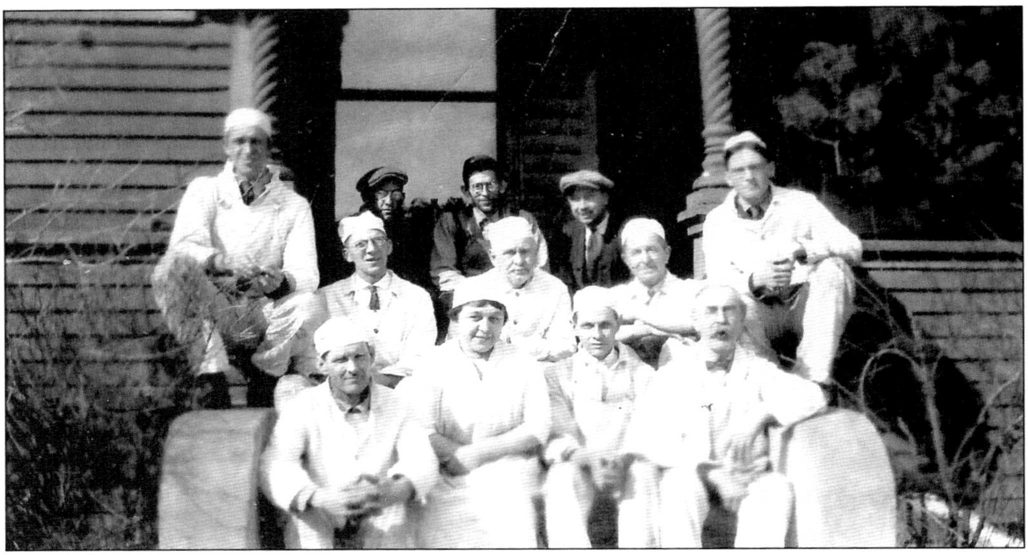

The creamery produced dairy products for local sale as well as for the Boston hotel market. In this 1924 photograph, creamery workers pose on the front steps of the building. They are, from left to right, as follows: (front row) Atwood Demary, Ruby Odekirk, Sherman Woodbury, and Bert Ball; (middle row) Brainard Newton, John Bond, and Dexter Green; (back row) unidentified, Charlie Brown, George Sheldon, Albert Kane, and Guy Bailey. (Donated by M. Woodbury.)

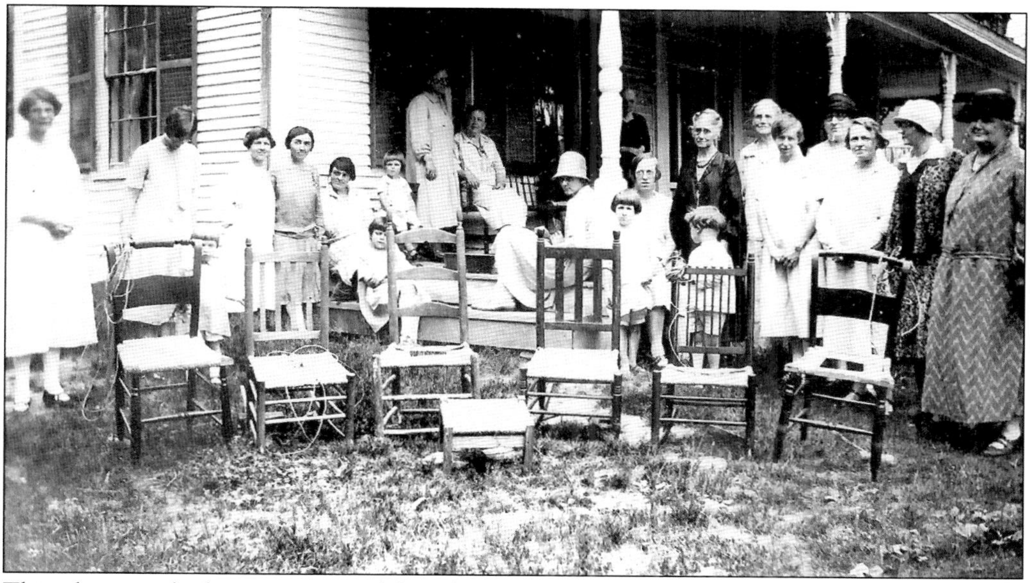

This photograph shows a group of farm bureau ladies caning chairs. Among them are Belle Wason, Gladys Mansfield, Joyce Michaud, Hattie Sheldon, Mrs. Grant, Hazel Wilson, Augusta Bartlett, Blanche Proctor, and Helen Dotey. (Donated by E. Gagnon.)

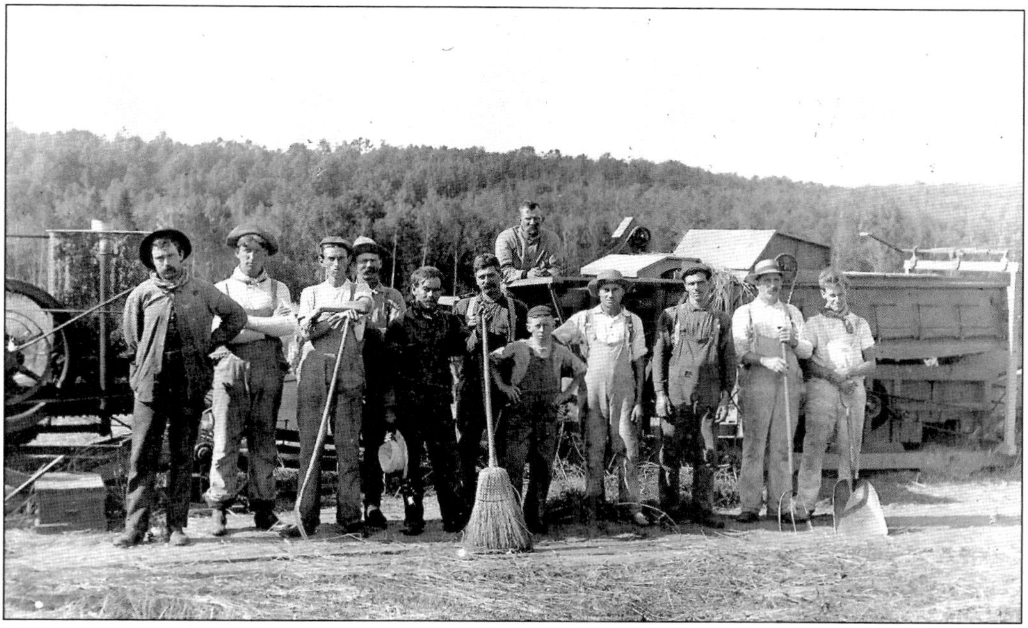

Here is a group of hardworking municipal workers. They are, from left to right, James Igo, Vince Igo, Jake Varney, Frank Hanson, Fred Hanson, Frank Rogers, Jah Jarfer, Feng Newill, George Johnson, Charlie Barr, Ashal Stearn, and Fred Watson.

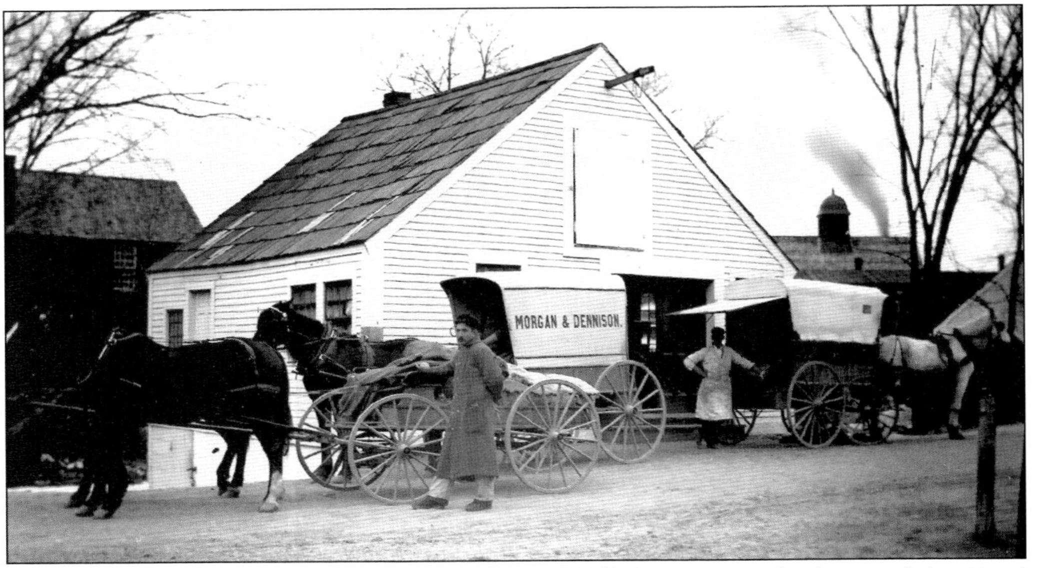

Here is Morgan and Dennison's Meat Market on Mill Street, now the home of the Good Neighbor Café. The structure that housed the meat market is on the banks of the Piscataquog River and has experienced much flooding over the years.

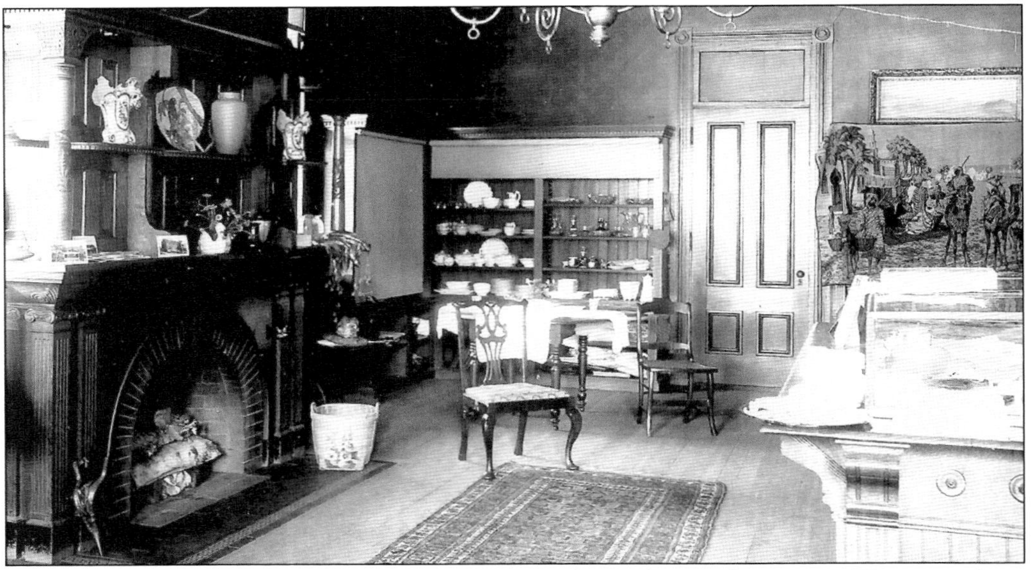

This postcard shows the interior of a gift shop once located in Dodge's Store. This space later became New Boston's post office and, subsequently, a private business.

A typical New England enterprise is the making of maple syrup. Here are both exterior and interior shots of Peirce Syrup House on River Road. Outside are Leslie Byam, Maurice Briere, and George Peirce. Inside are Maurice Briere, Grace and George Peirce, and two customers. (Courtesy of C. Davis.)

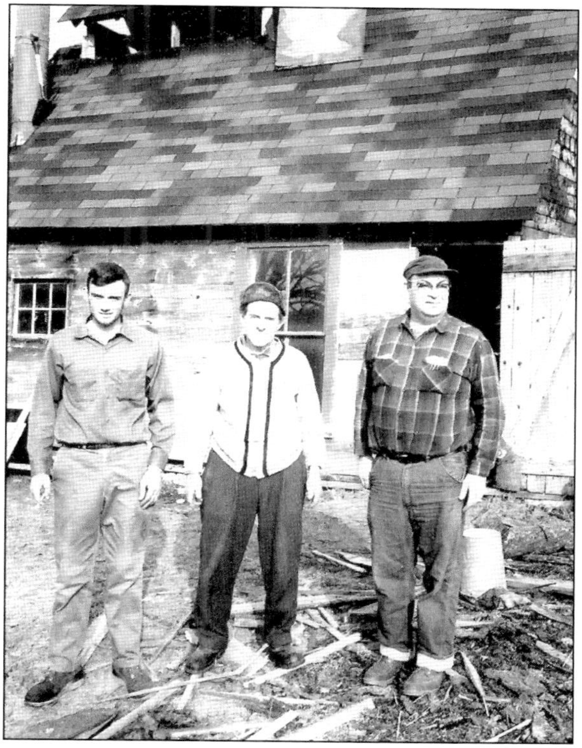

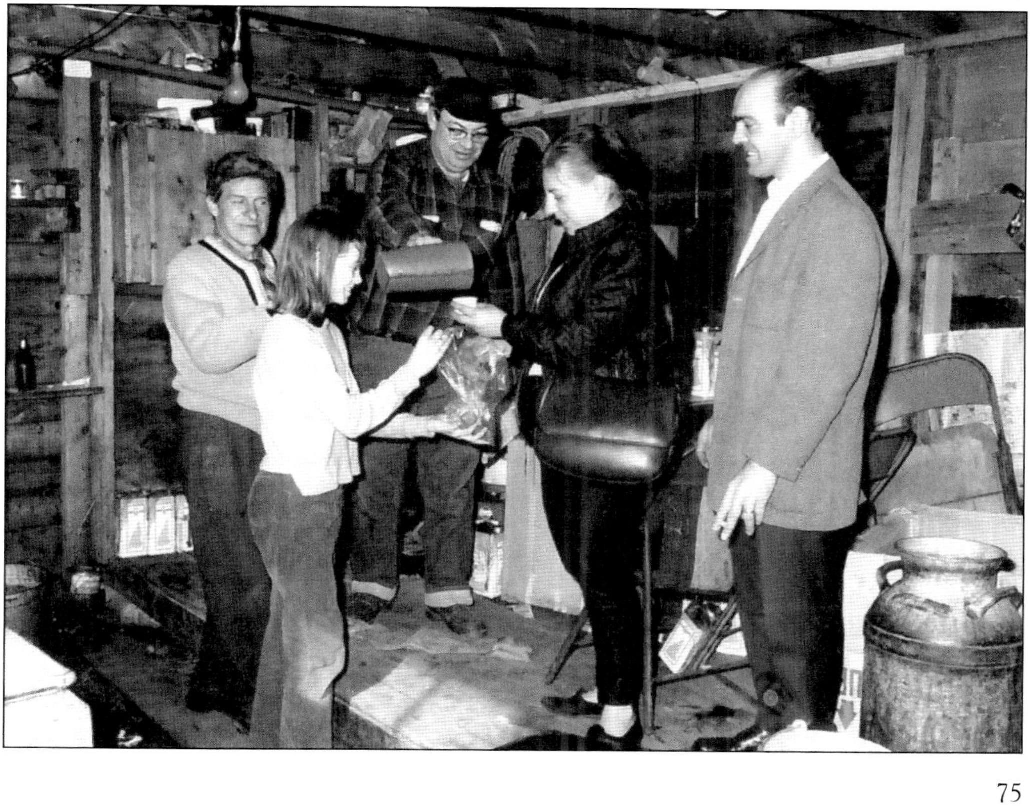

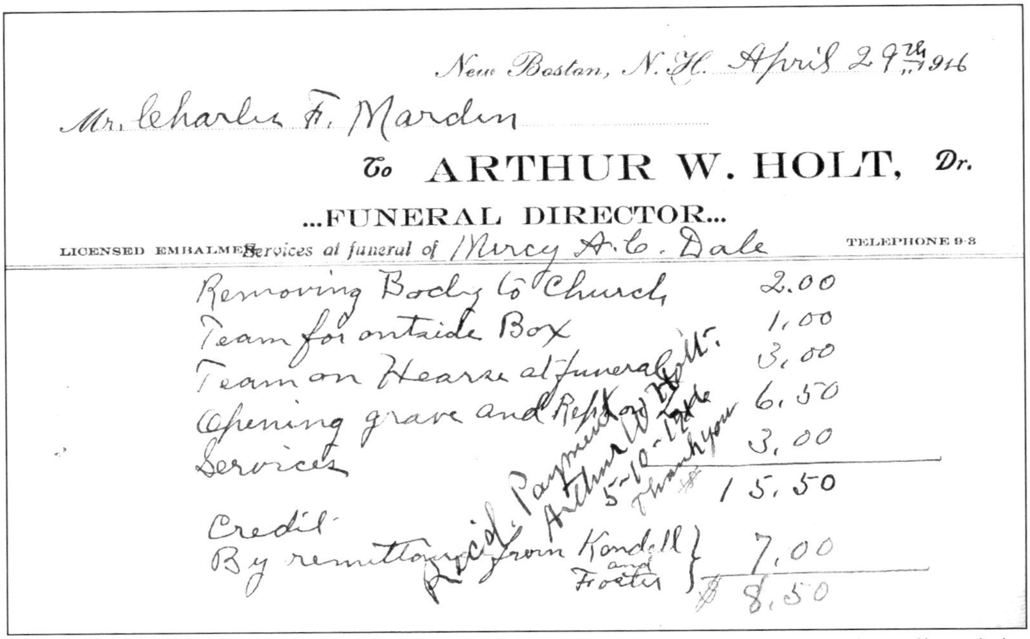

New Boston, N. H. April 29th 1916

Mr. Charles F. Marden

To ARTHUR W. HOLT, Dr.

...FUNERAL DIRECTOR...

LICENSED EMBALMER Services at funeral of Mercy A. C. Dale TELEPHONE 9-3

Removing Body to Church	2.00
Team for outside Box	1.00
Team on Hearse at funeral	3.00
Opening grave and Refit	6.50
Services	3.00
	15.50
Credit By remittance from Kendall and Foster	7.00
	$ 8.50

Rec'd. Payment Arthur W. Holt 5-10-1916 Thank you

This bill from New Boston funeral director Arthur Holt shows how inflation has affected the burial business. In 1916, the total for services rendered equaled $15.50.

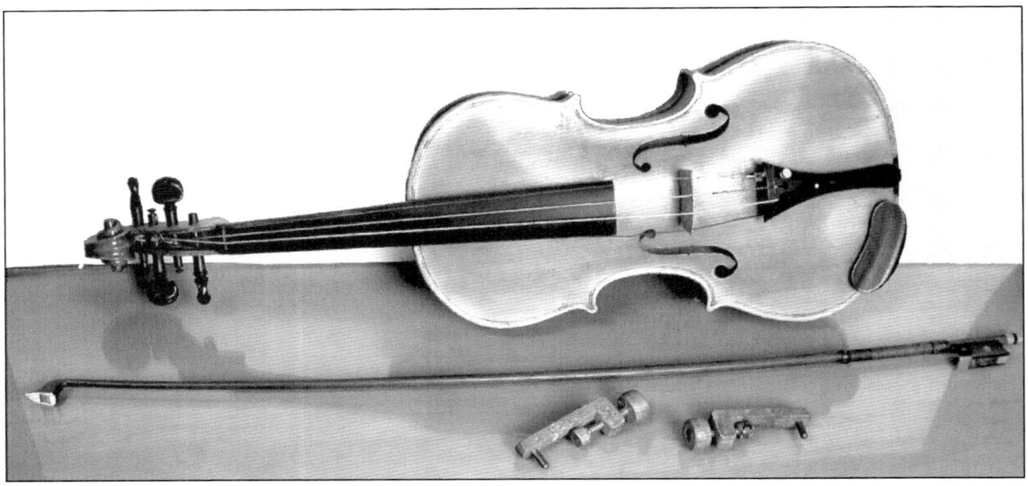

Charles Farley was a maker of violins and violas here in New Boston in the 19th century. Here is a photograph of violin No. 13, manufactured in 1885. Farley also made violin mutes and dealt in violin strings and trimmings as well. (Photograph by J. Hansen.)

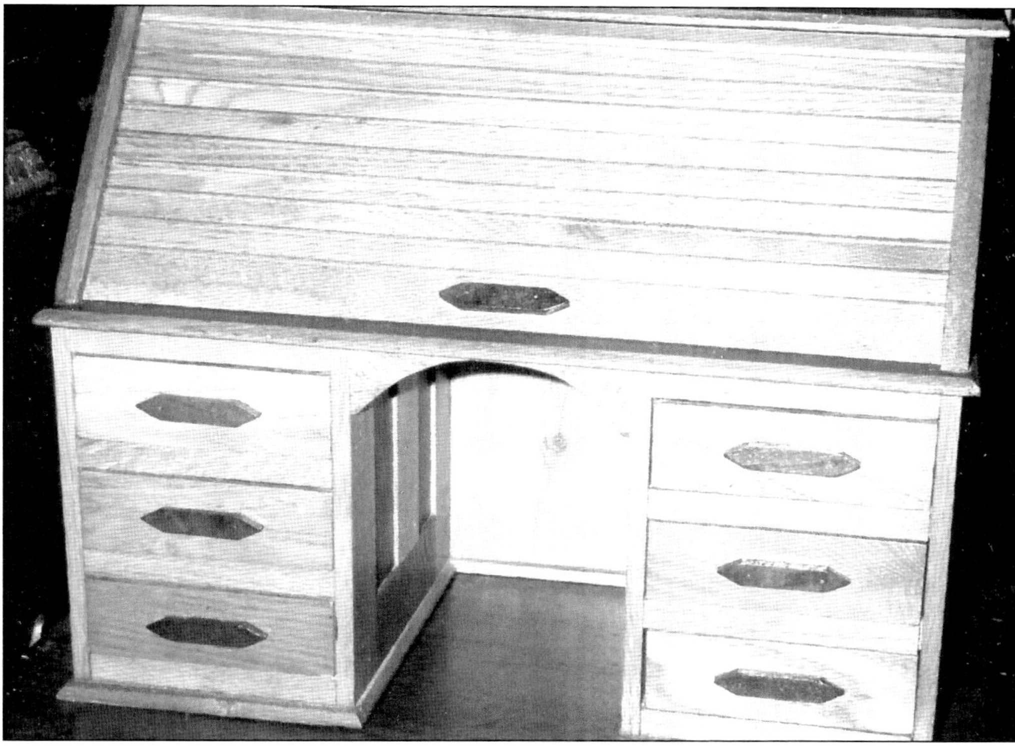

Here is a sample rolltop desk made by W. J. "Willie" Heath at his workshop in New Boston. Heath was a maker of medicine cabinets, rolltop cabinets, clothes bars, and desks. Heath made large desks to order but, during the winter, fashioned smaller sample desks, which he would peddle around town on his bicycle come spring. Between 1897 and 1907, a customer could purchase one of these toy-sized desks, complete with manufacturer's label, for $1.

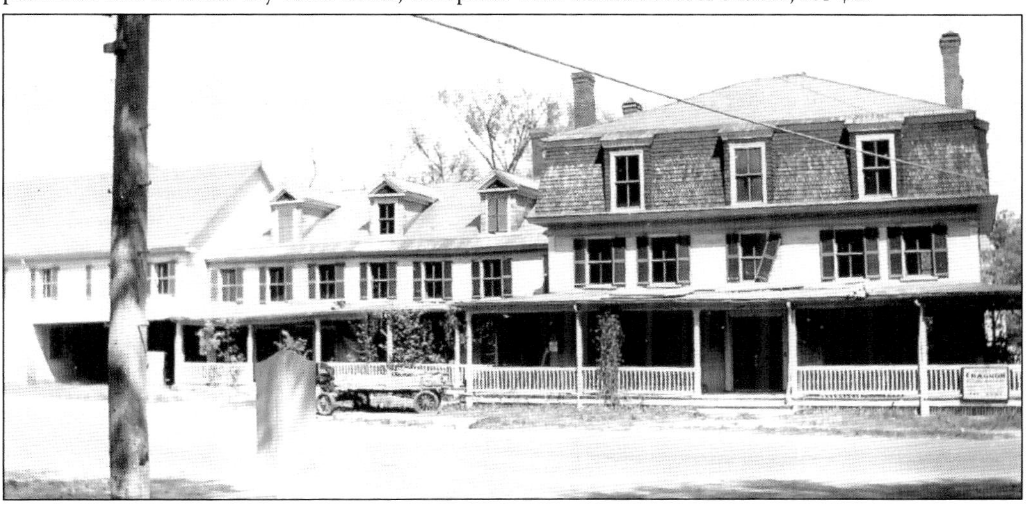

This photograph shows the famous Tavern as it looked shortly before its demolition in the 1940s. The Tavern had many rules that guests had to follow. One such rule was that no spitting was allowed on stoves, beds, furniture, or carpets. At one point in the Tavern's history, a guest could vacation for $14 a week. (Courtesy of C. Davis.)

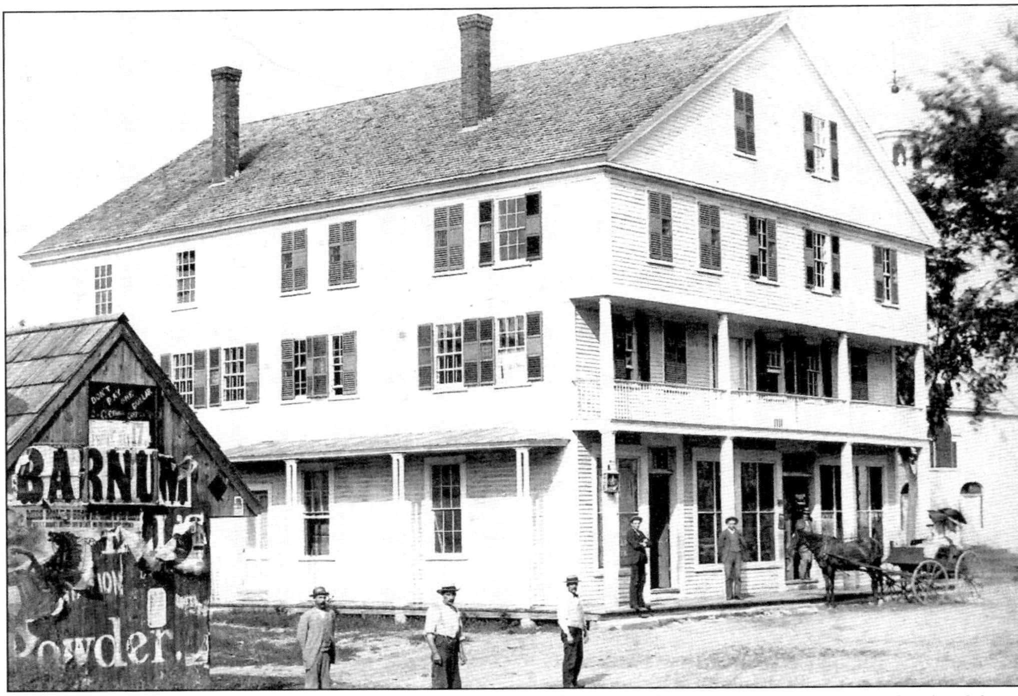

Here is an August 1885 photograph of New Boston's general store. This is one of the buildings that were destroyed by fire in 1887. Storekeeper Solomon Atwood raised this structure to three stories before moving his goods from a nearby store into the newly created space. Clarence Dodge also kept a store here for many years.

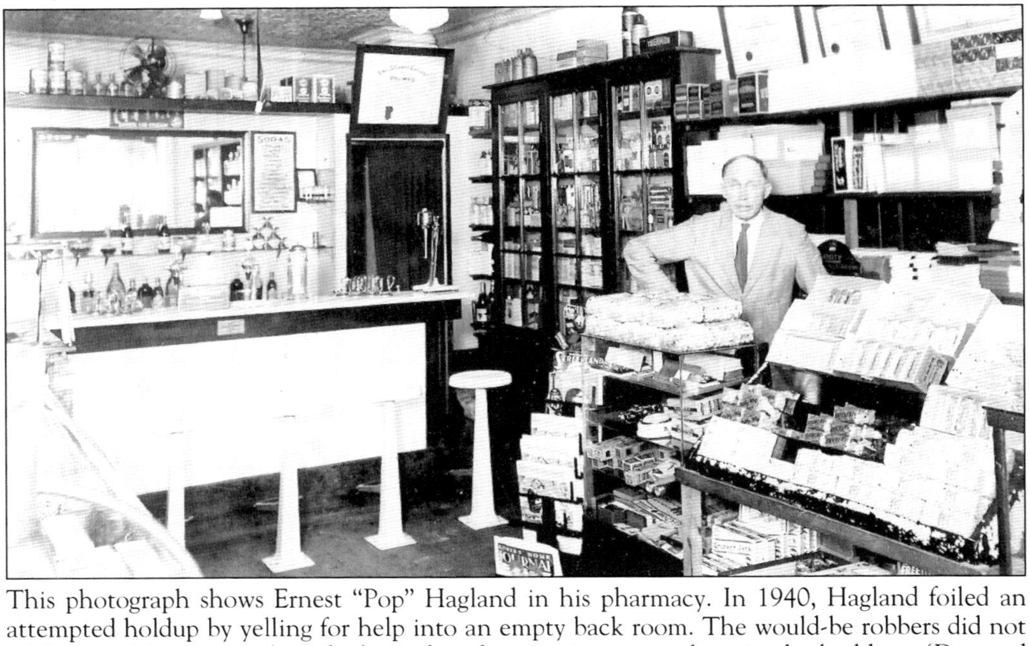

This photograph shows Ernest "Pop" Hagland in his pharmacy. In 1940, Hagland foiled an attempted holdup by yelling for help into an empty back room. The would-be robbers did not stick around long enough to find out that the proprietor was alone in the building. (Donated by S. French.)

Pictured here is a bottle of cider vinegar from the Saltmarsh cider mill. Paul Saltmarsh, the inventor of apple syrup, produced cider from 1944 until 1975 in the mill originally built by J. R. Whipple. Whipple never sold his cider to the public. Instead, it was used in his Boston hotels as sweet cider and cider vinegar. (Photograph by J. Hansen.)

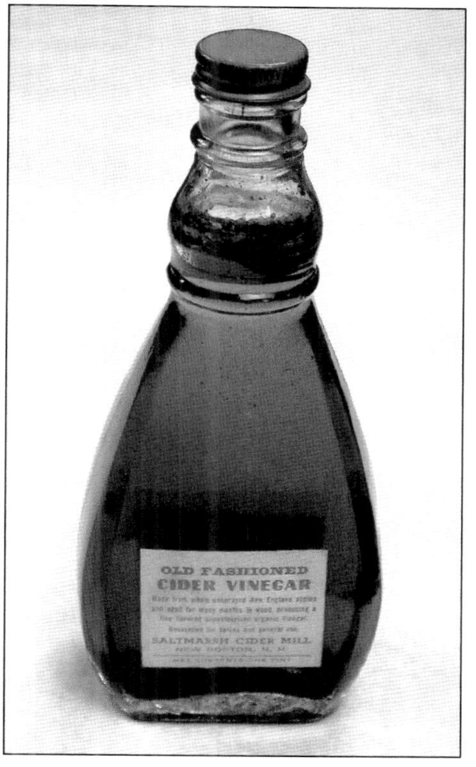

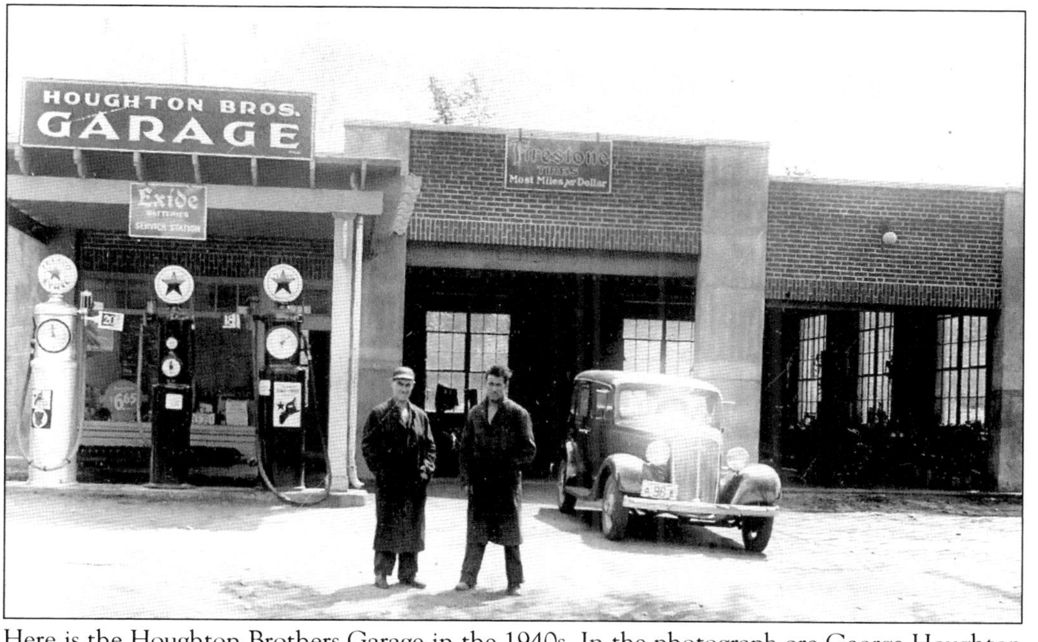

Here is the Houghton Brothers Garage in the 1940s. In the photograph are George Houghton (in the cap) and Les Tower. (Donated by L. Rollins.)

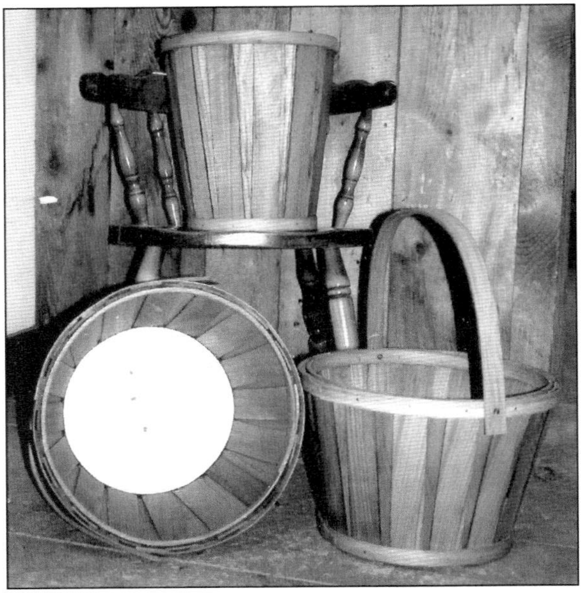

Although big industry is virtually nonexistent in New Boston today, a number of cottage industries still exist. One is the Butternut Basket Works, founded in 1990. Tom Speck's handmade baskets are crafted from slats cut from the butternut tree, then rubbed with linseed oil to enhance the wood's grain. According to the craftsman, customers have trouble choosing between one basket and another due to each one's interesting wood grain pattern. (Courtesy of M. Sipe.)

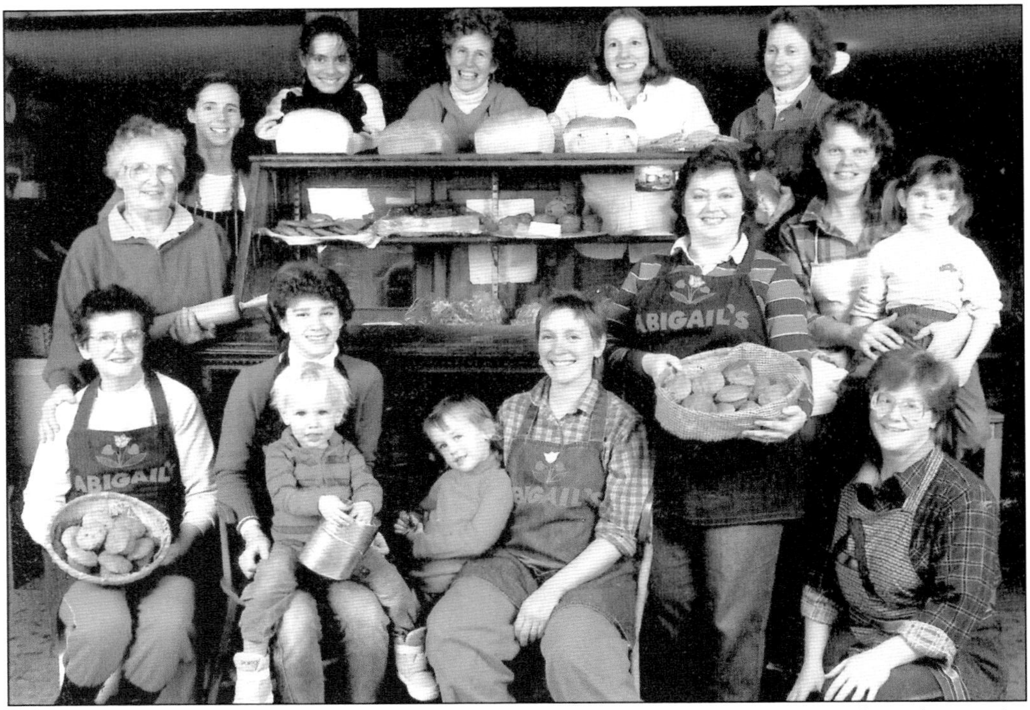

This photograph shows a variety of mouth-watering goodies made by Abigail's Bakery. The workers are, from left to right, as follows: (front row) Josephine Cummings, Jennifer Olson holding Benjamin Ballard, Cyndie Ballard holding Anna, Donna Magarian (standing), owner Debbie Gilligan (standing) holding Erin, and Cheryl Smith; (back row) Doris Byrer, Linda Granger, Daisy Foote, Candy Woodbury, Diane Olson, and Jean Cummings. Smith once lost her diamond engagement ring while kneading bread. It is not known whether the ring turned up on the dinner table of some lucky New Boston resident.

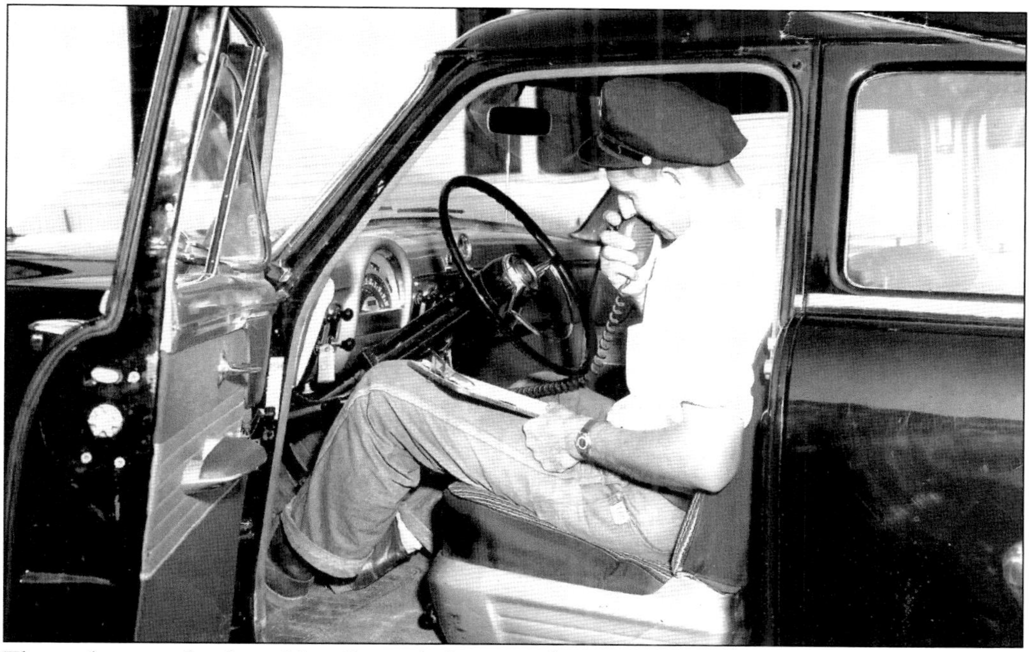

These photographs show New Boston's finest in the 1950s. Above is Charlie Davis, the first person in town to hold the title of chief of police. Below is the force as it was in 1957. Members are, from left to right, George St. John, Ray Pelchat, Chief Charlie Davis, Robert Barss, and Robert Bose. Although these men were not responsible for collecting taxes and dealing with tramps and stray dogs, as were their early predecessors, they did have to use their own vehicles, as the first police cruiser was not purchased until 1974.

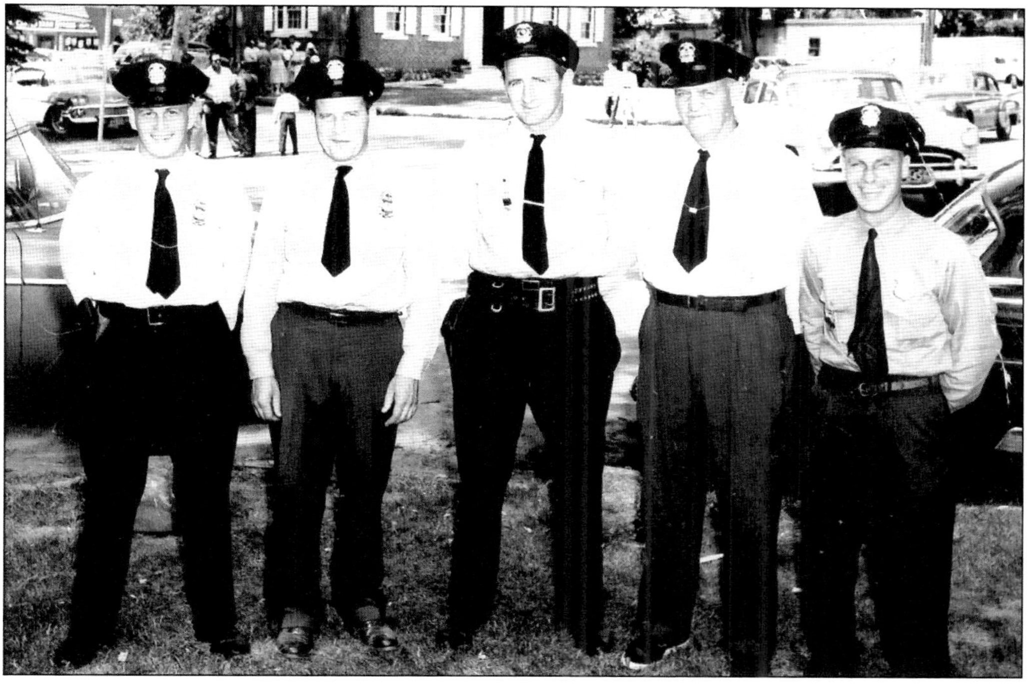

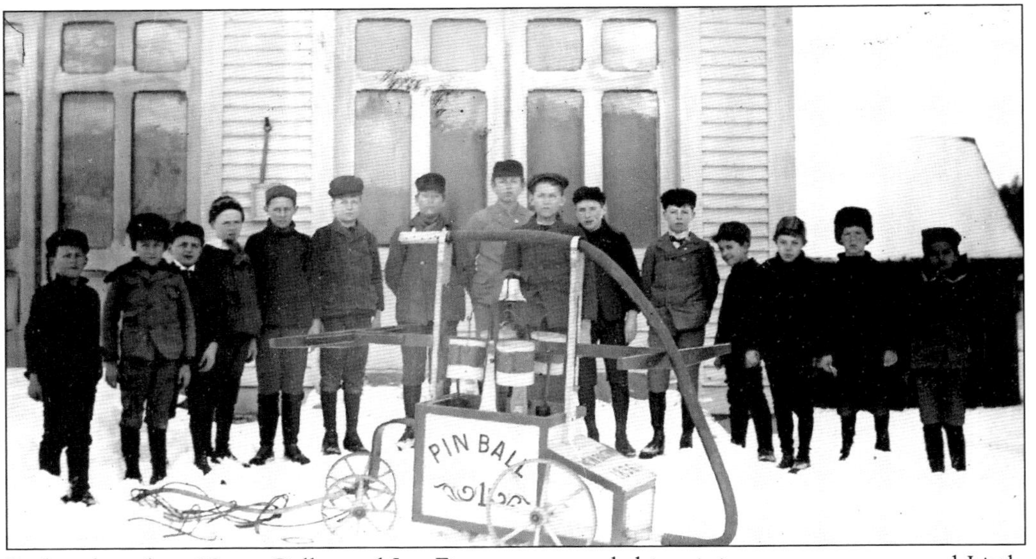

Railroad workers Harry Colby and Joe Fitts constructed this miniature pumper, named Little Pinball, for New Boston's junior firefighters. The device could pump quite a strong stream of water, and at a muster in 1899, it pumped a distance of 81 feet. Here, the youth group poses in front of New Boston's old fire station, now the home of the New Boston Historical Society.

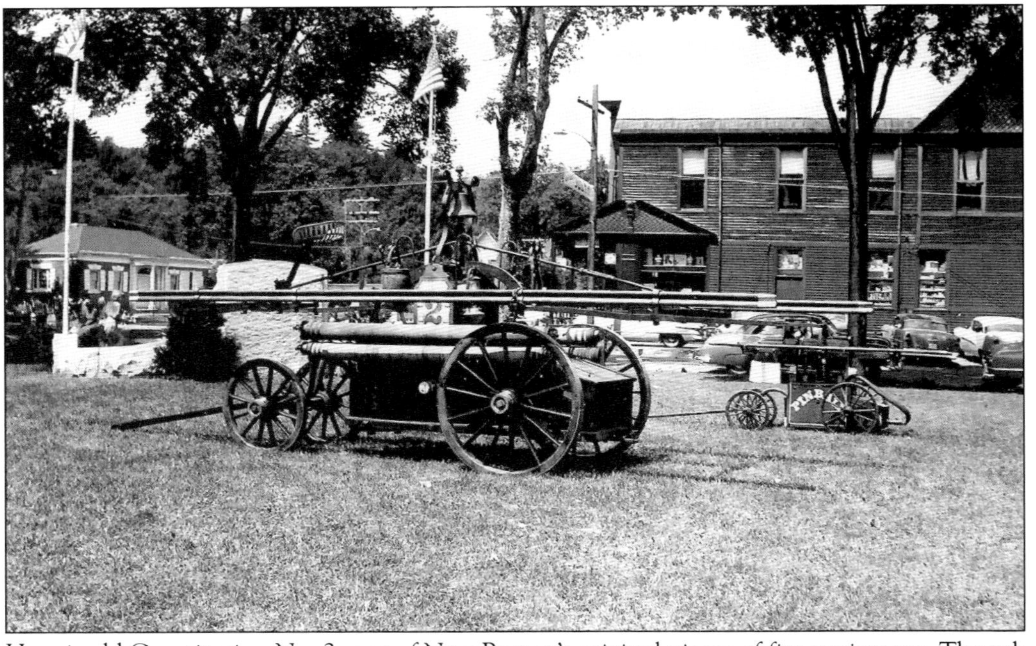

Here is old Constitution No. 2, one of New Boston's original pieces of fire equipment. The tub was made in Boston in 1851 and purchased in 1872 from Salem, Massachusetts, when Salem's fire company bought its first steam engine. It took 50 men to pump a stream of water 219 feet through 150 feet of hose. Old Constitution still participates in New Boston special events such as the Fourth of July parade.

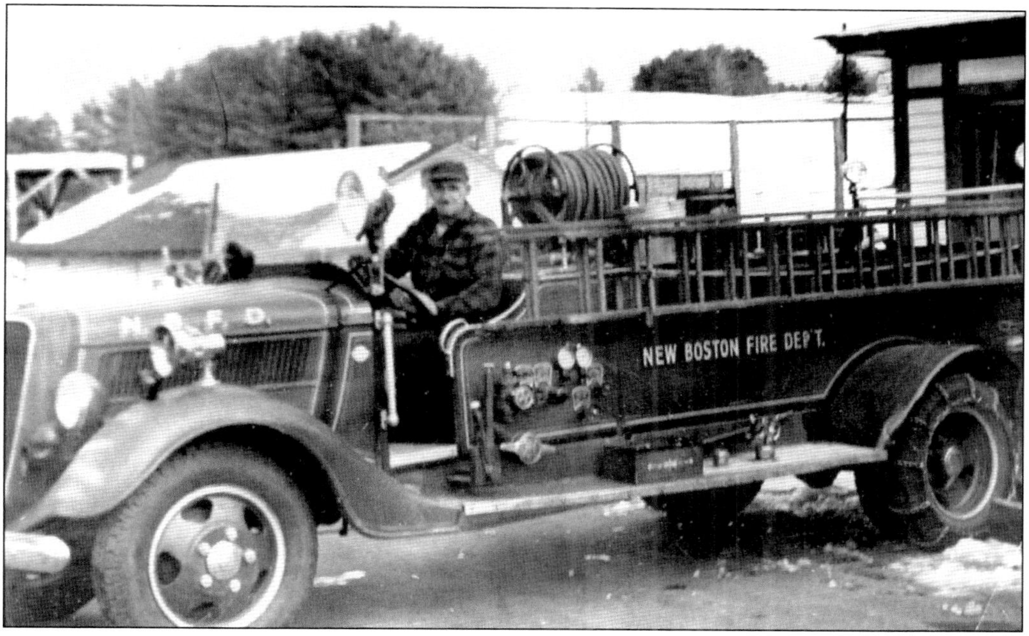

Here is Fire Chief Les Tower in one of New Boston's fire trucks. This 1937 Howe pumper was used by the department until a new one was purchased in 1964. New Boston's fire department consists mostly of volunteers. In the 1840s, firefighters here were exempt from militia duty and were paid an annual salary of between $30 and $36. (Donated by L. Rollins.)

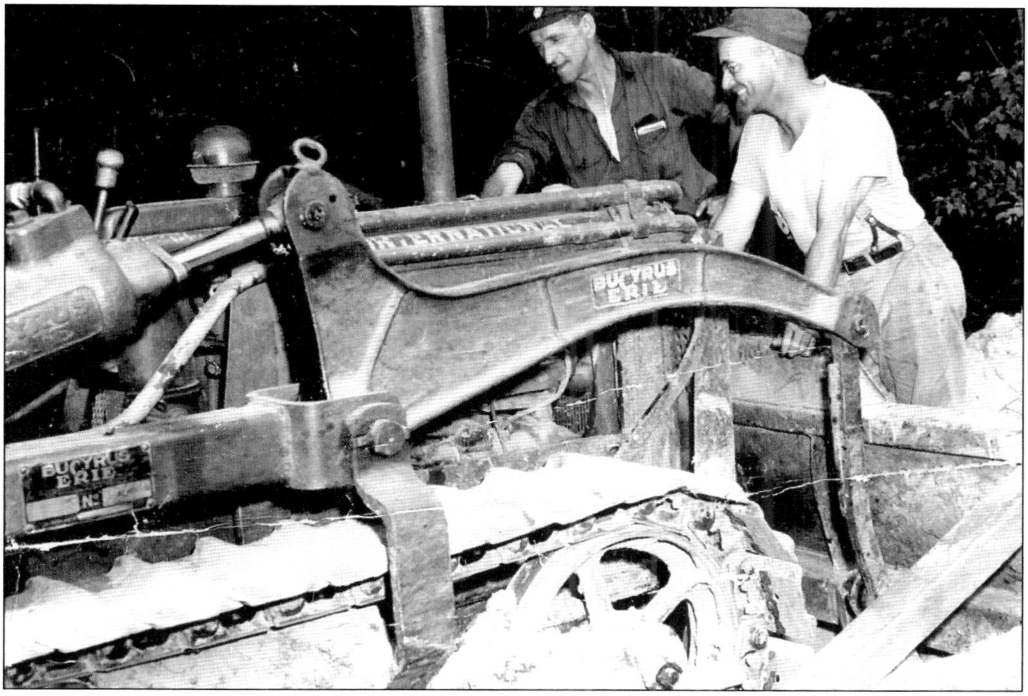

Here is a pair of hardworking men with Walt Kirsch's bulldozer. The men are Les Tower and Paul Barss (in the white shirt). (Donated by L. Rollins.)

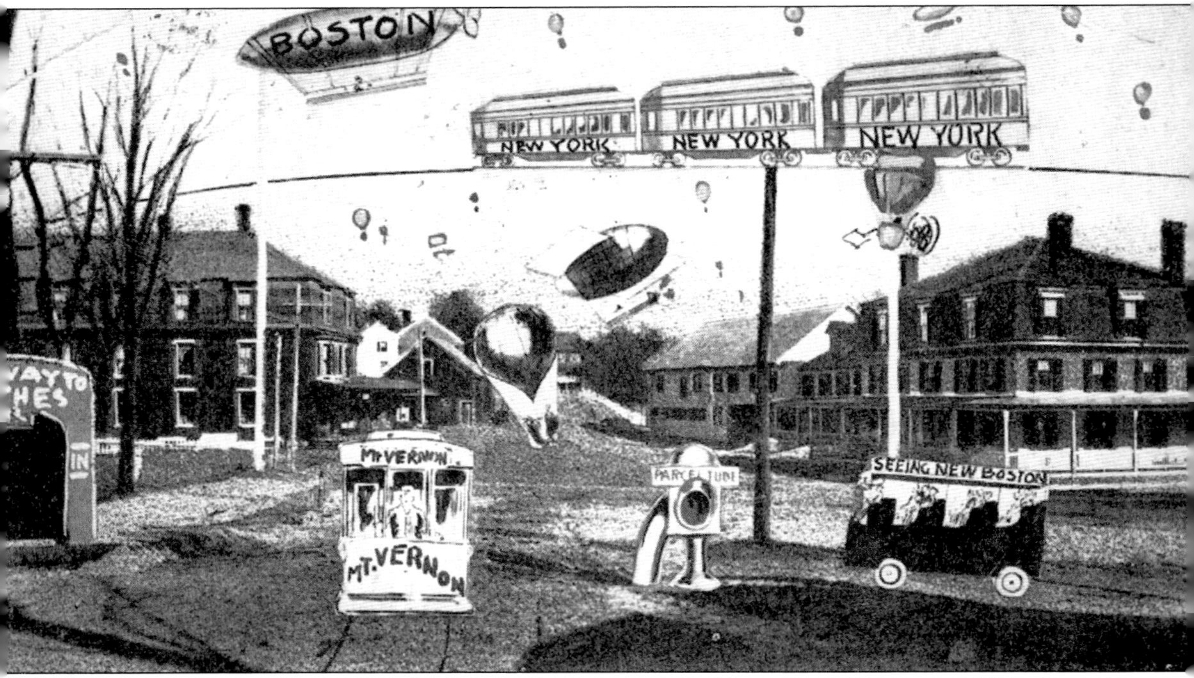

Here is an early postcard showing someone's vision of how New Boston would look in the future. As you can see, it was believed that a variety of public transportation options would take folks to places as close as neighboring Mont Vernon and as far away as New York.

Six

At Play

The object . . . is to conduct community sports, games, celebrations, etc., for the purpose of providing healthful and wholesome recreations for the citizens of New Boston.
—New Boston Playground Association, 1928

Aside from schoolyard games, organized sporting activities may have begun with the formation of the New Boston YMCA in the spring of 1869. But even if they did, the events were short-lived, as the last recorded meeting was in the fall of 1872. However, a subsequent Christian organization—the Community Church—under the direction of its new pastor, Rev. Louis W. Swanson, would become pivotal in organized town sports for generations. Due in large part to the efforts of one man, New Boston's church and the community became united in play.

By the early 1920s, two acres of the former Whipple land was bought with town funds and used as the area to host the first Community Day, coordinated by Reverend Swanson. He almost single-handedly inspired a large contingency of the population to build a community playground on the property (where the ball field still exists behind the current town hall). Remarkably, in little more than a single day, the land was cleared, a playground and refreshment stand were constructed, and grandstand seating for 600 people was built and finished (including painting). It is reported that by daybreak over 200 men, women, and children arrived with 22 horse teams.

Baseball in particular benefited the most from the formation of the playground association. Saturday afternoon games were a ritual. The Tri-Mountain League was established and named for mountains located in the participating towns of Goffstown (Uncanoonuc), Warner (Kearsarge), and Peterborough (Monadnock). It flourished as a wealth of amateur baseball talent in New Hampshire until World War II interrupted, for good, the league's schedule.

In the winter months during the Depression era, enterprising residents lured skiers to New Boston by towlines on groomed trails, such as the former Pinball Hill ski area. There has always been ample opportunity for other outdoor activities such as hunting and fishing, as both share a rich heritage in New Boston that remains to this day an excellent area for both sports. Additionally, the Boy and Girl Scouts and the 4-H youth group organizations were established in New Boston soon after their inceptions and remain active today.

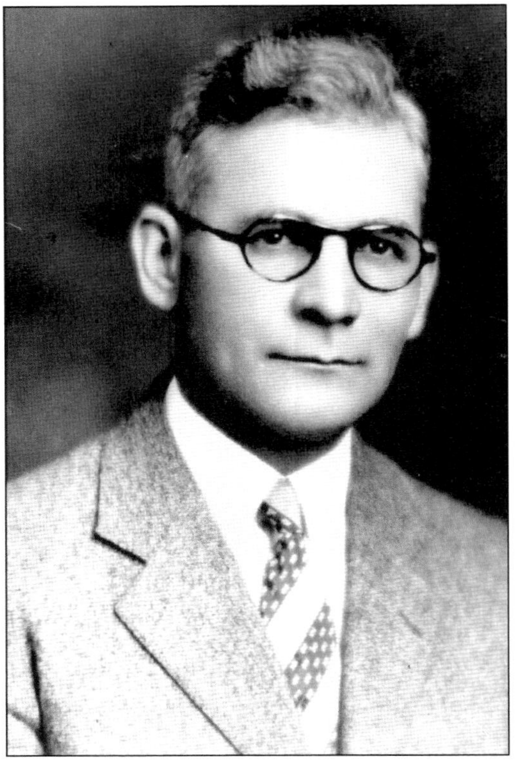

Rev. Louis Swanson was a minister in New Boston for many years and was taken into the hearts of the people. He came to town c. 1911 straight from theology school. His stay was expected to be for the summer only but extended to 35 years. He was the force behind the Community Church as well as many town projects such as the creation of the playground.

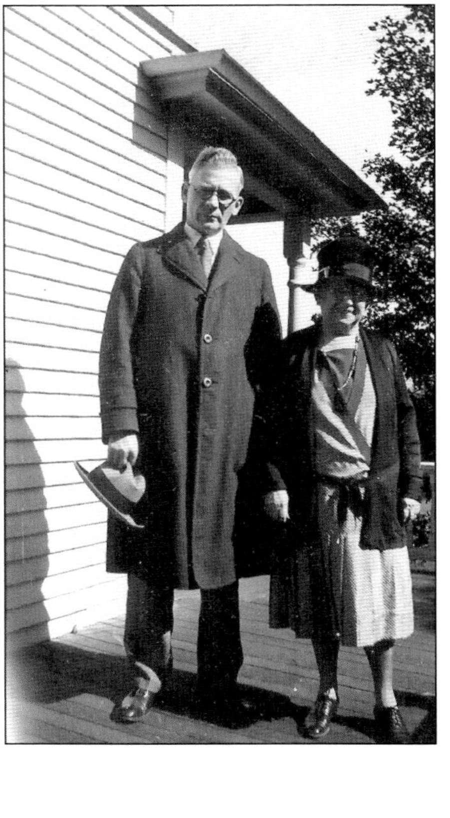

Reverend Swanson was married twice, both marriages ending in a heartbreaking loss. He never had children but claimed that the children of New Boston were his family. Both of his wives are buried in the New Boston Cemetery on the hill. There is a monument that bears his name as well, but the dates are blank. He never talked about where he came from and no relatives were known to have ever visited. One day he simply vanished.

Here is a picture of Reggie Hayes riding the first bicycle made in America. This original bone shaker was manufactured in 1861 by James Mahoney and consists of a wrought-iron frame, wood wheels, and iron tires. Hayes rode this bicycle 20 consecutive years at the Fourth of July parade. He and the bicycle once appeared in *Ripley's Believe It or Not*.

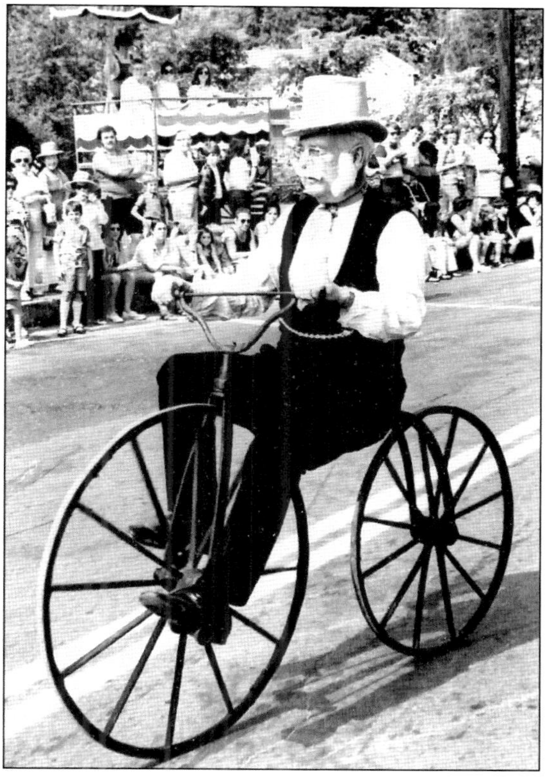

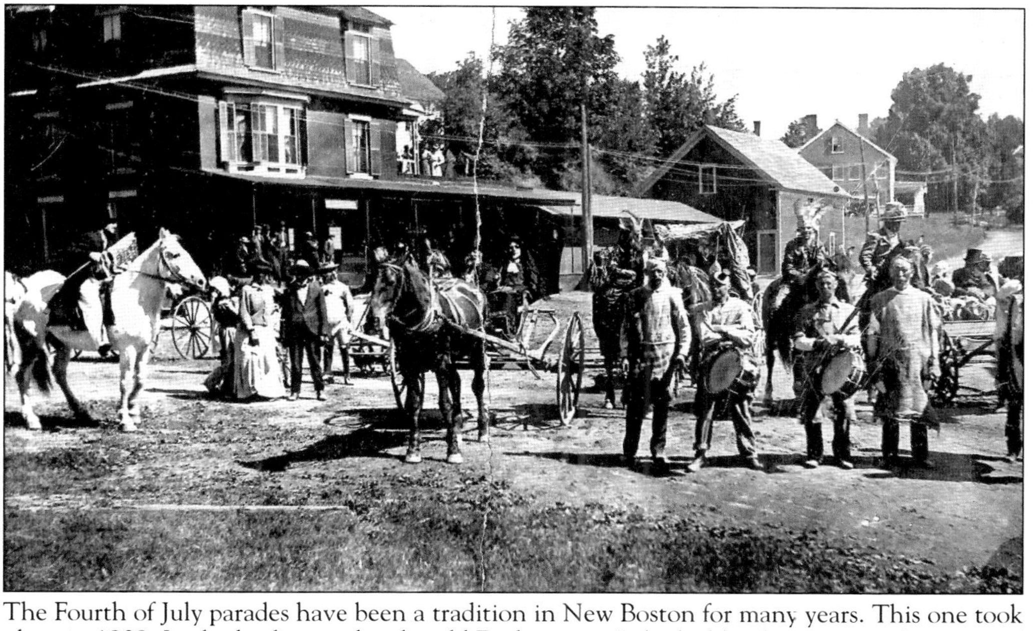

The Fourth of July parades have been a tradition in New Boston for many years. This one took place in 1909. In the background is the old Dodge store. It looks like the carriages, horses, and Indians are ready to roll.

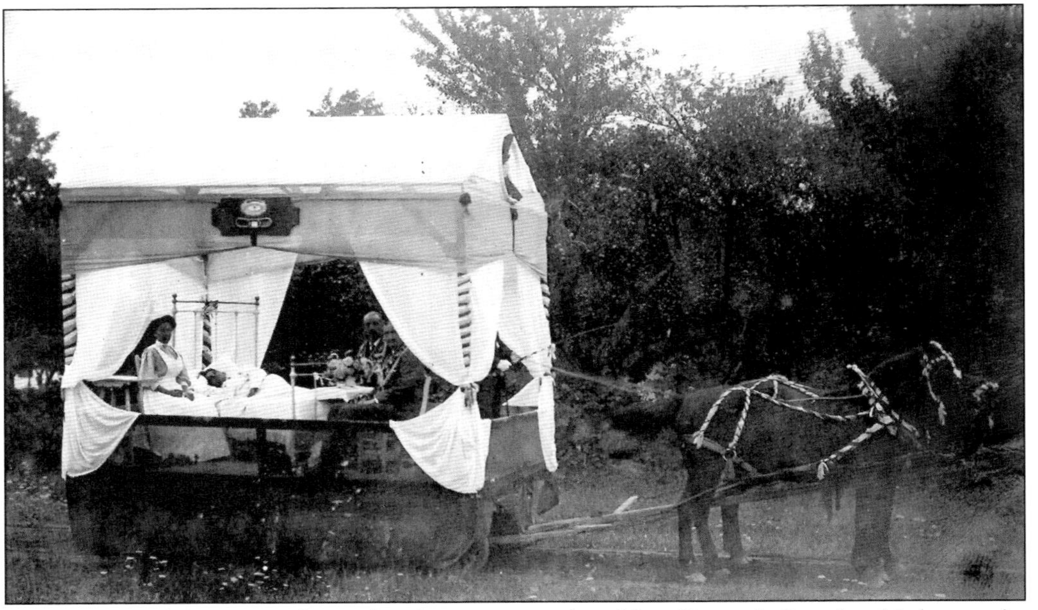

Here is one of the many floats that have appeared in New Boston's Fourth of July parade. This one depicts an ailing patient receiving nursing care. These early parades were always competitive, as recognition was given to the top three floats, a practice that continues today.

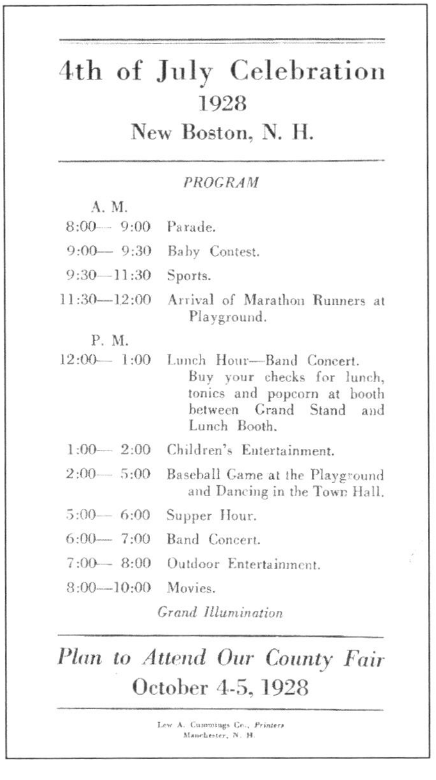

4th of July Celebration
1928
New Boston, N. H.

PROGRAM

A. M.

8:00— 9:00	Parade.
9:00— 9:30	Baby Contest.
9:30—11:30	Sports.
11:30—12:00	Arrival of Marathon Runners at Playground.

P. M.

12:00— 1:00	Lunch Hour—Band Concert. Buy your checks for lunch, tonics and popcorn at booth between Grand Stand and Lunch Booth.
1:00— 2:00	Children's Entertainment.
2:00— 5:00	Baseball Game at the Playground and Dancing in the Town Hall.
5:00— 6:00	Supper Hour.
6:00— 7:00	Band Concert.
7:00— 8:00	Outdoor Entertainment.
8:00—10:00	Movies.

Grand Illumination

Plan to Attend Our County Fair
October 4-5, 1928

Lew A. Cummings Co., *Printers*
Manchester, N. H.

Here is a program from the 1928 Fourth of July celebration. People still come from miles around to see New Boston's "grand illumination" on the Fourth.

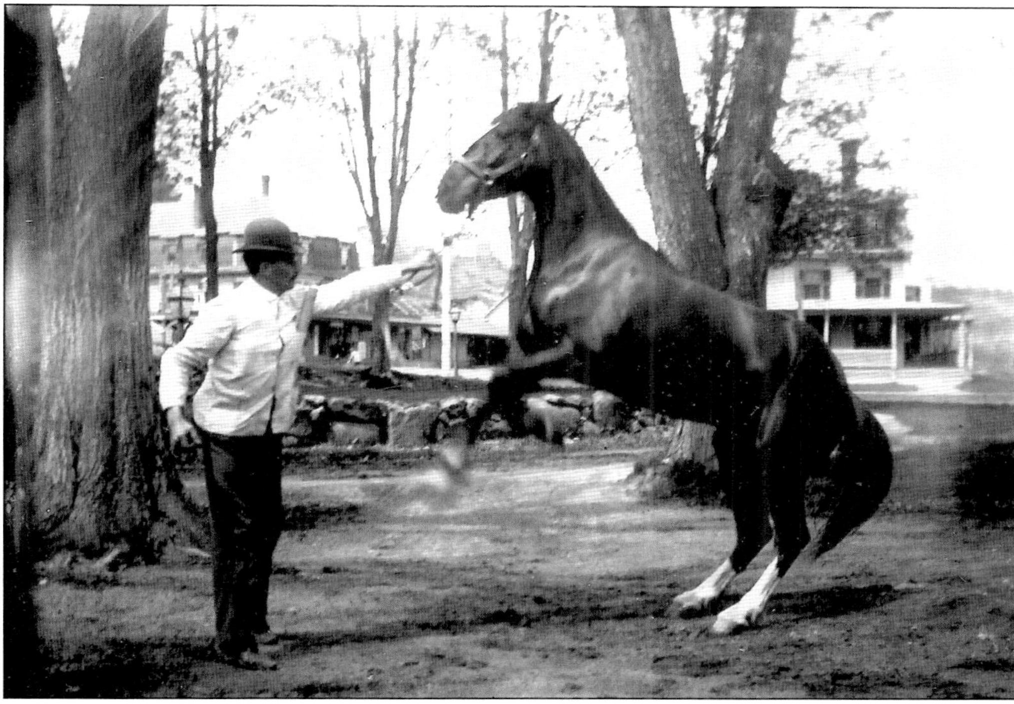

This is Arthur Holt and his frisky horse on the green in the center of town. In the background, one can see the old Dodge's Store on the left and the Tavern on the right. (Courtesy of M. Dodge.)

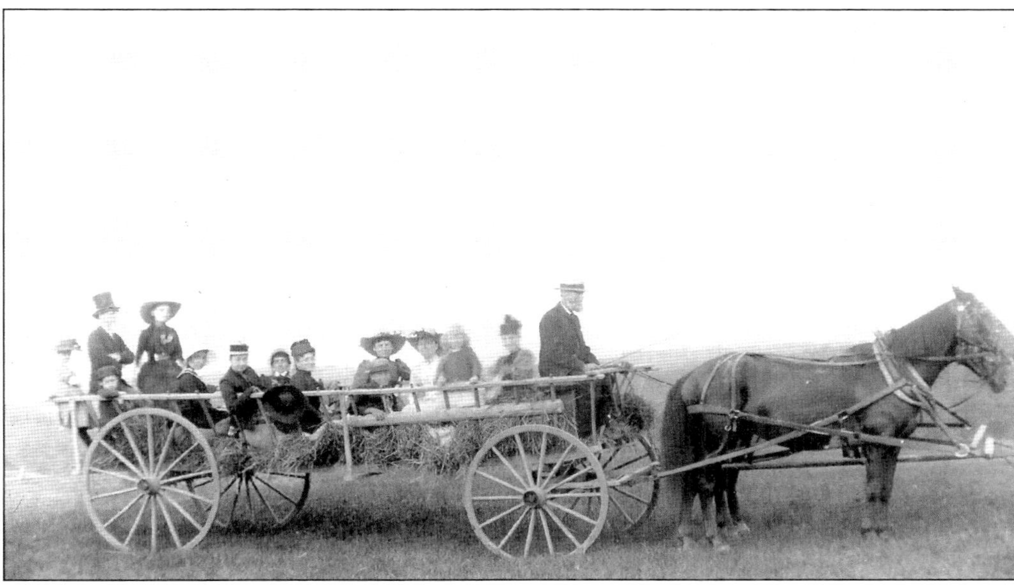

This photograph was taken c. 1892 and pictures Charles Shedd, a prominent New Boston resident, driving the wagon. The people are well dressed for a hayride, with the men in their stovepipe and straw hats and the ladies in their attractive bonnets.

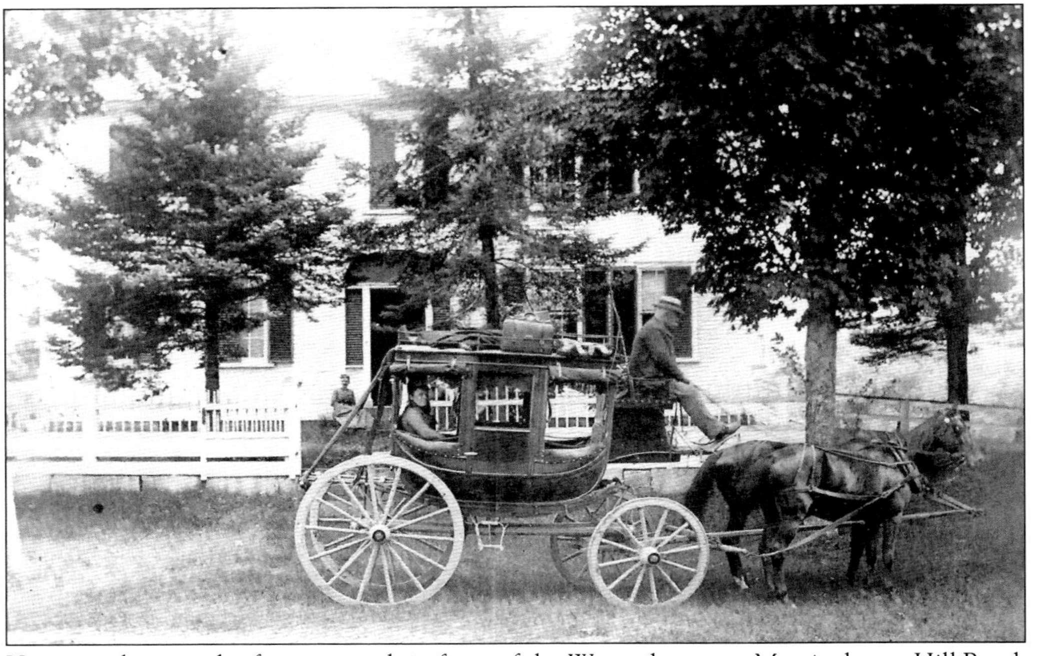

Here is a photograph of a stagecoach in front of the Wason house on Meetinghouse Hill Road. Charles Horace Chandler, the driver, carried passengers between Parker's Station and Weare for 23 years, until the railroad came to town and replaced the coach service.

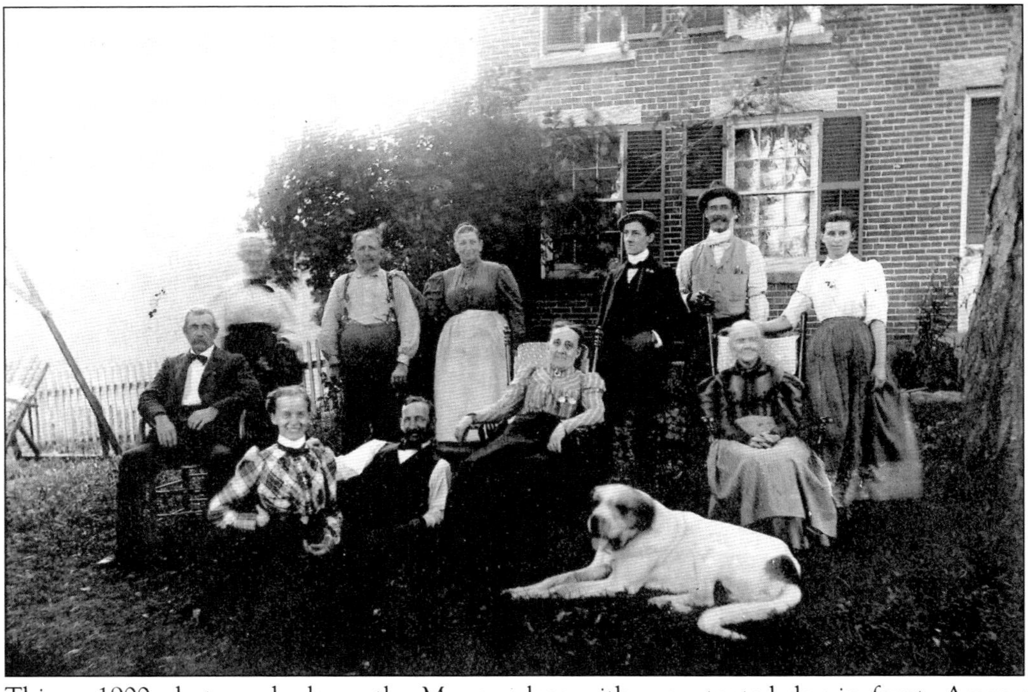

This *c*. 1900 photograph shows the Muzzey place with a contented dog in front. Among the humans in the picture are Mr. and Mrs. Muzzey, Helen and Charles Fletcher, and John, Elizabeth, and Herbert Todd.

Here is New Boston in the Gay Nineties. Pictured is a group of folks engaged in a game of cards, a popular form of entertainment from that era. The two people in the rear of the photograph are Merrill Todd's grandparents.

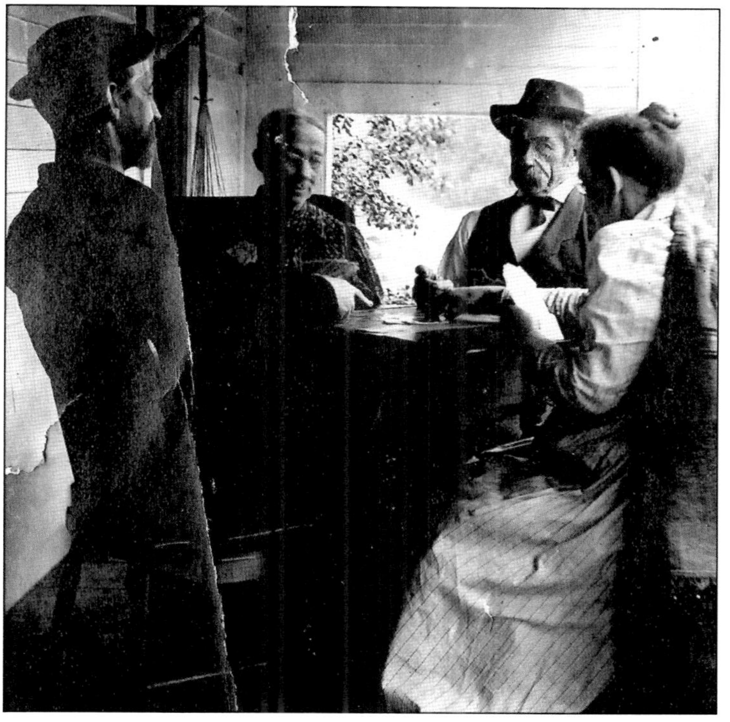

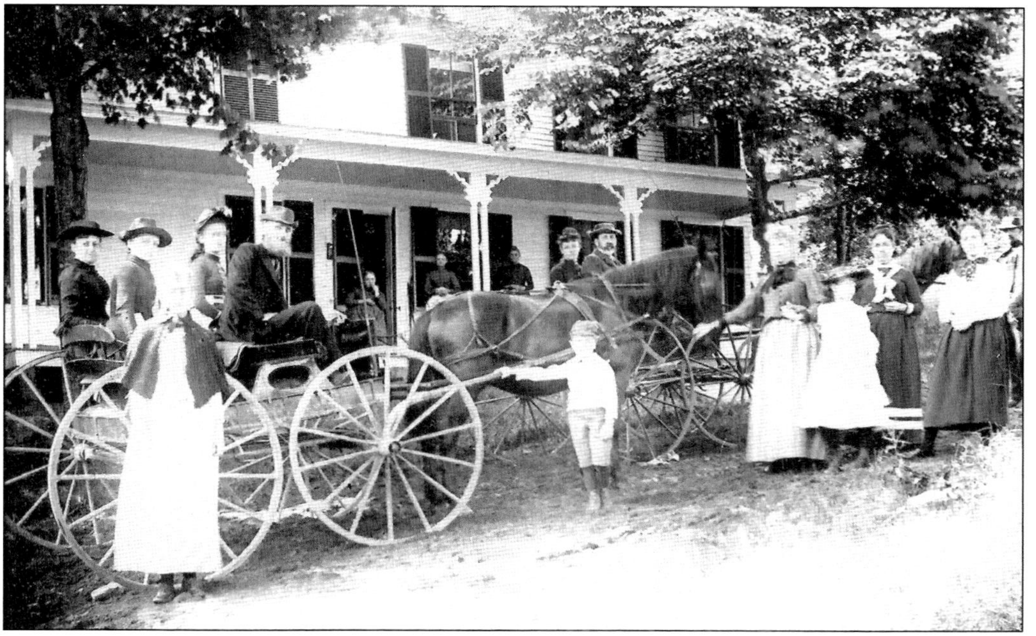

During the summer months, many citizens invited summer boarders into their homes. The railroad, with its passenger service, helped city people to come to New Boston and enjoy the country life. The boarders in this picture are at the Greenwood house, located on Meetinghouse Hill Road. Incidentally, it was in this house that the 1863 *History of New Boston* was written by Rev. Elliott Cogswell.

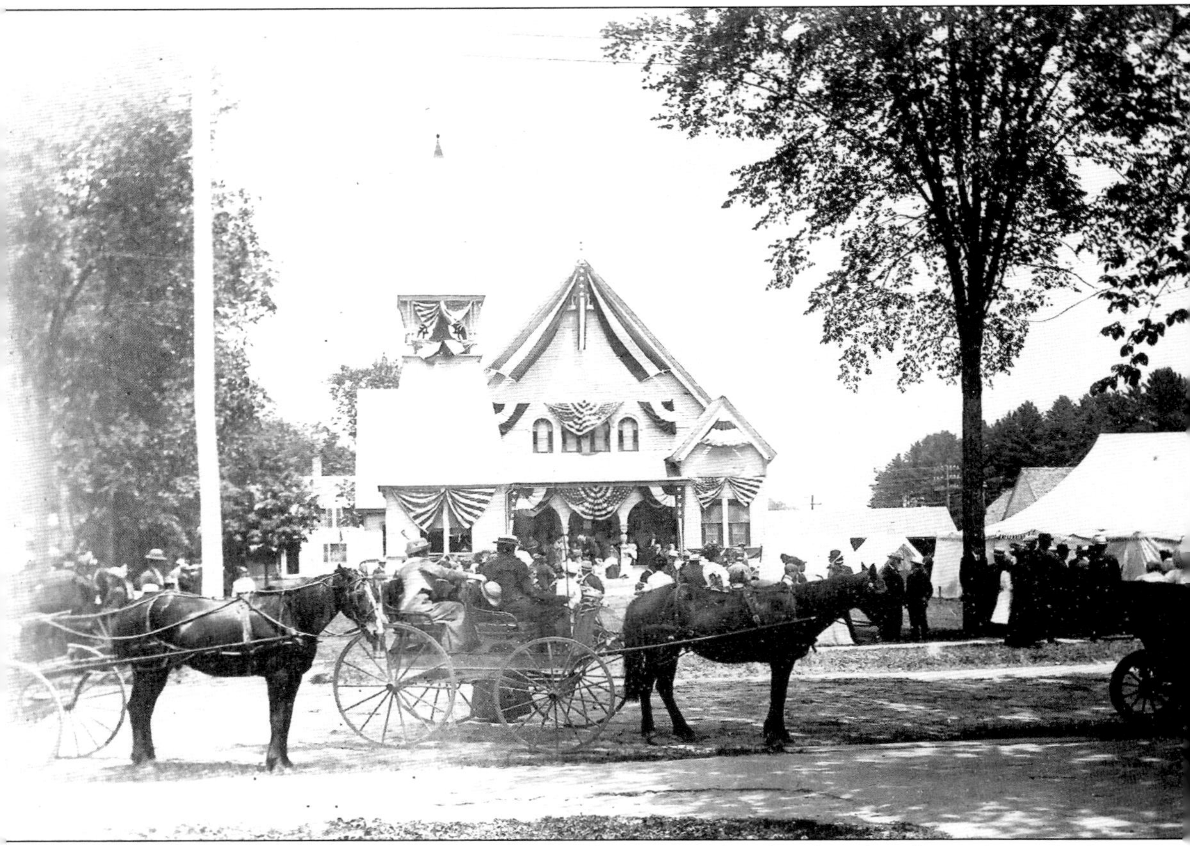

This picture of New Boston's center shows the Baptist church. This church was located where the gazebo now stands. The photograph was taken in 1913 and was part of the celebration of

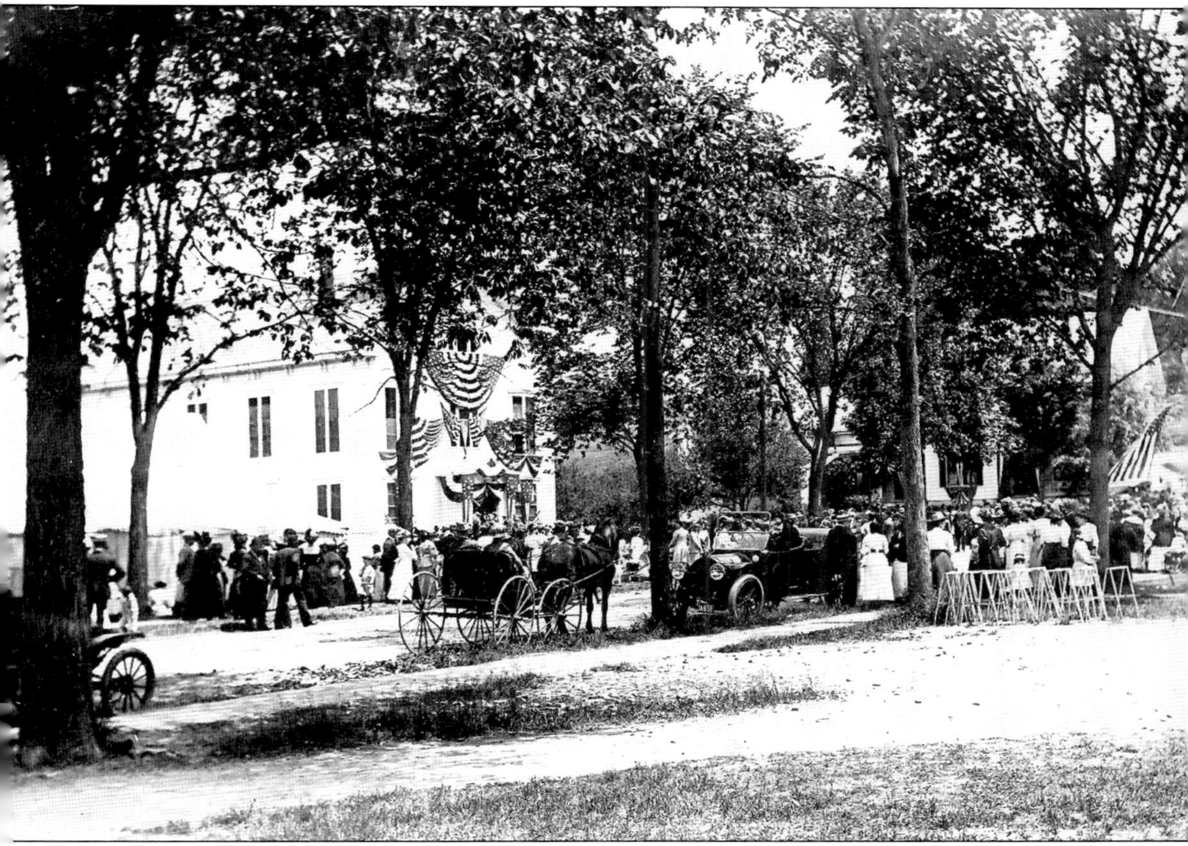

the town's 150th anniversary.

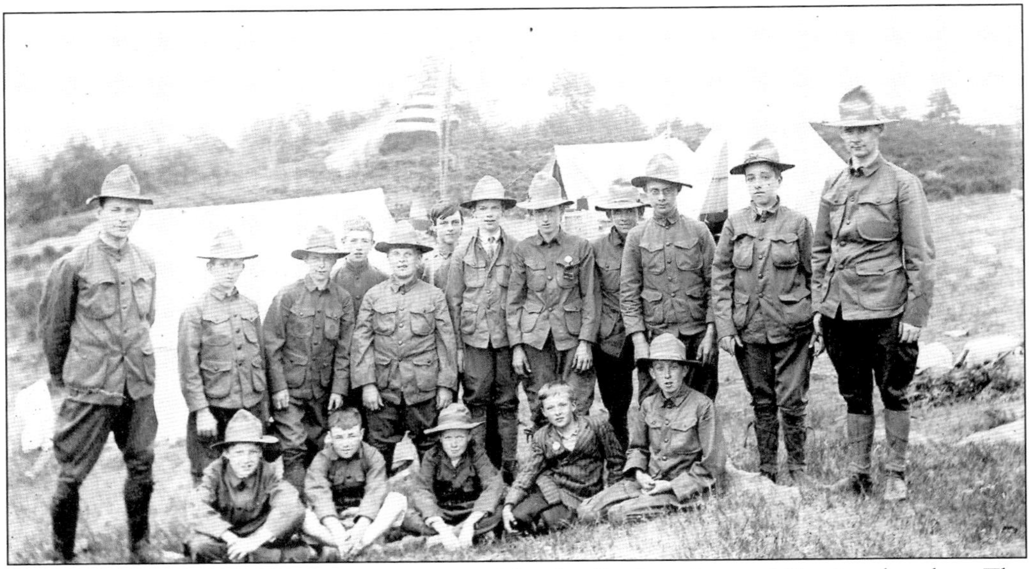

This c. 1912 Boy Scout troop was sponsored by the Presbyterian and Baptist churches. The group is camping near Scobie Pond in Francestown. Pictured are, from left to right, the following: (front row) John Bartlett, Frederic Orrell, Ted Fisk, Gale Andrews, and George Fisk; (middle row) scoutmaster Rev. Louis Swanson, Abner Woods, Archie Goodale, Amos Lyford, Aaron Todd, Lester Corliss, Fred Johonnett, Howard Marden, and assistant scoutmaster Rev. Gordon Warren; (back row) Lester Houghton and two unidentified scouts. (Donated by A. Lyford.)

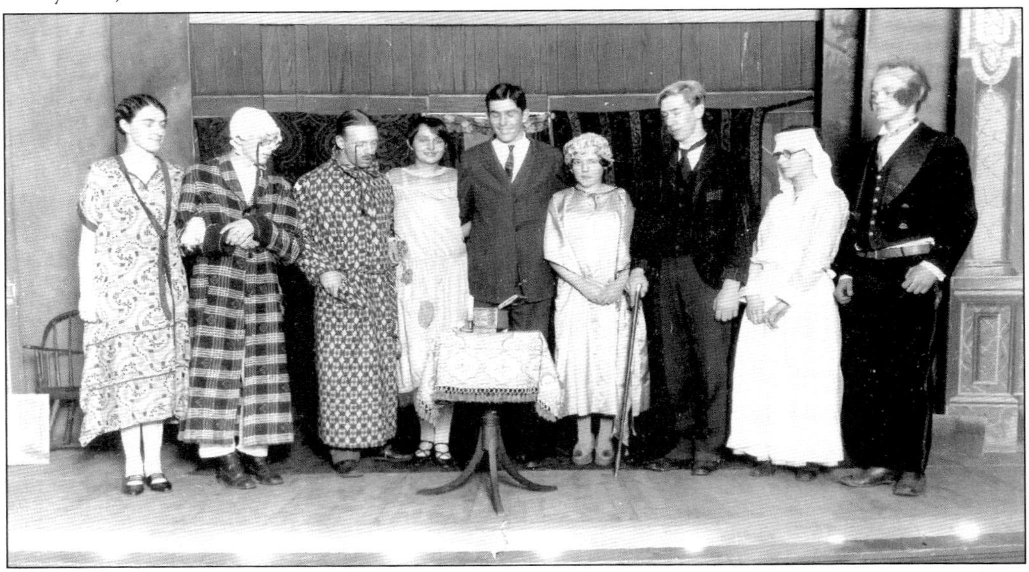

Pictured here is the cast of the 1927 senior class play, *The Tiger Earl*. Dorothy Kirsch, a junior, substituted for Dorothy Fraser, who had been injured in an accident two weeks before the production. The players are, from left to right, Ruth Carroll, unidentified, Donald Berry, Dorothy Kirsch, Russell Carroll, unidentified, Laban Todd, Sylvia Chandler, and Maurice Leland. The stage at the town hall was used for these high school productions. (Donated by W. Kirsch.)

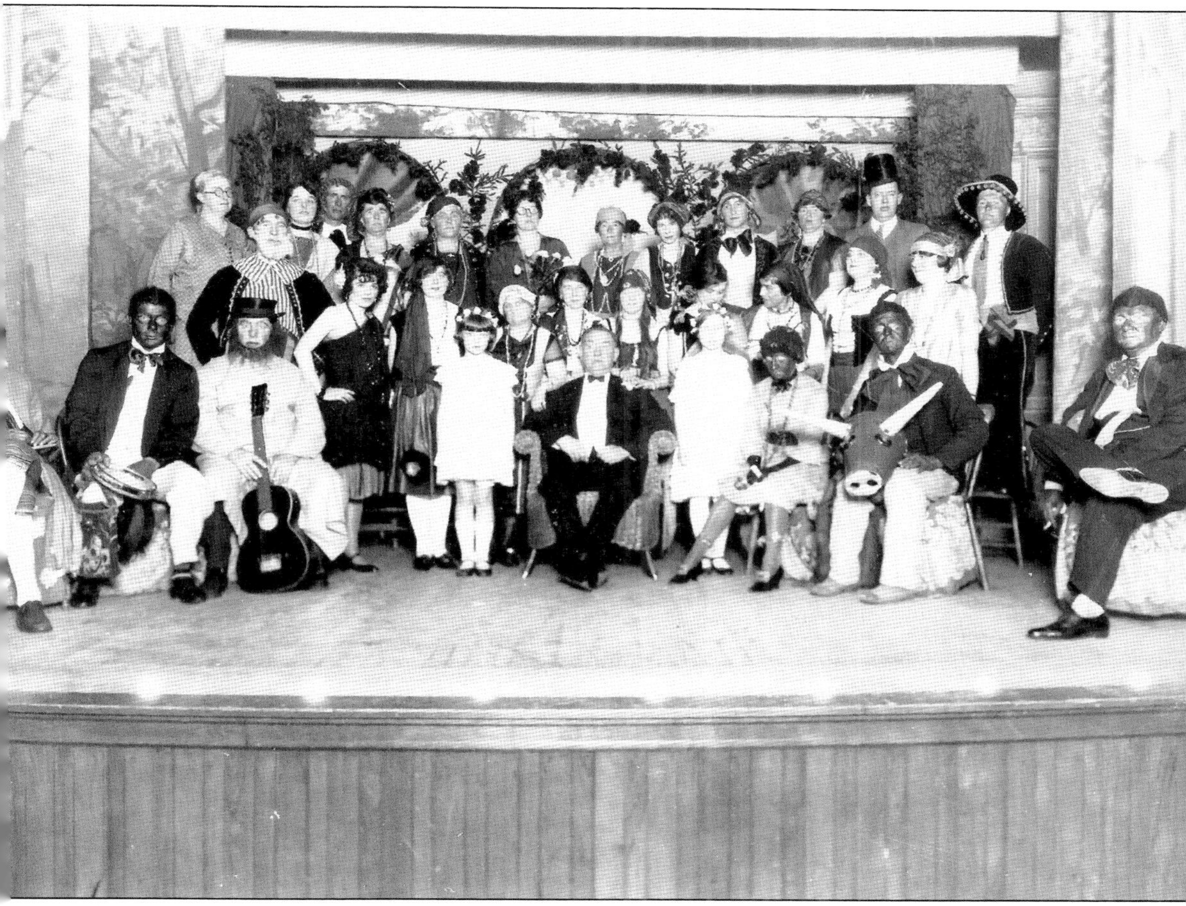

Without television and the forms of entertainment available today, people found other ways to amuse themselves. Depicted here is a typical minstrel show, popular in New Boston as well as other towns in the area. Adults could attend one of these shows for 60¢, and children for 30¢, tax included. (Donated by W. Dotey.)

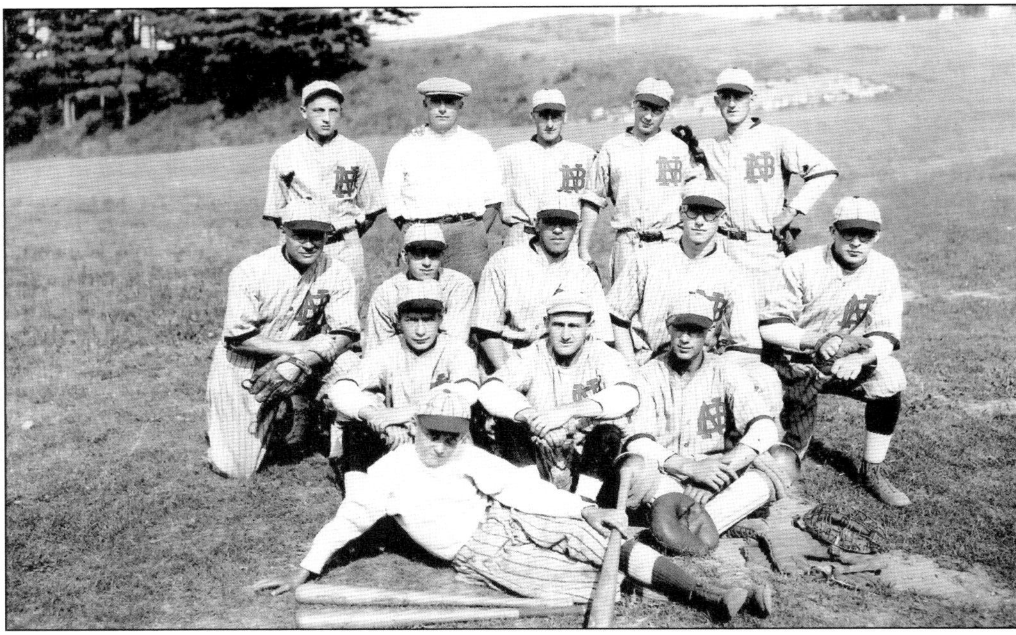

Baseball has been a popular sport in New Boston for many years. This photograph shows the town's team in 1924, when they won 21 straight games. Pictured here are, from left to right, the following: (first row) mascot Clint Smith; (second row) Walt Kirsch, "Doggie" Richards, and "Cider" Worden; (third row) Fred Cann, Earl Odekirk, Arthur Hill, John Todd, and Don Pettee; (fourth row) Winn Smith, Harlan Shedd, Ray Wheeler, Alvin Lewis, and Roger Eaton. (Donated by W. Kirsch.)

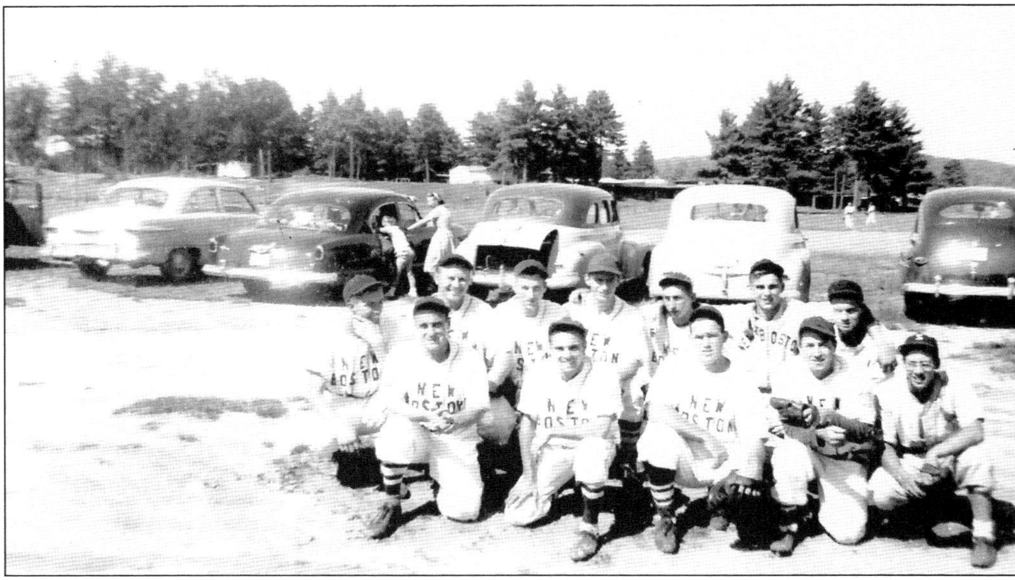

Another New Boston baseball team is seen at Hopkinton when they were members of the Tri-Mountain League. In this photograph are, from left to right, L. Daniels, W. Daniels, D. Cilley, V. Daniels, F. Allen, unidentified, D. Yost, unidentified, R. Sallada, W. Kirsch, R. Kennedy, and unidentified. (Courtesy of C. Davis.)

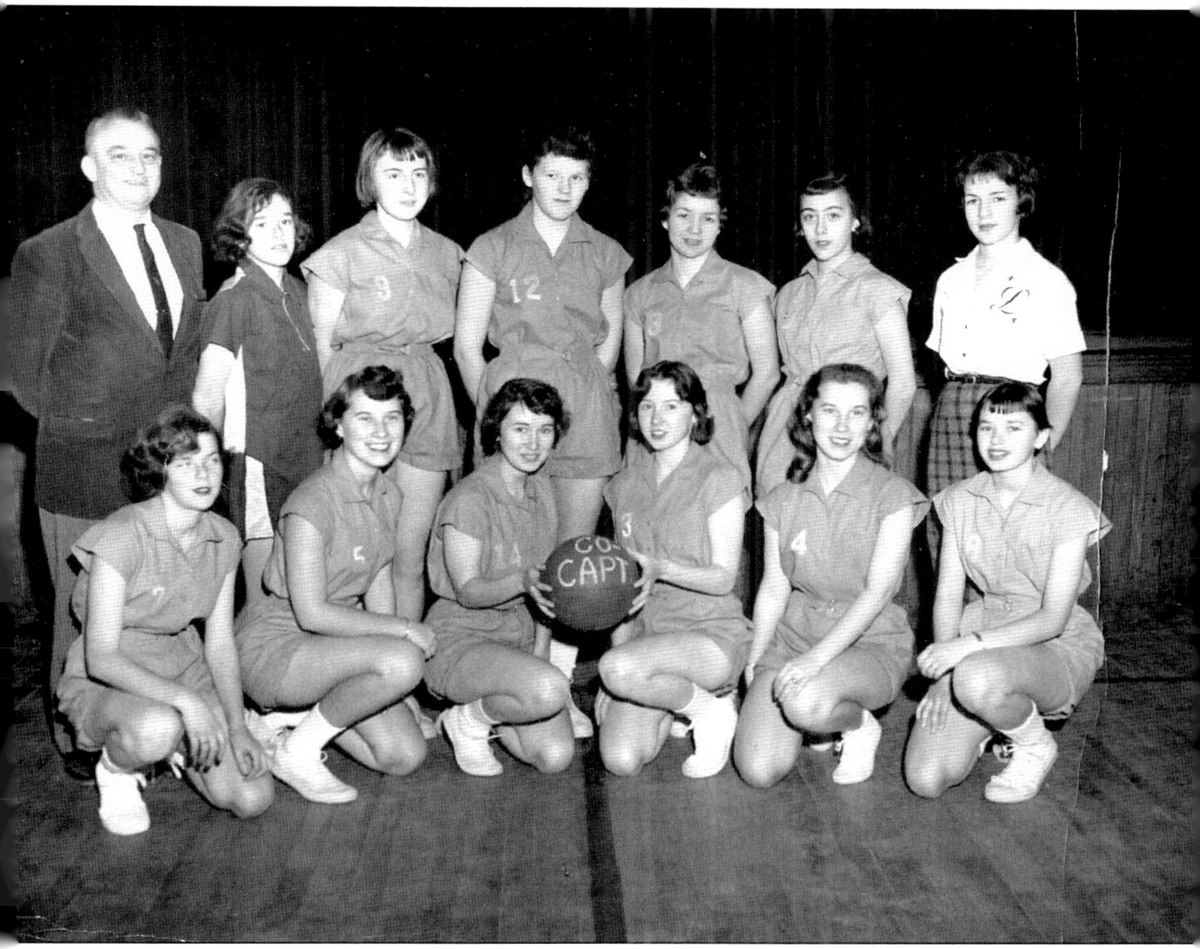

New Boston girls also enjoyed sports. Here is a 1960 photograph of a girls' basketball team. From left to right are the following: (front row) Andy Card, Barbara Kane, Arlene Kennedy, Dottie Daniels, Beverly Kane, and Marge Prince; (back row) coach George Kitridge, Ruth Houghton, Virginia Davis, Dottie Tower, Ginny Lehman, Justine Gagnon, and Lois Lehman. (Courtesy of A. Dodge.)

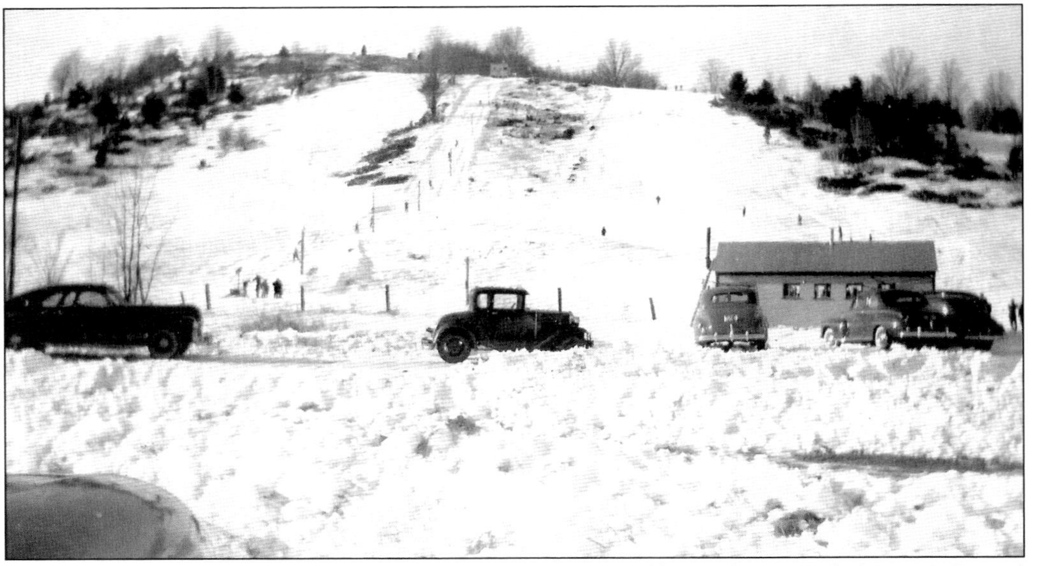

New Boston's Pinball Hill ski area was owned and operated by Walter Kirsch from 1947 until 1953. There was an engine house at the top of the hill that housed the V-8 Ford engine used to drive the rope tow. The area had three slopes, and the main run was to the right of the tow. At the bottom of the slopes, as pictured, was the warming hut.

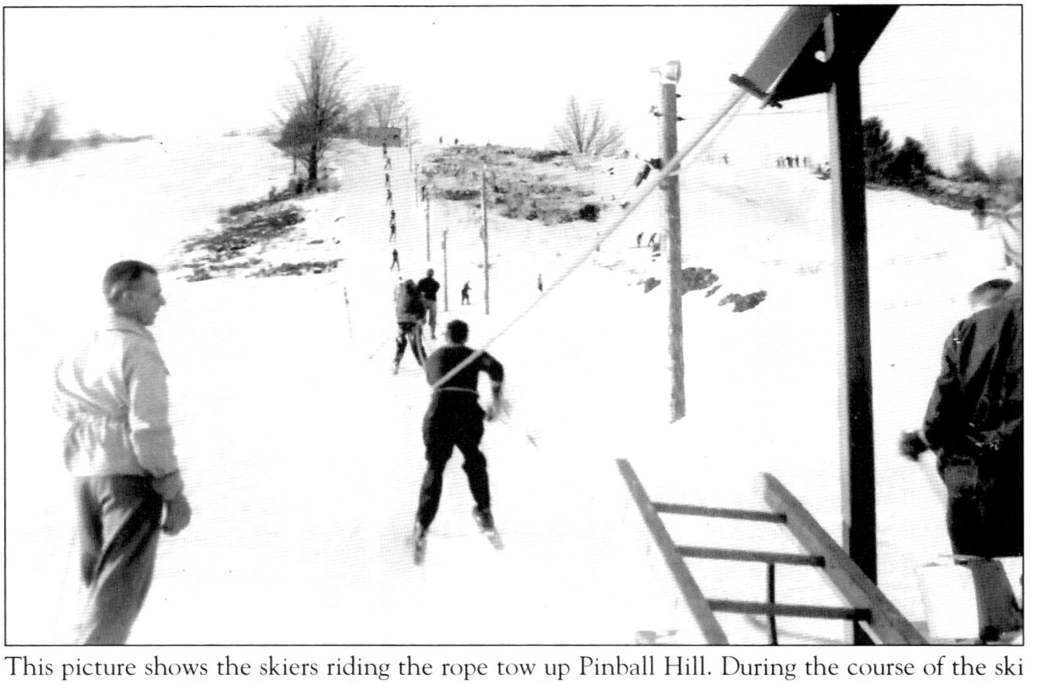

This picture shows the skiers riding the rope tow up Pinball Hill. During the course of the ski season, one would need to purchase many pairs of mittens, as gripping the rough rope took its toll. This hill is where the 4-H fairgrounds, home of the Hillsborough County fair, are located. (Courtesy of C. Davis.)

New Boston has been the home of the Hillsborough County Agricultural Fair since 1957. The fair was originally held on the ball field in the center of town but moved to the 4-H fairgrounds along Route 13 when that facility was completed in 1970. In this photograph, children take part in a sack race as spectators cheer them on. (Courtesy of B. Dodge and the Hillsborough County 4-H Foundation.)

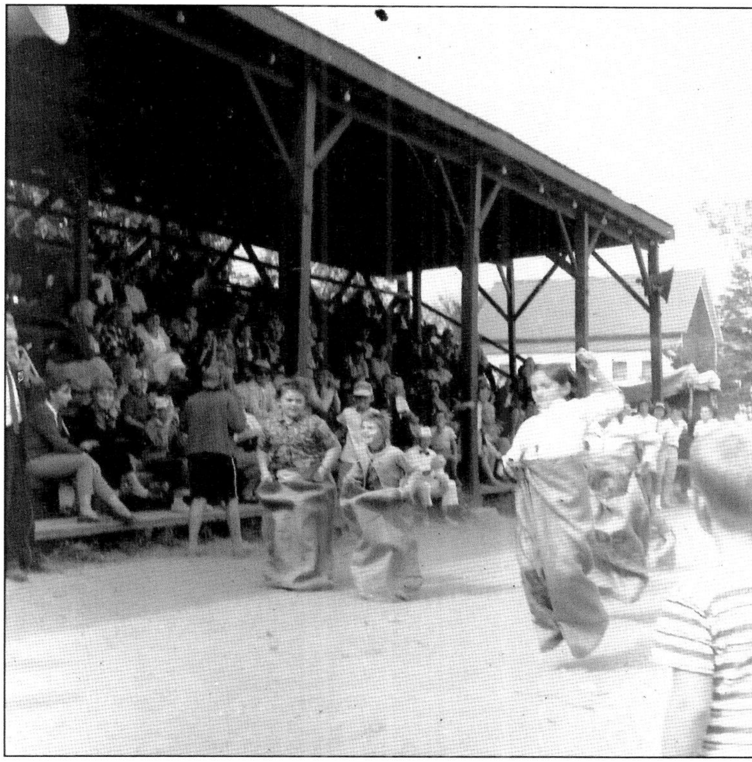

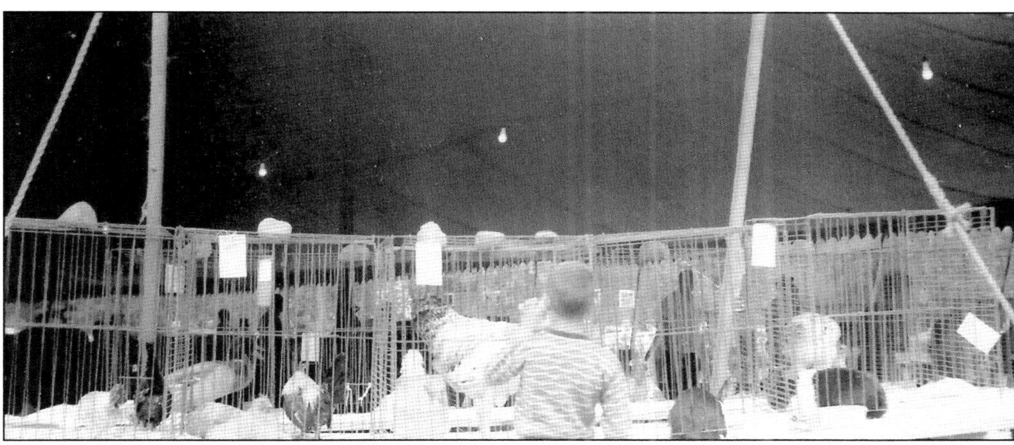

New Boston children can enjoy the satisfaction of raising their own livestock, such as these rabbits, or simply attending the county fair and enjoying the sights. A carnival midway also helps to keep the youngsters amused.

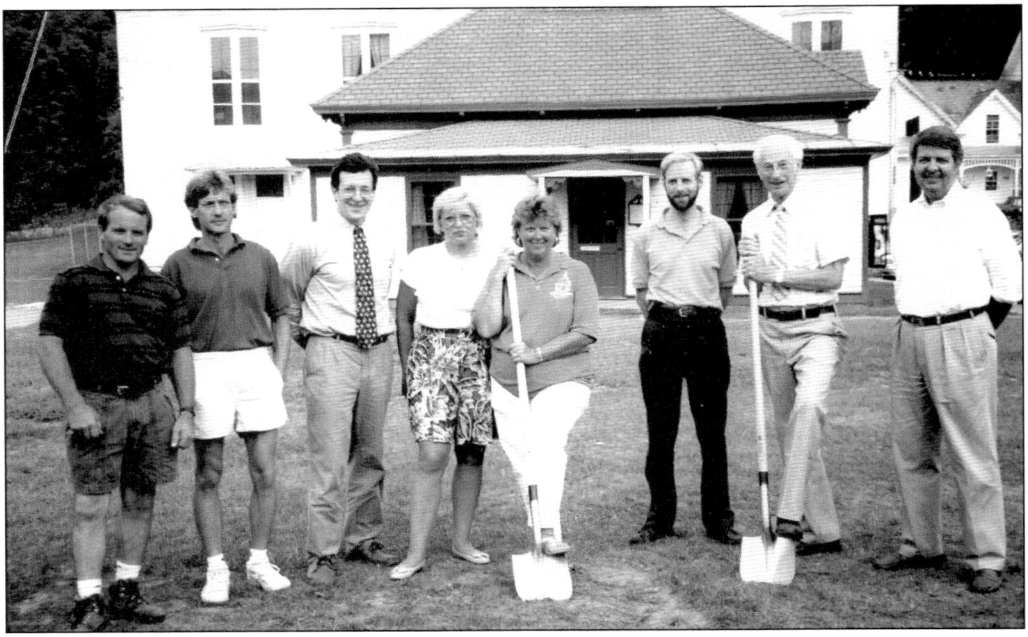

Here is a picture of the groundbreaking ceremony for the new gazebo built in 1994. This photograph was taken on July 20, 1994, and shows, from left to right, Tony Hall, Tom Condon, Steve Peach, Darlene Goodin, Sandy Gallup, David Hulick, Roland Sallada, and Bobby Dodge. Concerts and children's programs are held at the gazebo during the summer months.

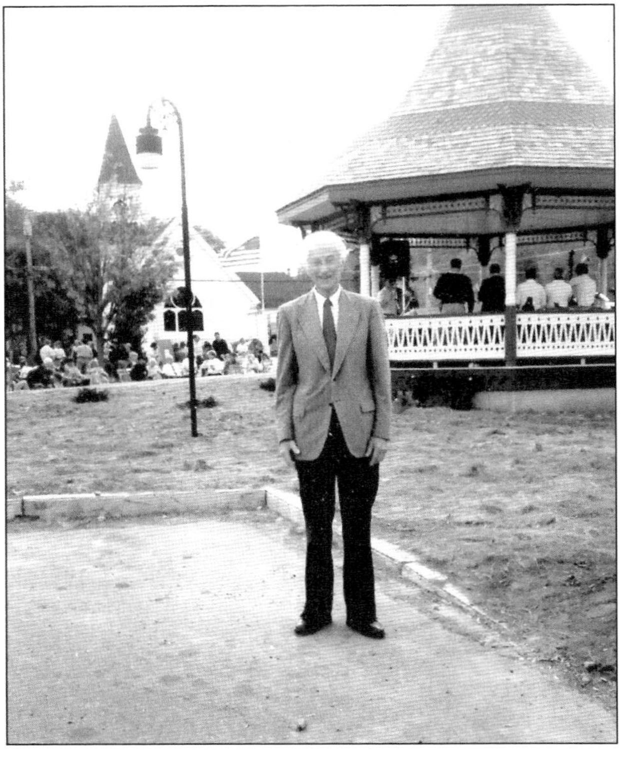

This is the 1994 dedication of the gazebo on the town common. The structure is certainly one of the most picturesque gazebos in the state. In the foreground is Roland Sallada, who contributed much to the town of New Boston and to the historical society and was a selectman for a number of years.

Seven

TROUBLED TIMES

Has the way sometimes seemed long and hard?
Have we often weary grown?
Through it all, above the darkest day,
God's unfailing love has shone.

—Introductory remarks at Old Folk's Day, 1905

Since its incorporation, major natural and man-made disasters have affected New Boston, including extraordinary flooding from the flood of 1936 and as a result of the Hurricane of 1938. However, the infamous fire of 1887 not only threatened to decimate the town center by destroying nearly 40 buildings but also destroyed forever some of the permanent records for the town. Many, if not all, of the gaps in the town's history are because of the documents and records lost in one day. And certain establishments in the town never fully recovered. By the 1930s, the Baptists had dissolved for good and a new church built after the fire was torn down. Fortunately, fate did not conspire to give New Boston more than it could bear. Whipple's farm was still a mainstay, and the railroad would be reaching town within a few years.

In addition to the challenges of living in seasonal, rural, northern New England, the political climate also varied and produced additional man-made trials such as the French and Indian War (three residents participated directly) before the town was even incorporated. Since then, New Boston has sent men in response to the call for arms whenever the need has arisen. Interestingly, more men participated in the Revolutionary War (136 men total) than during any other. From Bunker Hill and the previously discussed Battle of Bennington to the War of 1812 and the American Civil War to the world wars, patriots of many generations have represented New Boston with conviction and valor. The first women to enlist from New Boston served during World War II.

Through each troubling time, New Boston has been a community that shares its sorrows just as it shares its laughter and celebration. As observed by past events in New Boston, the effects of no disaster or other troubled time last forever in such a close community. Time after time, New Boston has proved its resiliency both as a town and a community.

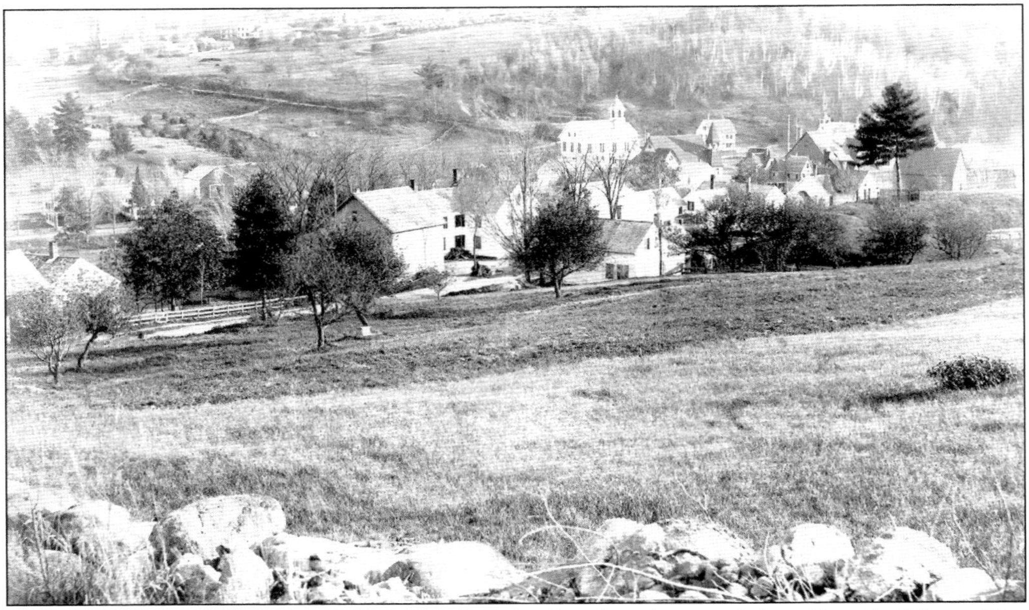

This is how New Boston center looked before the fire that destroyed the village buildings. The photograph was taken from a hill on High Street. River Road is in the center. The Baptist church, town hall, and Tuttle home are on the right. Meetinghouse Hill Road winds up the picture toward the cemetery. On May 11, 1887, all of the buildings from lower Meetinghouse Hill Road to the Piscataquog River were lost due to a fire caused by a spark from the Wason cooper shop.

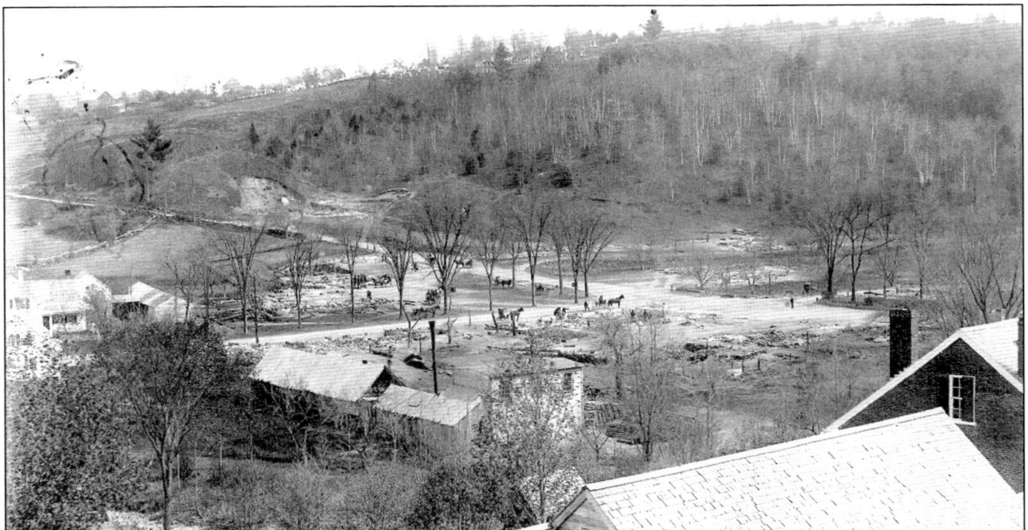

The spark from the Wason cooper shop set the Atwood barn on fire. The fire spread quickly due to a strong northwest wind, and all was lost in an hour and a half. When J. R. Whipple later built the creamery on the site of Wason's shop, he ran pipes from its water supply to a hydrant and then ran a hose from the hydrant to his steam pump. The hydrant was so useful that in 1895 a town warrant was passed to connect to Whipple's system for fighting town fires. The Wason cooper shop is seen toward the bottom of this photograph.

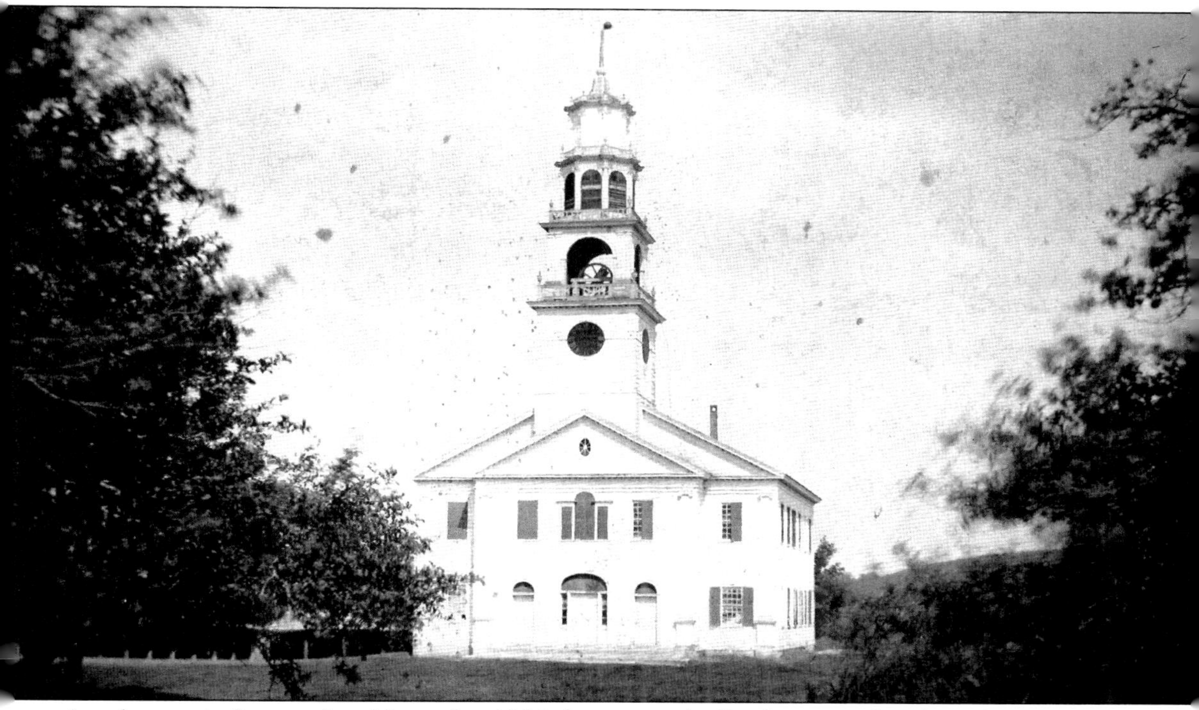

Another tragic fire struck in November 1900, destroying the Presbyterian church in the Upper Village. This church had been built in 1823 on two acres of land purchased from Ammi Dodge for $420. The meetinghouse was abandoned at some point and sold to Lydia Atwood for $650. In November 1900, its spire was struck by lightning, which caused a steeple fire that eventually destroyed the building.

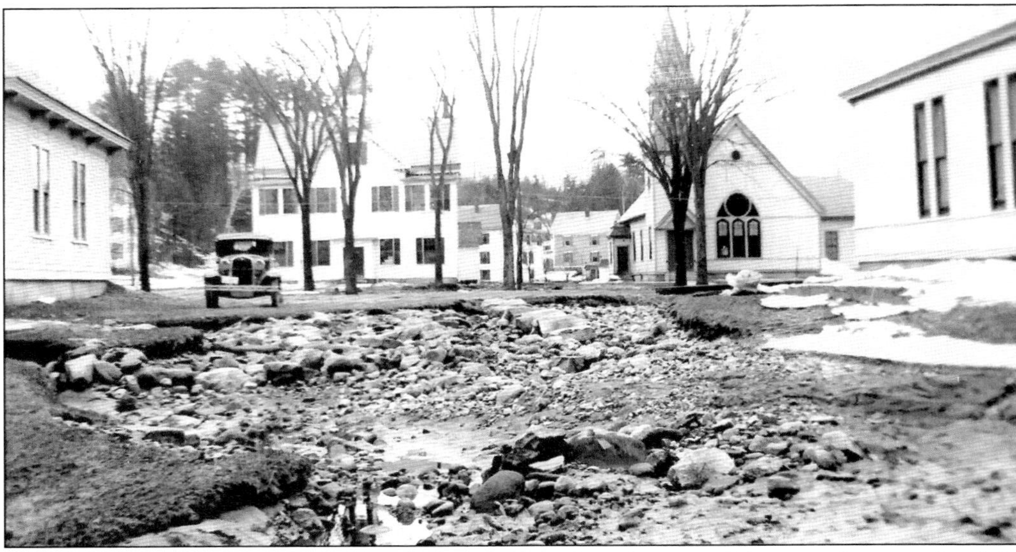

Flooding is another hazard for those living on the edge of a river. This is a photograph of the village during the flood of 1936. The rock wall in the center of the picture is the foundation of the Baptist church that burned in 1888. The high school and the Presbyterian church can be seen across the street. (Donated by G. Merrill.)

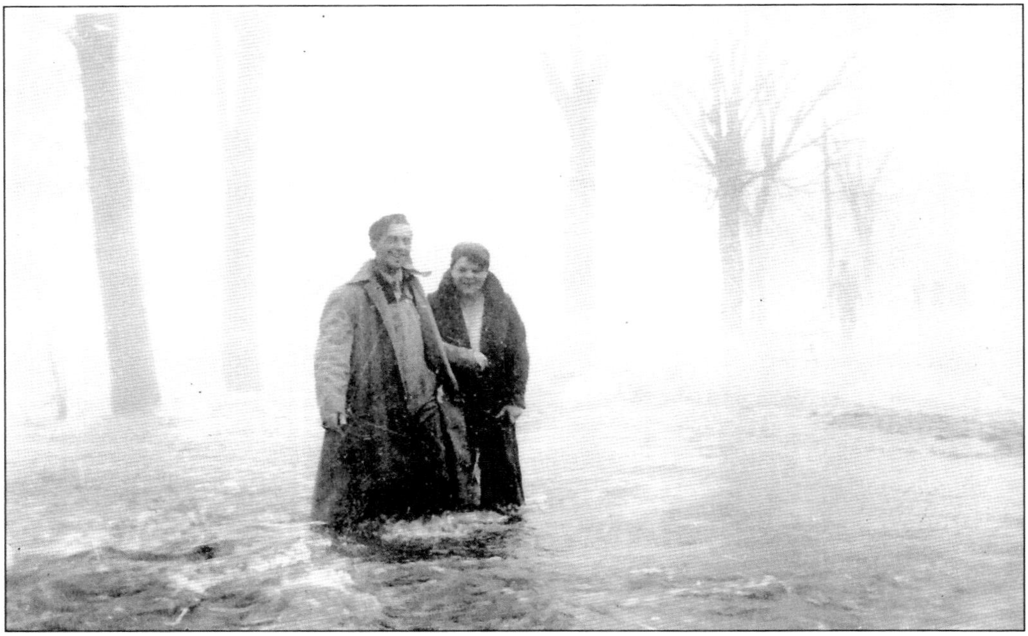

This photograph shows two people braving the floodwaters in March 1936. (Donated by A. Grant.)

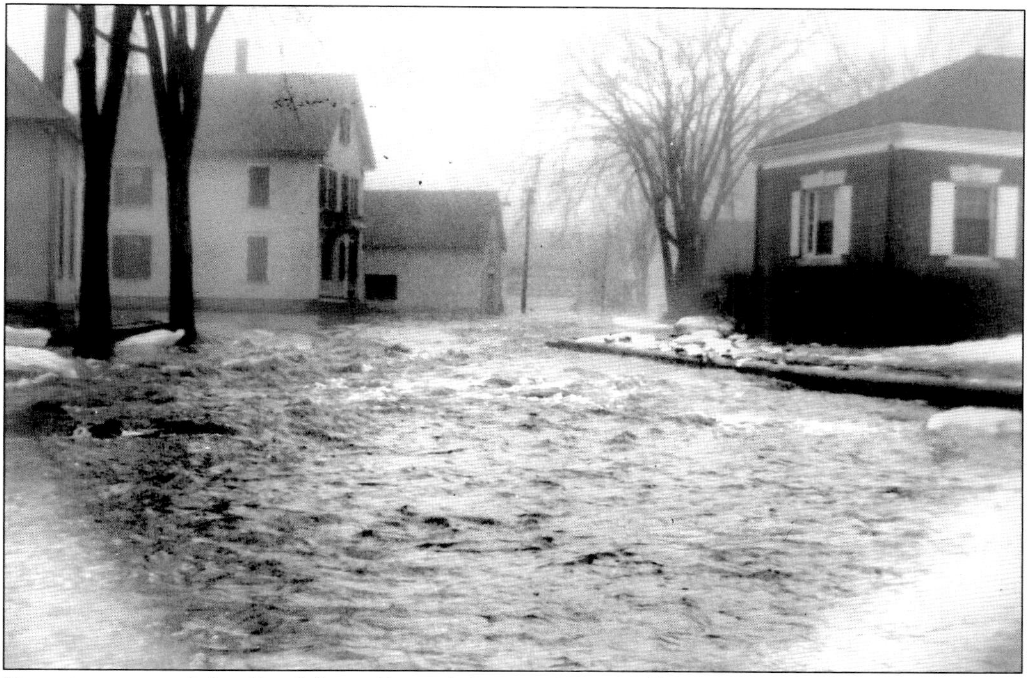

Here is a view of the flood from Central Square down Mill Street on March 19, 1936. The Whipple Free Library is on the right. (Courtesy of C. Davis.)

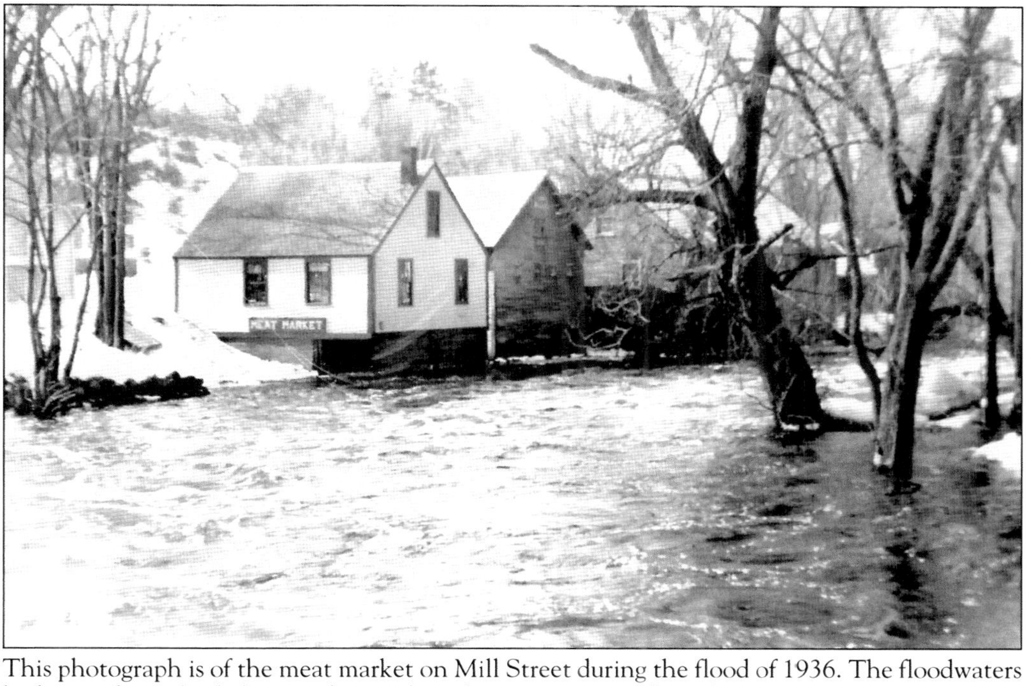

This photograph is of the meat market on Mill Street during the flood of 1936. The floodwaters had started to subside by March 22, when this picture was taken. (Courtesy of C. Davis.)

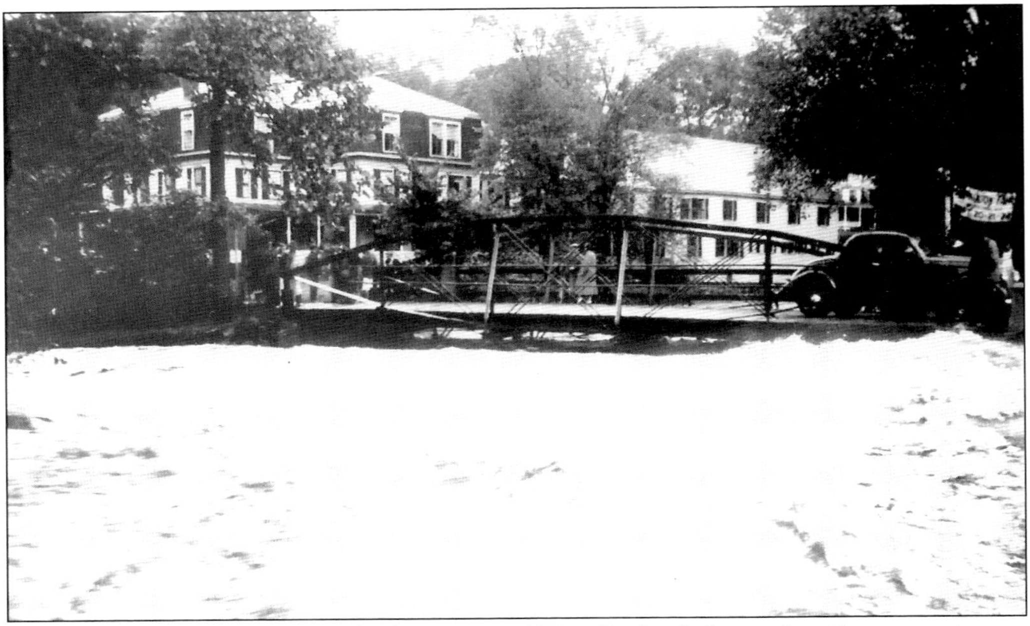

The Hurricane of 1938 affected a large part of New England. It struck without warning on September 21. This photograph shows the iron bridge in Central Square being washed out by the flood that resulted. The picture was taken at 10:00 a.m. on that day. (Courtesy of C. Davis.)

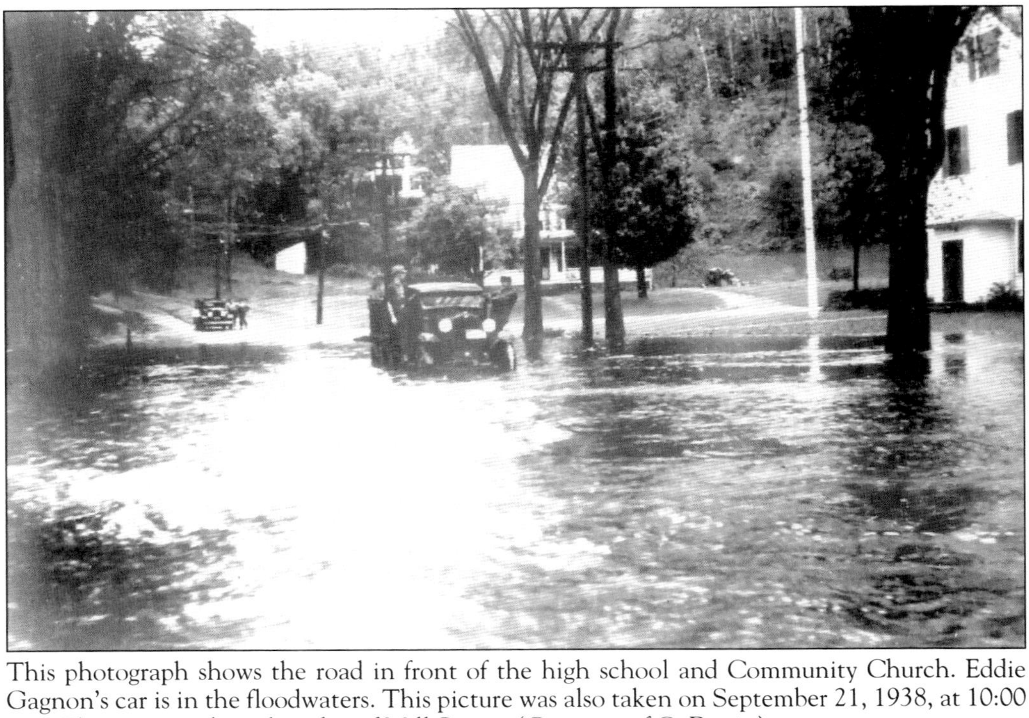

This photograph shows the road in front of the high school and Community Church. Eddie Gagnon's car is in the floodwaters. This picture was also taken on September 21, 1938, at 10:00 a.m. The water ends at the edge of Mill Street. (Courtesy of C. Davis.)

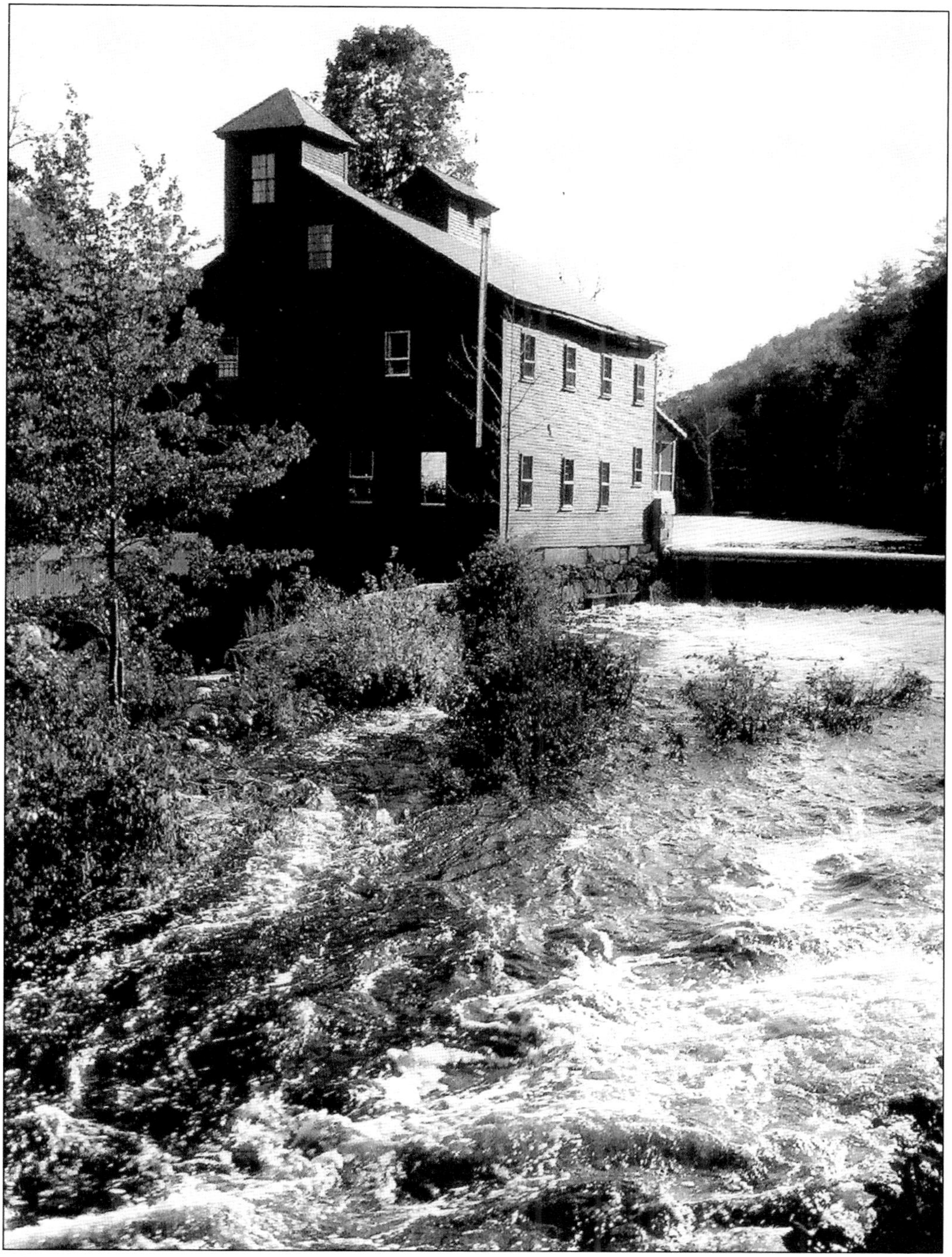

This photograph shows the Parker Mill dam on the Piscataquog River just off Central Square. This building was on the cover of the 1997 town report and has been the subject of many scenic photographs and stories. The dam was washed away in the flood of October 1996. It was not rebuilt because of the cost and the environmental impact of a replacement dam. (Courtesy of R. Parker.)

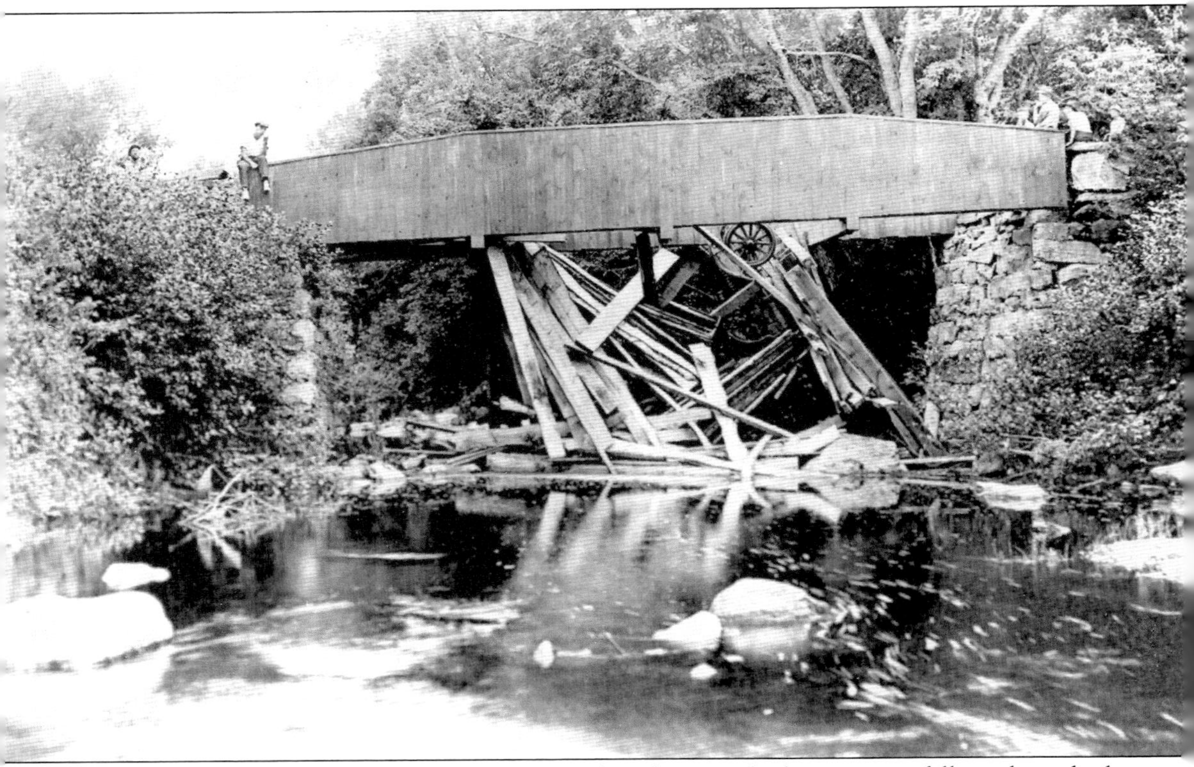

Where there is a river, there are bridges. This photograph shows a cart falling through the Butterfield Bridge sometime in the mid-1920s. There was some controversy over where this incident occurred. Some thought the bridge was located in Lyndeborough, but it was later determined that it was in New Boston near the Lyndeborough line.

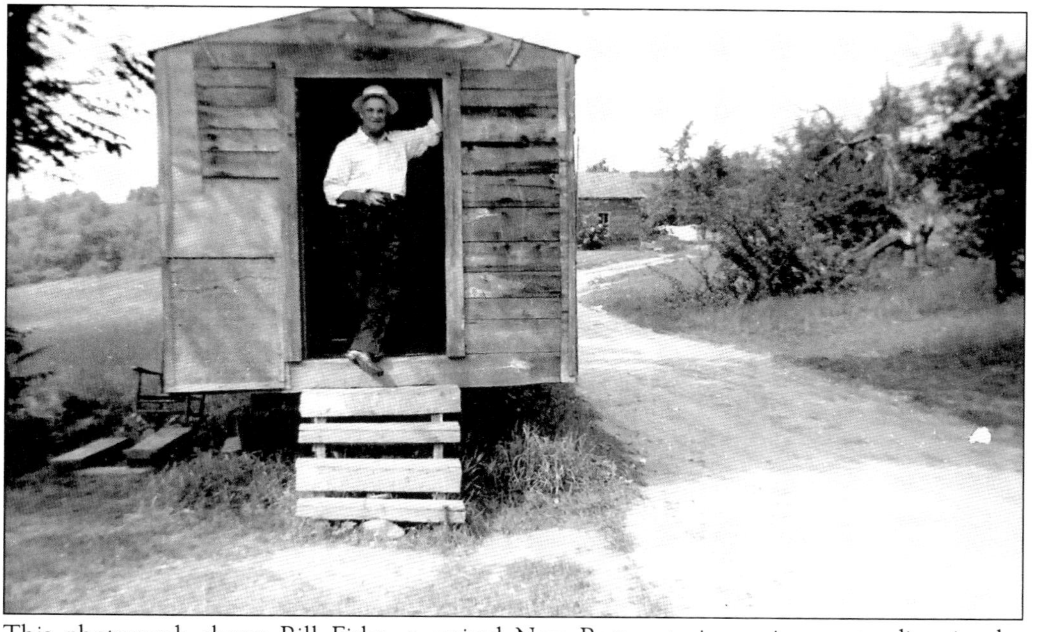

This photograph shows Bill Fiske, a retired New Boston train engineer, standing in the doorway of the first World War II observation post in town. The post was an old Work Projects Administration shack on wheels, known as the Caboose. It was moved to an area off Molly Stark Lane during a gas shortage after residents complained of having to drive too far to do their watch. The photograph was taken by Clem Lyon Jr. on July 18, 1942.

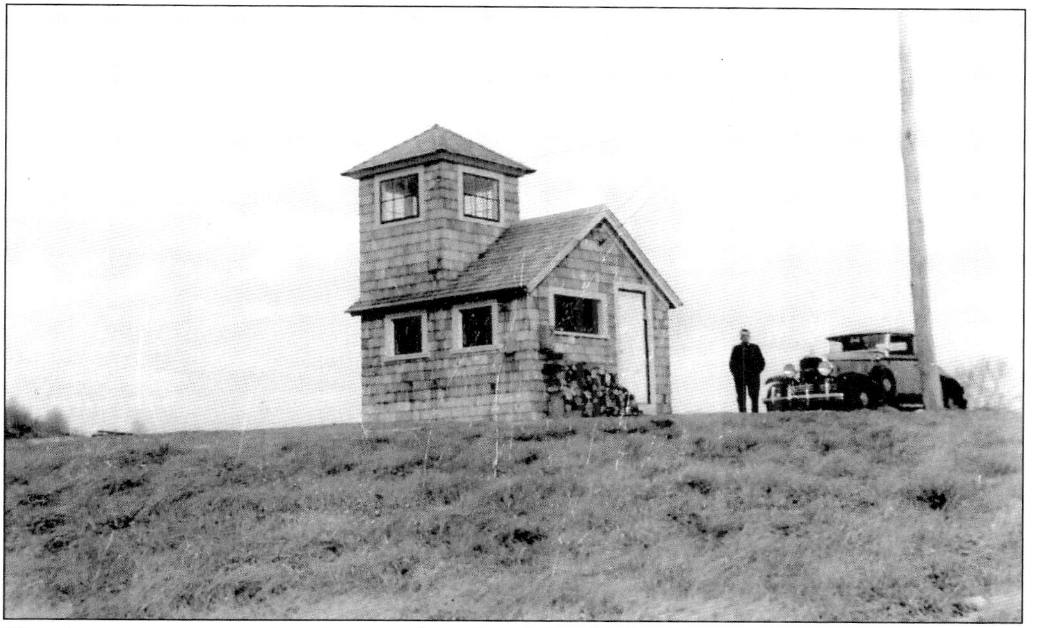

The observation post in this photograph replaced the old shack pictured above. Town residents staffed these posts, watching for enemy aircraft. The women worked in pairs and did two-hour shifts. The men did three- or four-hour shifts at night. This photograph was taken in 1944. (Courtesy of C. Davis.)

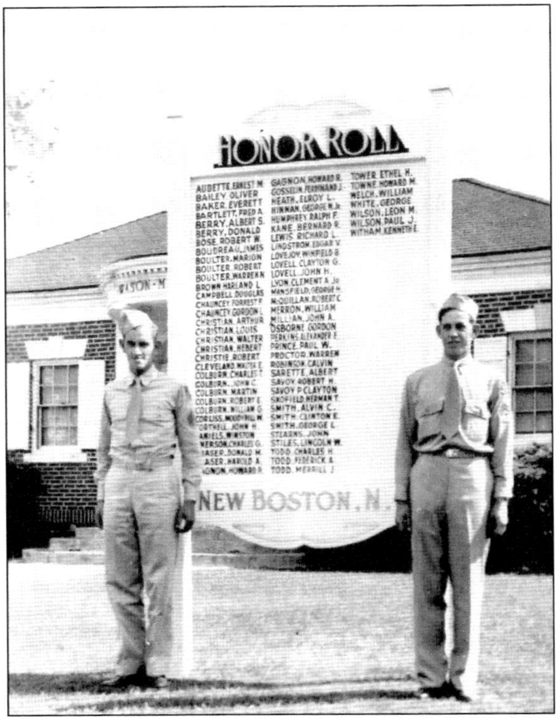

This 1943 or 1944 photograph shows Arthur Gagnon and Charles Todd standing in front of the World War II honor roll. The sign was placed on the front lawn of the library.

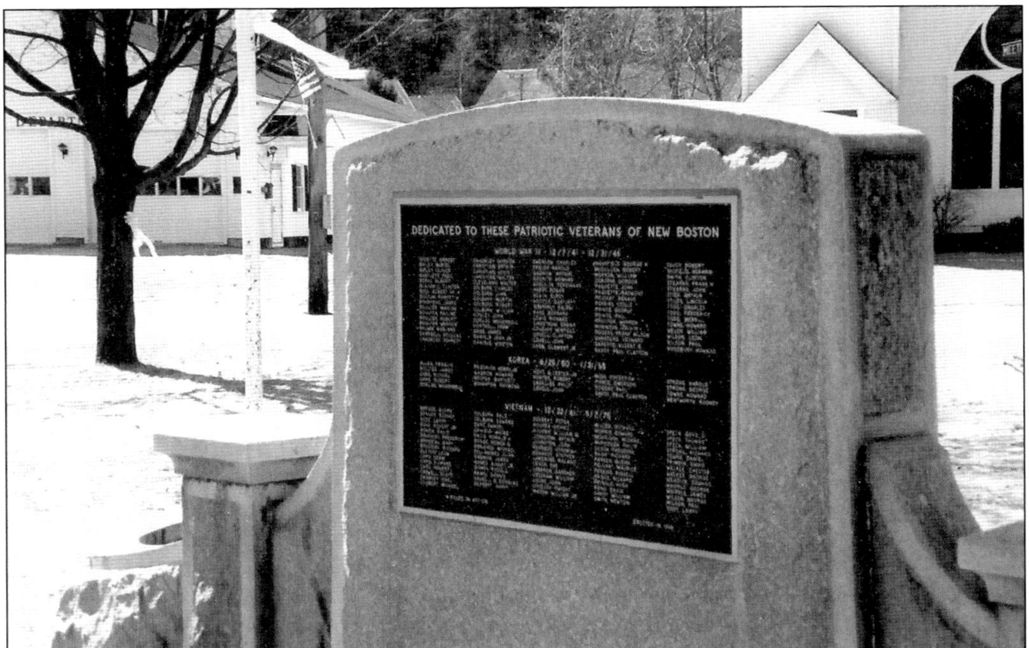

This photograph shows the monument on the town common that honors the New Boston soldiers who have died in service to the country during wartime. Frank French created the memorial with a bequest of $2,000 from Eben Dodge in 1921. Its original location was on the triangle on Route 13. It was moved to the town common in 1947.

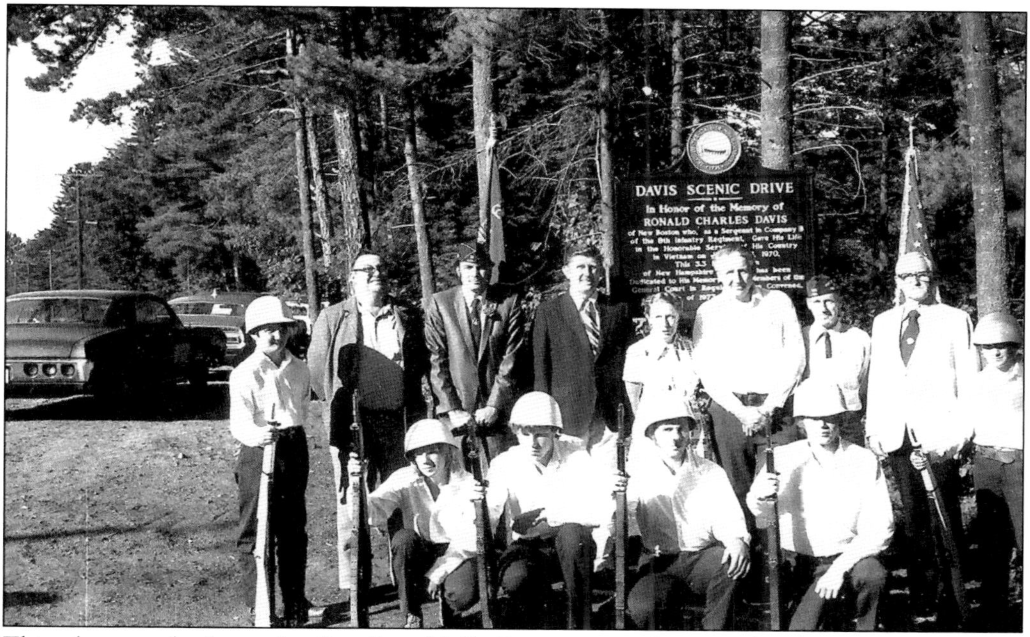

This photograph shows the Sgt. Ronald C. Davis scenic drive marker located southerly on Route 13. This photograph, taken in 1974, shows, from left to right, the following: (front row) Mike Shallow, Ronald Corey, Allen Corey, and John Dukirk; (back row) Kenny Belanger, Greg Peirce, Robert Erskine, Dave Nixon, Rena and Charles Davis, Wilfred Corey, John Howell, and Eddie Belanger. (Courtesy of C. Davis.)

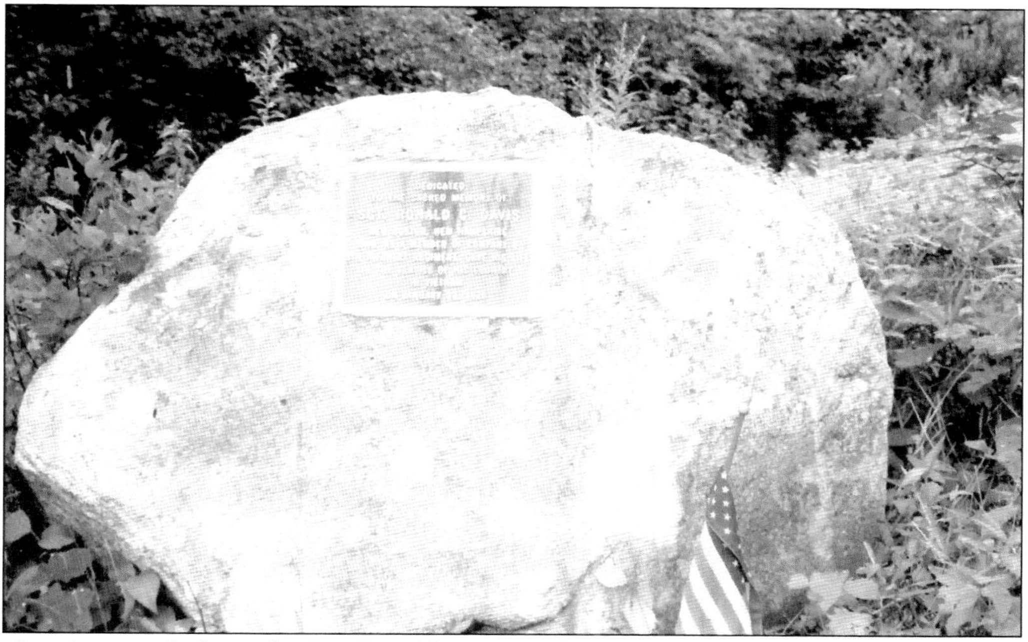

This photograph shows the Sgt. Ronald C. Davis plaque mounted on a rock on the corner of Route 13 and Gregg Mill Road. The plaque is in memory of Sergeant Davis, who gave his life in the service of his country in Vietnam on January 23, 1970. (Photograph by B. Poltrack.)

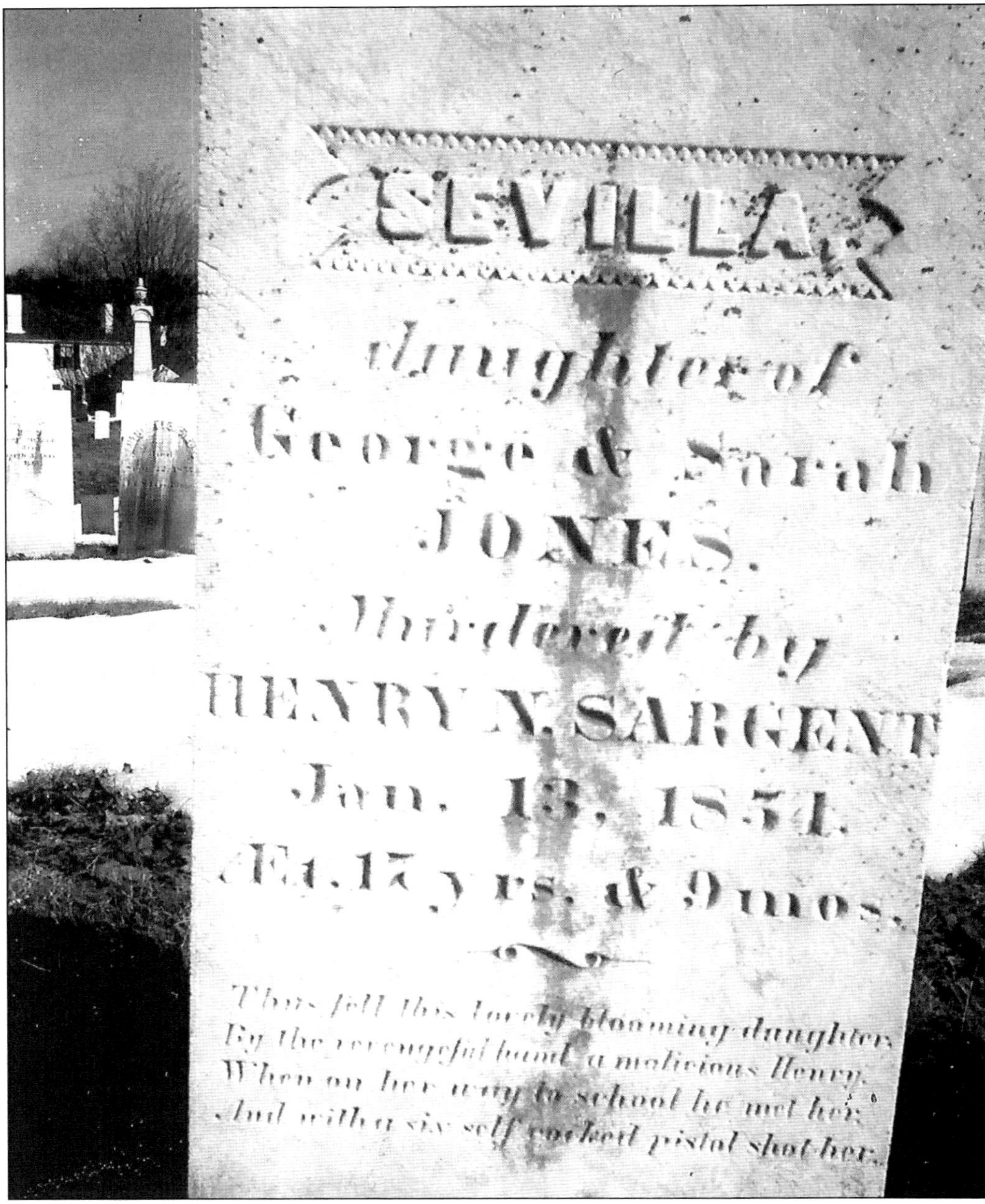

The Sevilla Jones story is a tragic love story. Jones was 17 years old when she was murdered by her spurned boyfriend, Henry Sargent. In a letter he wrote about his murder plans, he stated that she had lost interest in him due to the intervention of others. In his sorrow, he committed murder-suicide on January 13, 1854, on a remote wooded road near Joe English Hill. His request was that they be buried together, for he was sure she loved him as much as he loved her. They were together in the town tomb only until spring, when they were buried about 100 feet apart in their family lots. Jones's gravestone inscription reads, "Thus fell this lovely blooming daughter by the revengeful hand, a malicious Henry when on her way to school he met her and with a six self cocked pistol shot her." (Courtesy of C. Davis.)

Eight

THE GRAVITY CENTER OF THE WORLD

I more and more see the need both of courage to stand fast and the willingness to change. One is the lock and the other is the key; either without the other becomes useless.
—Roger Babson, *Before Making Important Decisions*, 1943

On his deathbed in 1727, Isaac Newton refused to accept the Anglican Church's sacraments, as he had privately decided that they did not reflect a true understanding of Christianity. More than 200 years later, Newton's bed (though probably not the one he actually died in) could be found in New Boston. Roger Babson established the Gravity Research Foundation near the center of town in 1948, and by 1963, it included a public display to honor not Newton's theories on religion but rather his attempts to understand the power and potential of gravitational forces. Inspired by his friend Thomas Edison, Babson also included a display of approximately 5,000 gravity-defying birds.

Requiring somewhere safe from the effect of a potential nuclear war, Babson chose New Boston as the ideal self-sustaining locale just beyond his required 60-mile distance from Boston, a presumed high-profile target. It would be perfect for research and annual conferences—the gravity center of the world. He even wanted a sign proclaiming New Boston to be the safest place in North America if World War III occurred, but the town selectmen did not agree. Ironically, despite Babson's earlier predictions, most people would observe with humor that the U.S. Air Force satellite-tracking station constructed in New Boston c. 1960 would probably cause the former Soviet Union to specifically aim nuclear warheads at their small New England town during the Cold War.

Originally intending to research ways to block or reduce the effect of gravity (with antigravity aircraft wings to prevent crashes or walking shoes with special soles to make one feel lighter, for example), Babson ultimately fostered research and discussions to simply better understand it. An annual essay contest routinely drew entries from such individuals as the physicist Stephen Hawking. The Gravity Research Foundation left town shortly after Babson's death in 1967. Can gravity be harnessed like water or electricity for power, or can its effects be reduced? Still no one knows, but there remains in the center of town a small stone memorial that celebrates those who attempted to find out.

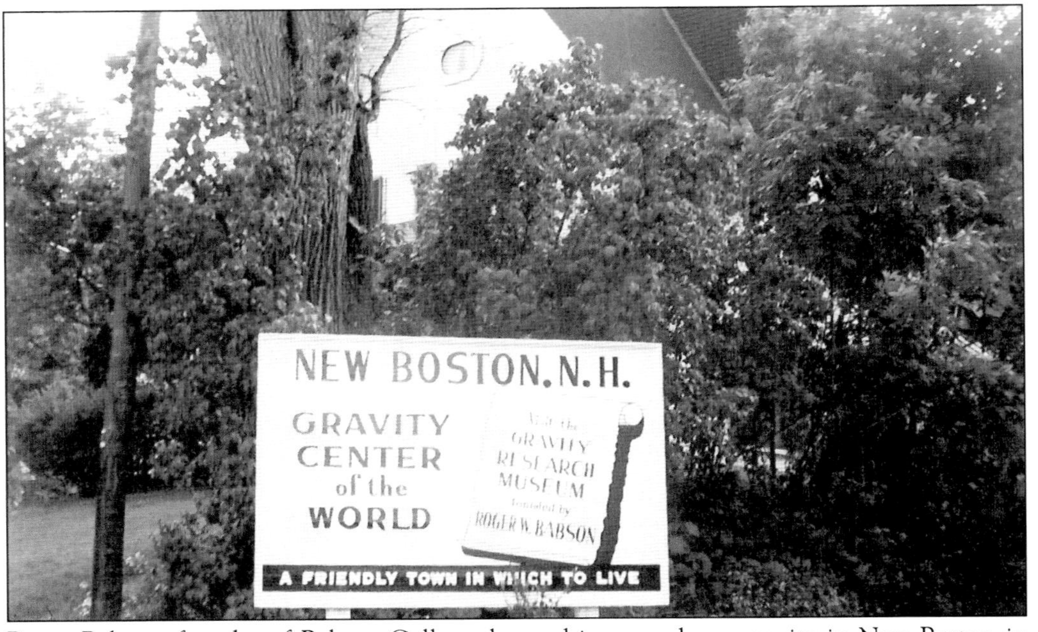

Roger Babson, founder of Babson College, began his research on gravity in New Boston in 1948. He felt that the town's rural location protected it from the threat of atom bombs in the event of World War III. The Gravity Research Foundation was housed in an old farmhouse purchased by Babson, now the location of the Molly Stark Tavern.

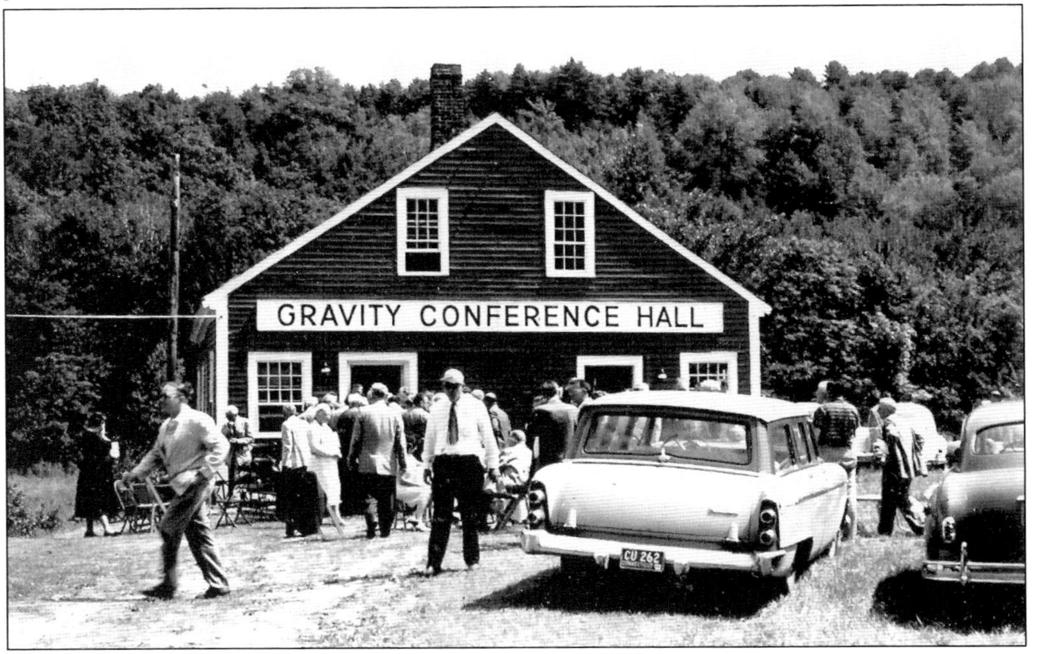

Annual conferences on the subject of gravity were held here at the Gravity Research Foundation. Awards were given for outstanding essays on the subject. A 1,000-year-old bed from Warwick Castle in England once used by Sir Isaac Newton was on display. Attendees complaining of arm and leg pains could hear about Babson's antigravity pill called priscolene.

Here is a typical schedule of events from one of Babson's summer conferences, in August 1960. The original intent of the group was to find ways to counteract the effects of gravity, but later the focus changed to simply trying to understand it.

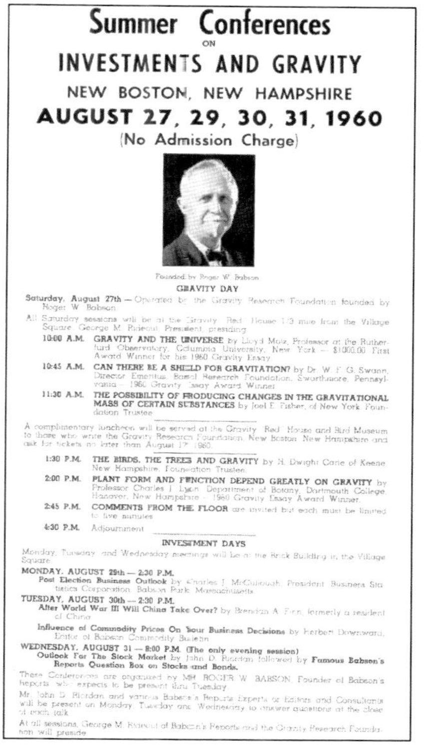

Summer Conferences

ON

INVESTMENTS AND GRAVITY

NEW BOSTON, NEW HAMPSHIRE

AUGUST 27, 29, 30, 31, 1960

(No Admission Charge)

Founded by Roger W. Babson

GRAVITY DAY

Saturday, August 27th — Operated by the Gravity Research Foundation founded by Roger W. Babson.

All Saturday sessions will be at the Gravity "Red" House 1/3 mile from the Village Square. George M. Rideout, President, presiding.

10:00 A.M. **GRAVITY AND THE UNIVERSE** by Lloyd Motz, Professor at the Rutherfurd Observatory, Columbia University, New York — $1000.00 First Award Winner for his 1960 Gravity Essay.

10:45 A.M. **CAN THERE BE A SHIELD FOR GRAVITATION?** by Dr. W. F. G. Swann, Director Emeritus, Bartol Research Foundation, Swarthmore, Pennsylvania — 1960 Gravity Essay Award Winner.

11:30 A.M. **THE POSSIBILITY OF PRODUCING CHANGES IN THE GRAVITATIONAL MASS OF CERTAIN SUBSTANCES** by Joel E. Fisher, of New York. Foundation Trustee.

A complimentary luncheon will be served at the Gravity "Red" House and Bird Museum to those who write the Gravity Research Foundation, New Boston, New Hampshire and ask for tickets no later than August 17, 1960.

1:30 P.M. **THE BIRDS, THE TREES AND GRAVITY** by H. Dwight Carle of Keene, New Hampshire, Foundation Trustee.

2:00 P.M. **PLANT FORM AND FUNCTION DEPEND GREATLY ON GRAVITY** by Professor Charles J. Lyon, Department of Botany, Dartmouth College, Hanover, New Hampshire — 1960 Gravity Essay Award Winner.

2:45 P.M. **COMMENTS FROM THE FLOOR** are invited but each must be limited to five minutes.

4:30 P.M. Adjournment

INVESTMENT DAYS

Monday, Tuesday, and Wednesday meetings will be at the Brick Building in the Village Square.

MONDAY, AUGUST 29th — 2:30 P.M.
Post Election Business Outlook by Charles J. McCullough, President, Business Statistics Corporation, Babson Park, Massachusetts.

TUESDAY, AUGUST 30th — 2:30 P.M.
After World War III Will China Take Over? by Brendan A. Finn, formerly a resident of China.

Influence of Commodity Prices On Your Business Decisions by Herbert Downward, Editor of Babson Commodity Bulletin.

WEDNESDAY, AUGUST 31 — 8:00 P.M. (The only evening session)
Outlook For The Stock Market by John D. Riordan followed by **Famous Babson's Reports Question Box on Stocks and Bonds.**

These Conferences are organized by MR. ROGER W. BABSON, Founder of Babson's Reports, who expects to be present thru Tuesday.

Mr. John D. Riordan and various Babson's Reports Experts or Editors and Consultants will be present on Monday, Tuesday and Wednesday to answer questions at the close of each talk.

At all sessions, George M. Rideout of Babson's Reports and the Gravity Research Foundation will preside.

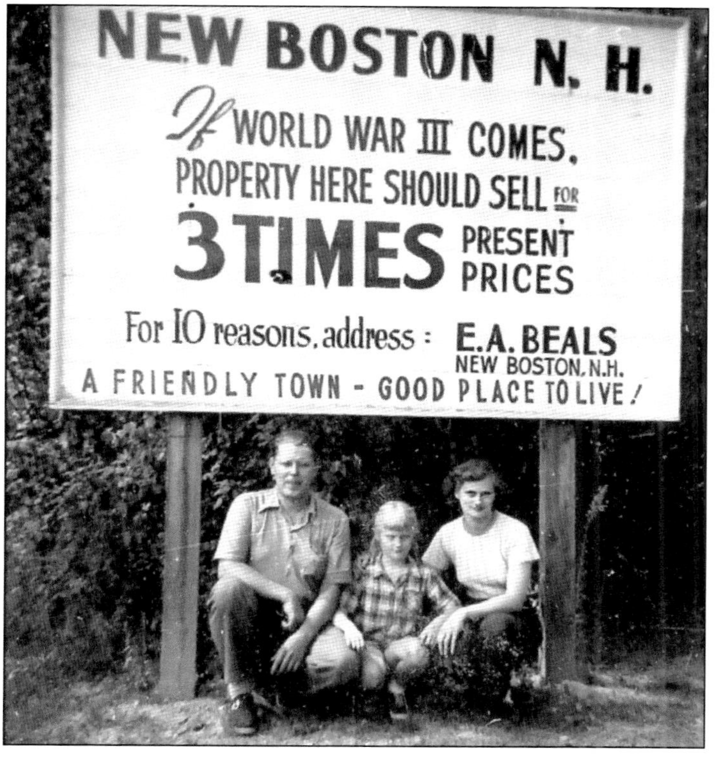

Roger Babson's interest in New Boston attracted a lot of attention to the town. It appears that a local real-estate agent used that attention to his advantage in an advertising campaign. Beneath the sign is the Wilke family, William, June, and Helen, c. 1950. (Donated by J. Edwards.)

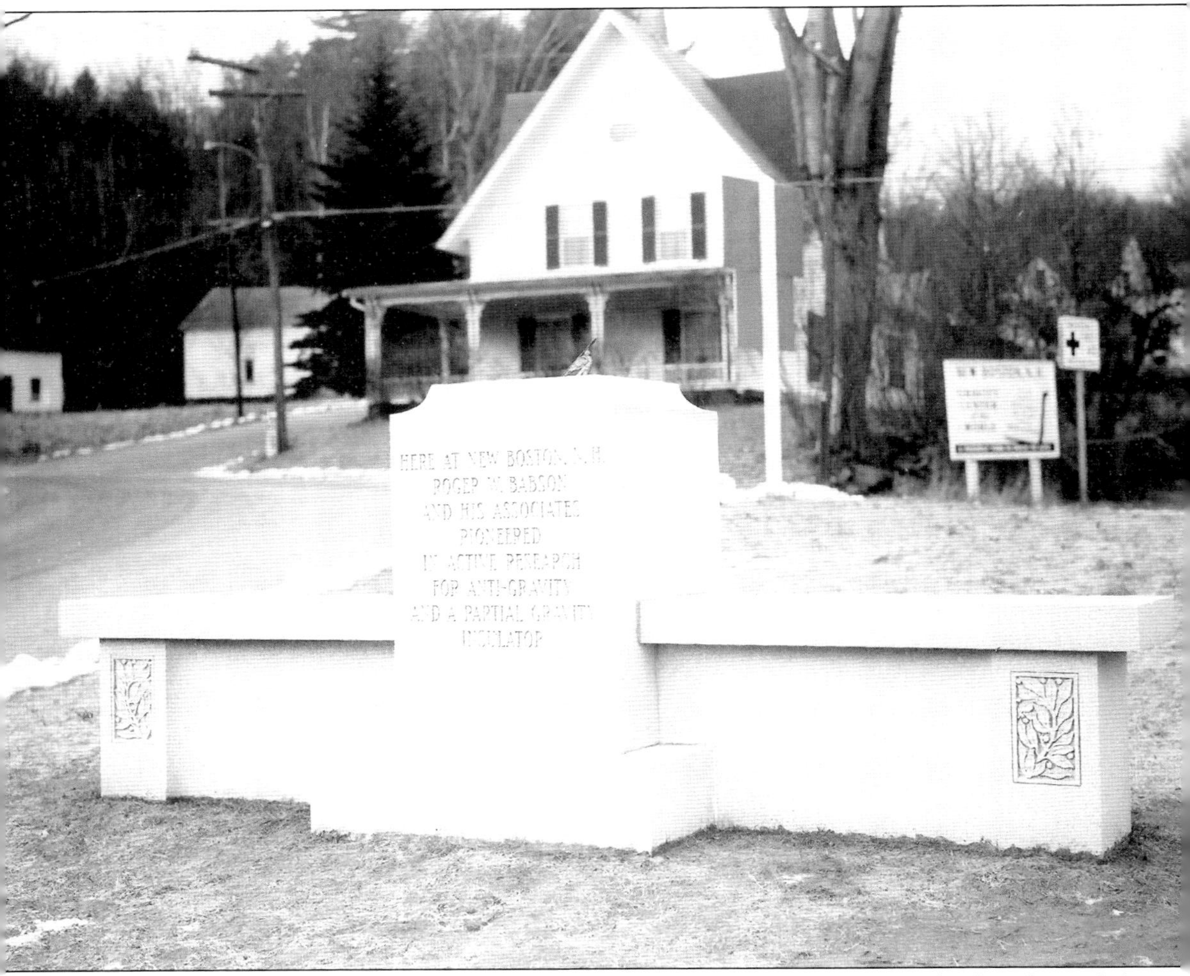

A stone monument in the center of town commemorates Babson's work. The foundation left New Boston sometime after Babson's death in 1967. The essay contests continue to take place, however, and are administered out of Wellesley, Massachusetts.

Nine

Around Town

This is a charming town; Nature has been lavish in her bestowal of attractions.
—Robert O. Fuller, New Boston Old Folk's Day, 1897

Perhaps the phrase "around town" is misleading when speaking of New Boston, since its 43 square miles are laid out in a near perfect square, with the exception being a small nip annexed from the northeast boundary to the neighboring town of Goffstown in 1836. Regardless of the method or description of traveling its roads, New Boston offers something for either the casual Sunday driver (evidenced by the curious Sunday Driver Rock on Bedford Road) passing through or the individual specifically searching for historical or natural beauty. Within its boundaries, New Boston is a remarkable combination of picturesque landscape and human artifacts.

The best-known natural landmarks and oddities are chiefly products of the fierce but sometimes whimsical glacial activities that occurred approximately 12,000 years ago. Although no mountains exist within New Boston proper, there are numerous preglacial hills that resisted total flattening during glacial advance and retreat. For their resistance to the ice sheets that advanced southeasterly to the ocean, a portion of each hill's leeward slope was plucked away, sometimes gently, as in the case of Pinball Hill, or dramatically, as is the case with Joe English Hill. A much smaller but more entertaining example is the ever-vigilant Frog Rock, which still resides in the southwestern portion of town. Practically speaking, the same glaciers also left behind valuable pockets of sand and gravel, numerous ponds, and the lifeblood of the early town—the winding Piscataquog River.

Long after the glaciers departed, residents from near and far have also added to the scenery of New Boston. For example, a satellite-tracking facility operated by the federal government is tucked inconspicuously (except for the 20-foot-high domes that resemble golf balls and are used to house specialized equipment) near Joe English Hill and Joe English Pond, targeted as a former bombing range during World War II. Careful observation will note numerous plaques describing points of interest such as the Davis Scenic Drive or the site of the first Baptist church. And for those visiting or traveling by foot, walking paths along the river and through town-maintained forests are available for enjoyment at any time.

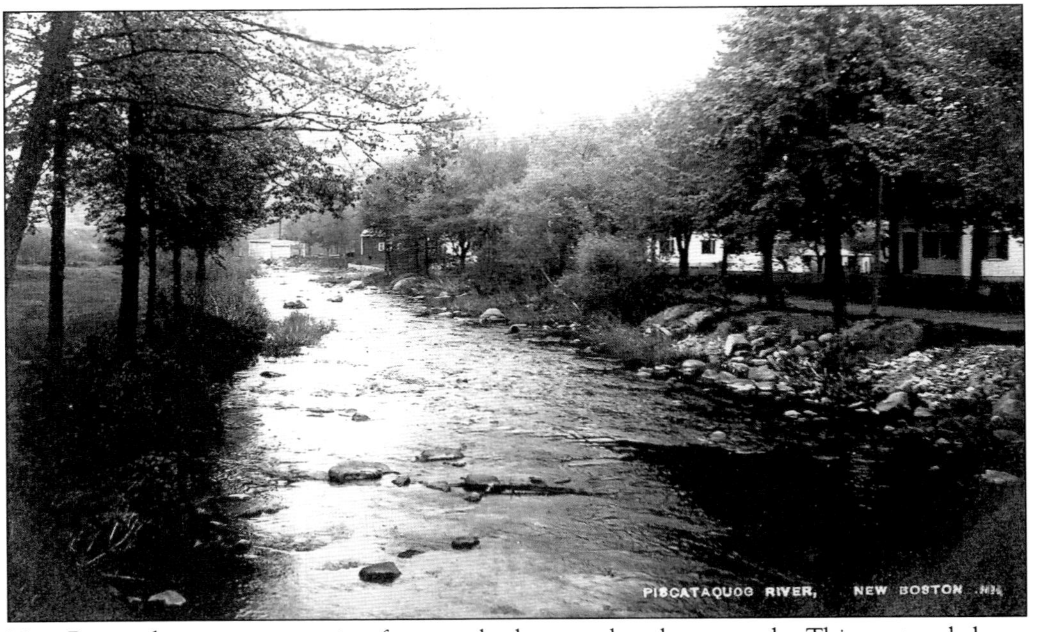

New Boston has many attractive features, both natural and man-made. This postcard shows a road following along the Piscataquog River, one of the town's more picturesque attractions. Piscataquog is an American Indian word meaning "great deer place." Citizens and visitors can enjoy the river's beauty or take advantage of its bounty of salmon, trout, and freshwater bass.

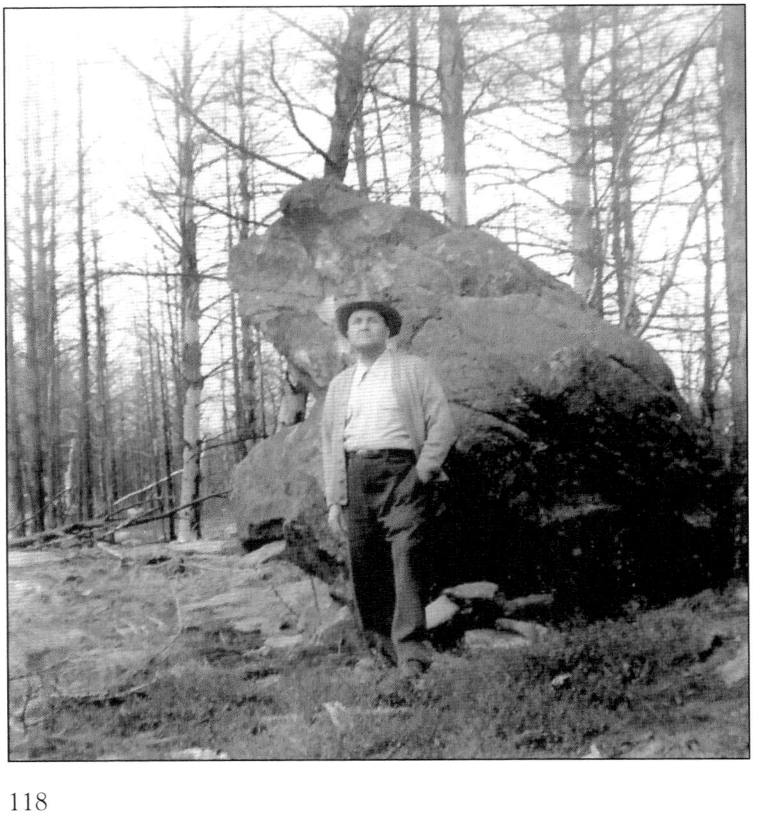

Bill Dotey stands in front of a rock formation that resembles a frog. This picture was taken after a fire burned the woods in the area, making the rock easier to find. Frog Rock has also been depicted on postcards.

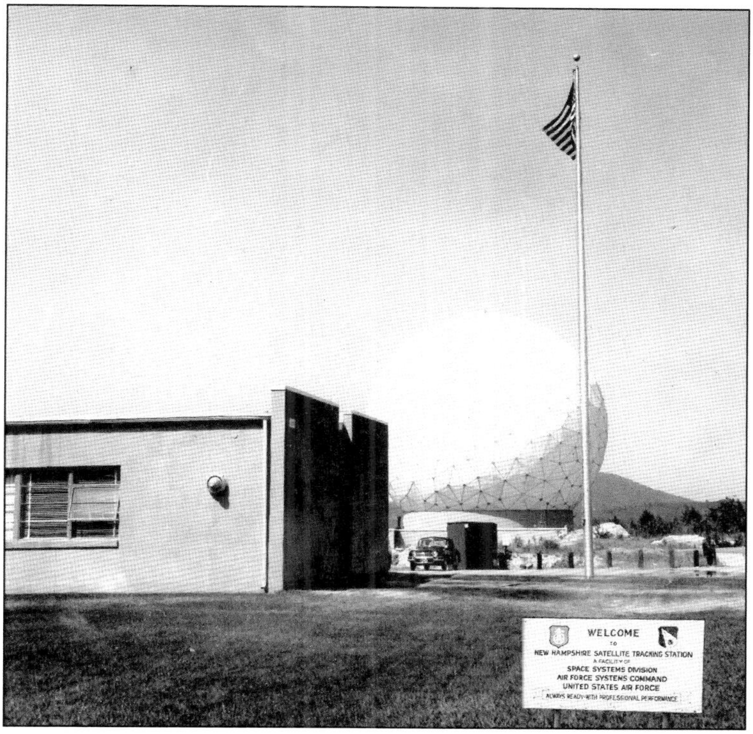

This photograph shows the U.S. Air Force tracking station in its early years. Today, it is a large campus with many buildings. At the entrance to the facility is the fire station, which is now staffed by the New Boston Fire Association and is known as the Hilltop Station. The equipment at the Hilltop Station is maintained by the U.S. Air Force and is available for use by the town.

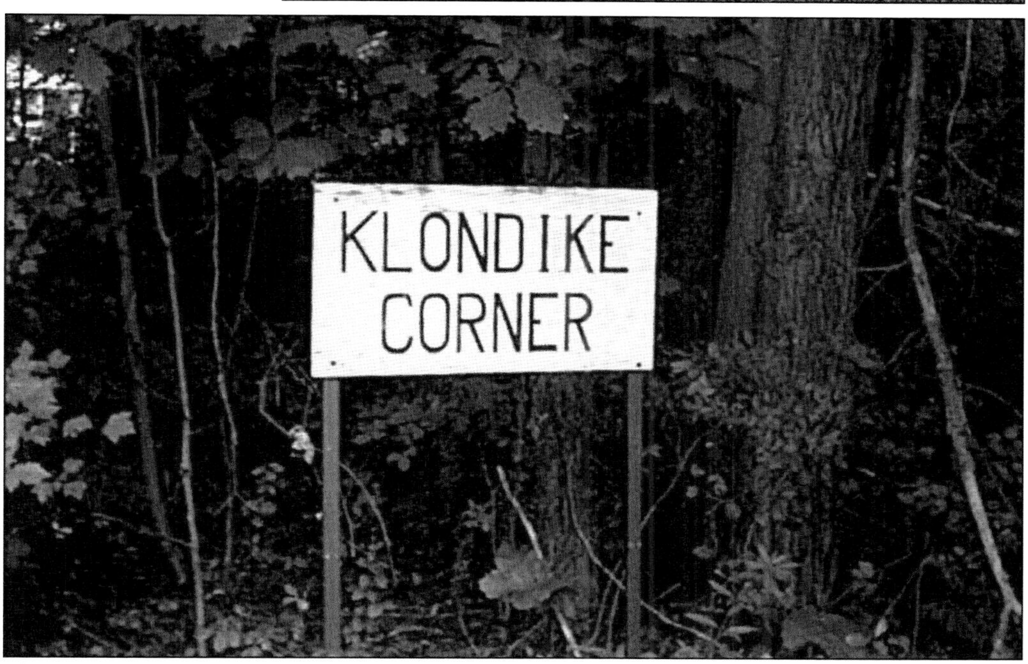

This sign on the corner of Chestnut Hill and Bedford Roads commemorates New Boston's participation in the gold rush. Gold seeker Clifford Dawson lived nearby and named the corner in remembrance of his Alaskan adventures. Dawson was killed in 1915 while painting a train trestle.

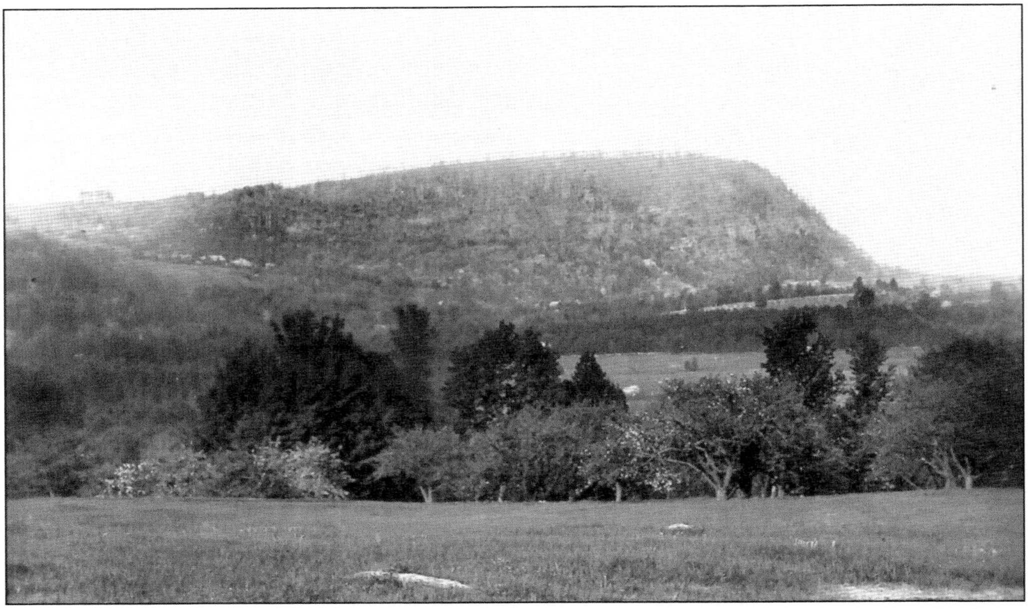

This postcard shows a view of Joe English Hill from the west. The hill was named after a legendary Native American who was called Joe English because of his friendly association with the settlers. The hill has a lake, which was once the center of summer cottages. The area was taken over by the U.S. Air Force for bombing practice in World War II and is now the home of the satellite-tracking station.

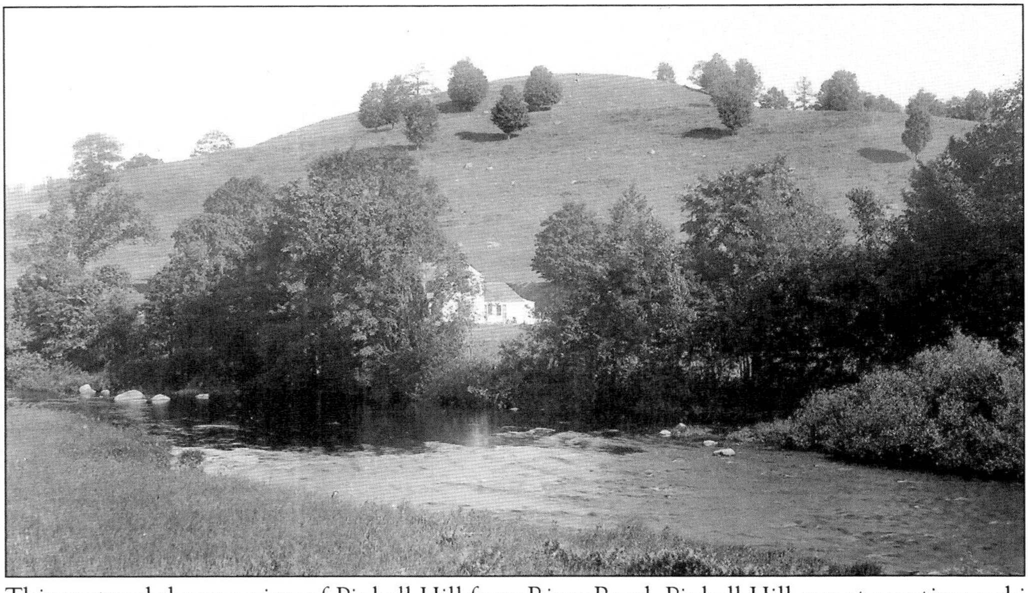

This postcard shows a view of Pinball Hill from River Road. Pinball Hill was at one time a ski hill. At the bottom of the hill are the Hall house and a bridge over the Piscataquog River. The Hall house still sits at the entrance to the 4-H fairgrounds.

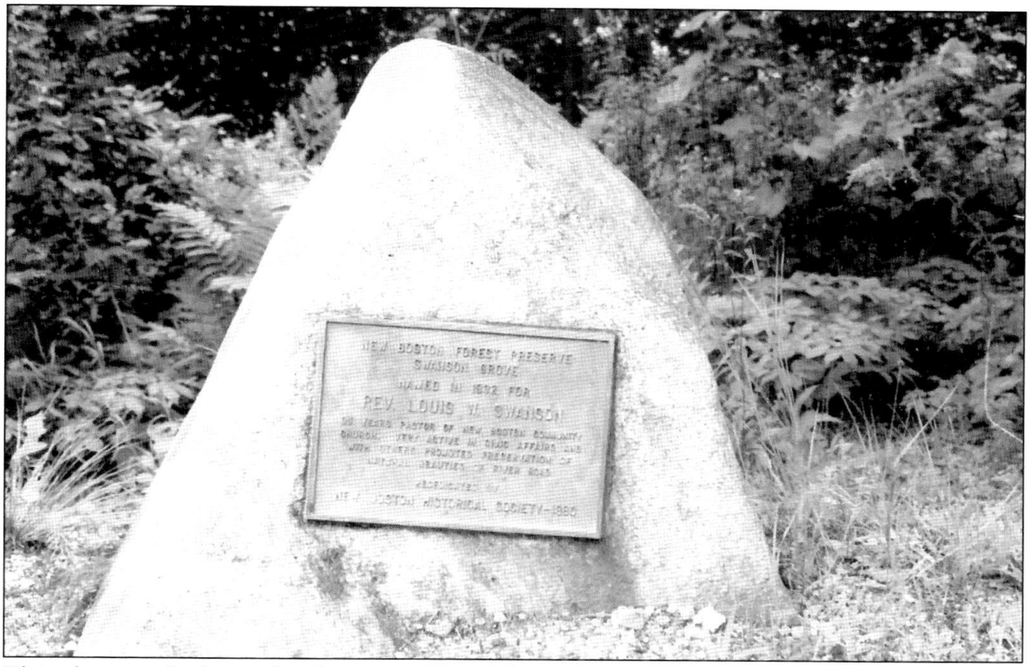

This photograph shows the Swanson Grove plaque mounted on a rock on the side of Route 13. This tract of land was named in 1932 after Rev. Louis Swanson, who served as pastor of the Community Church for 35 years. The historical society dedicated the rock and plaque to Reverend Swanson in 1980. (Photograph by B. Poltrack.)

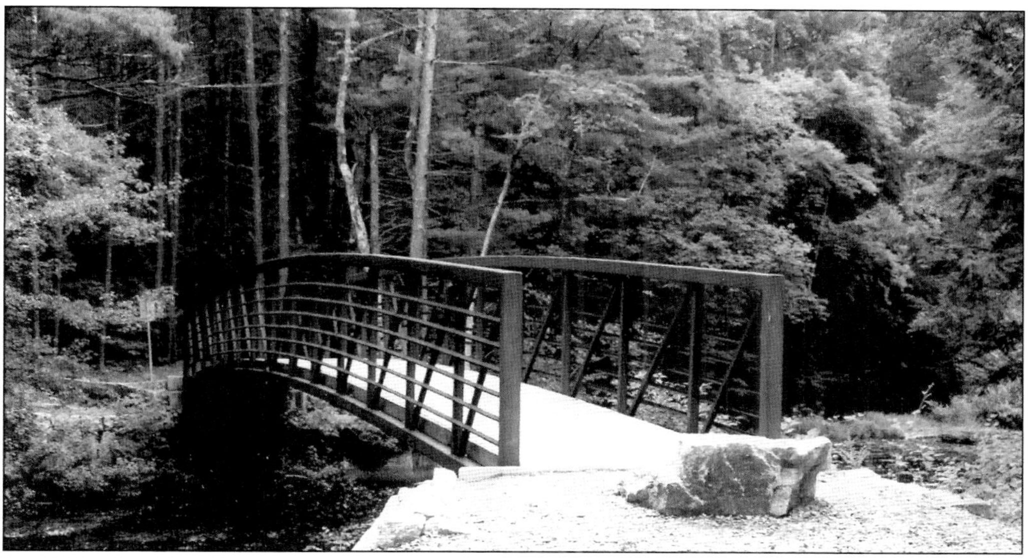

In 2000, the New Boston Conservation Commission realized a long-held wish to build this footbridge, connecting trails separated by the middle branch of the Piscataquog River. The project, funded by Conservation Commission funds, grants, and private donations, enables hikers, snowshoers, cross country skiers, and equestrians to traverse the old railroad bed between the 4-H fairgrounds and the Goffstown line for a distance of approximately four miles (Photograph by Betty Poltrack.)

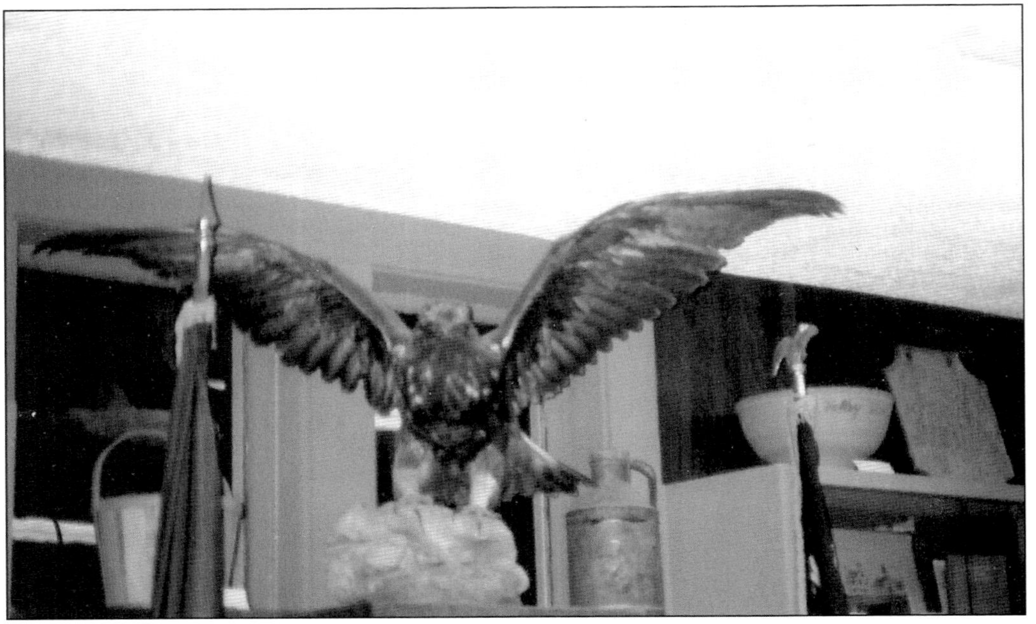

This golden eagle was donated to the historical society by Roland St. Onge, who was rabbit hunting with his beagle pup on Bog Road one October Sunday in 1961 when the dog was captured by the eagle. St. Onge shot the bird before it got too far and was thus able to save his dog. The bird has a 6½-foot wingspan, weighs 12 pounds, and measures 32 inches from beak to tail.

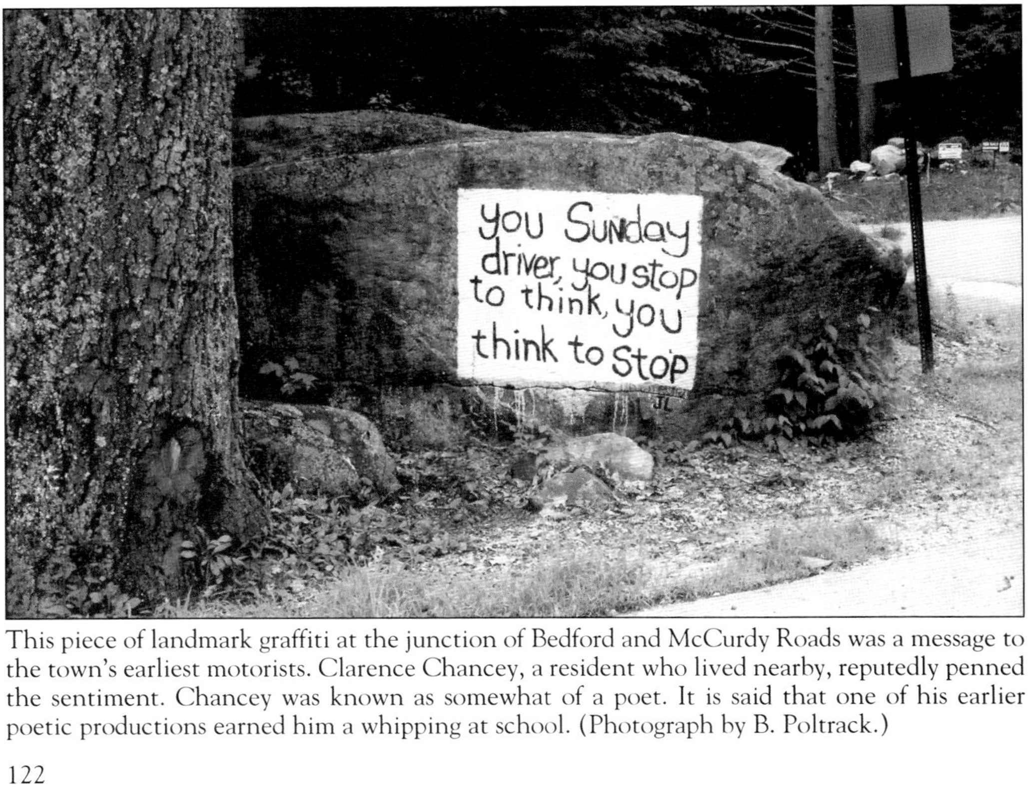

This piece of landmark graffiti at the junction of Bedford and McCurdy Roads was a message to the town's earliest motorists. Clarence Chancey, a resident who lived nearby, reputedly penned the sentiment. Chancey was known as somewhat of a poet. It is said that one of his earlier poetic productions earned him a whipping at school. (Photograph by B. Poltrack.)

Ten

Still Standing

Your old historic granite hills I hope to see again;
The meadows, brooks and little rills
And landmarks that remain.
—New Boston native John Bachelder, 1897

Like most small New England towns, New Boston has changed remarkably to keep up with the modern world, and it shows. But in more subtle ways, one is hard-pressed to provide evidence that almost 250 years have passed since its incorporation. Well-traveled state highways lined with vital utility poles curve smoothly throughout town, passing modern homes and developments, occasional stores, engineered bridges, and the like. Yet, remnants of an agriculture heritage are seen in former barns, pastures, and occasional dirt roads dotting the landscape.

The most obvious evidence of agriculture, and particularly the Whipple era, is the former cement barn near the center of town. The Whipple creamery is now a private residence. And although the train route that whistled into town during this time has not been in passenger service since 1931, the former train station has changed hands several times and is privately owned. Although there is only one school (a modern school) active today, several former schoolhouses remain in use as private residences. Other historic buildings that still exist structurally and are in reuse include the old firehouse and the former pharmacy. Of course, the natural landmarks and oddities that have resulted from geologic processes should remain standing even after any evidence of New Boston and its residents have vanished.

New Boston is once again a town experiencing rapid growth, as it did over 100 years ago. But it seems unfathomable today that even if a catastrophic event such as the fire of 1887 occurred again, it surely could not again wipe clean so many records and documentation of a town. Or could it? The community spirit that exists in New Boston is something that has stayed fundamentally present from generation to generation and does not appear to have been adversely affected or wounded by the passing of time in the nearly 250 years of New Boston history. The character of a town such as New Boston cannot be destroyed, torn down, or ravaged with age. Indeed, it will be the last characteristic still standing.

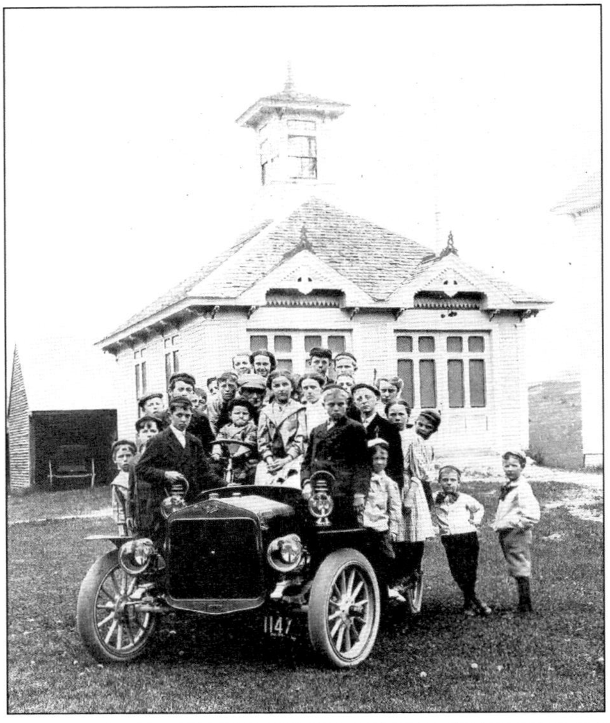

This tiny building next to the town hall was originally the town's fire station. It was built in 1889, two years after the great fire destroyed the original engine house. The two bays facing the street were sufficient to house the town's fire equipment until 1973, when the new fire station across the street was built. In 1989, the building was turned over to the New Boston Historical Society and underwent some restorations in keeping with its original appearance.

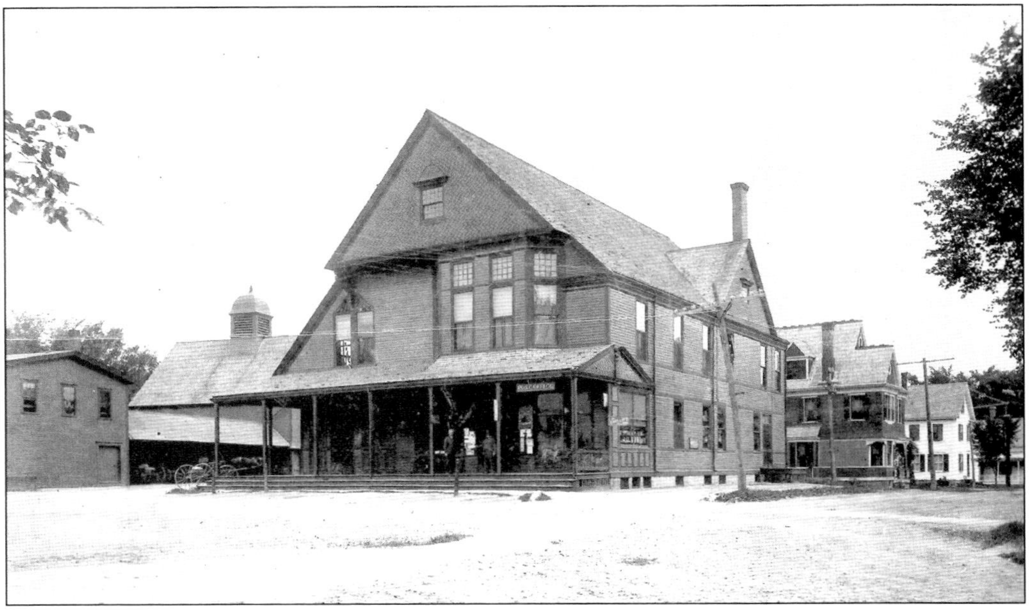

There has been a store at this location since the early 1800s. The original structure burned during the town's great fire of 1887 but was rebuilt thanks to a loan from the generous J. R. Whipple. The building also housed Valley Hall, where town activities were held. At other times, the Whipple Free Library and the post office were located there. The business has been known as Dodge's Store since 1920, when Clarence Dodge moved his goods here. Although it passed from Dodge family hands in 1995, the name remains. (Donated by B. Armstrong.)

Here is a photograph of Joe English Grange No. 53 and the town hall. The Grange was formed in 1875, and at the second meeting, it was decided that all future meetings would be held monthly, "on or before the full of the moon." The current building was erected sometime after the fire of 1887, which destroyed the lower town hall. The Grange continues to operate today, doing good and worthy deeds for the community. New Boston town offices are still located here.

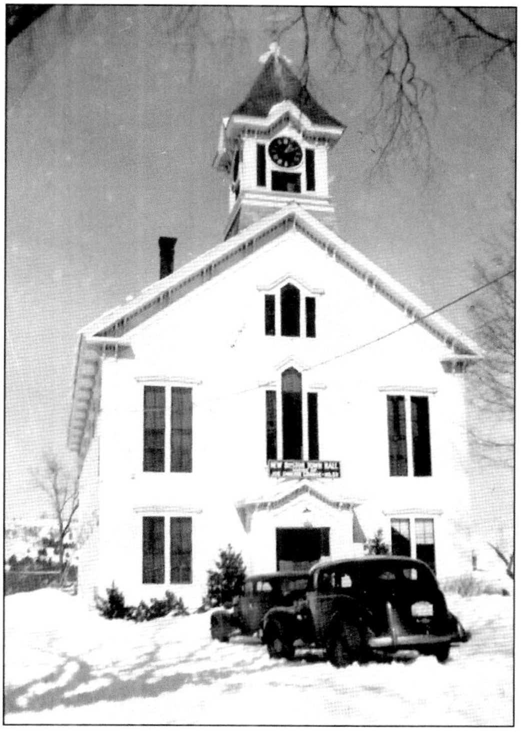

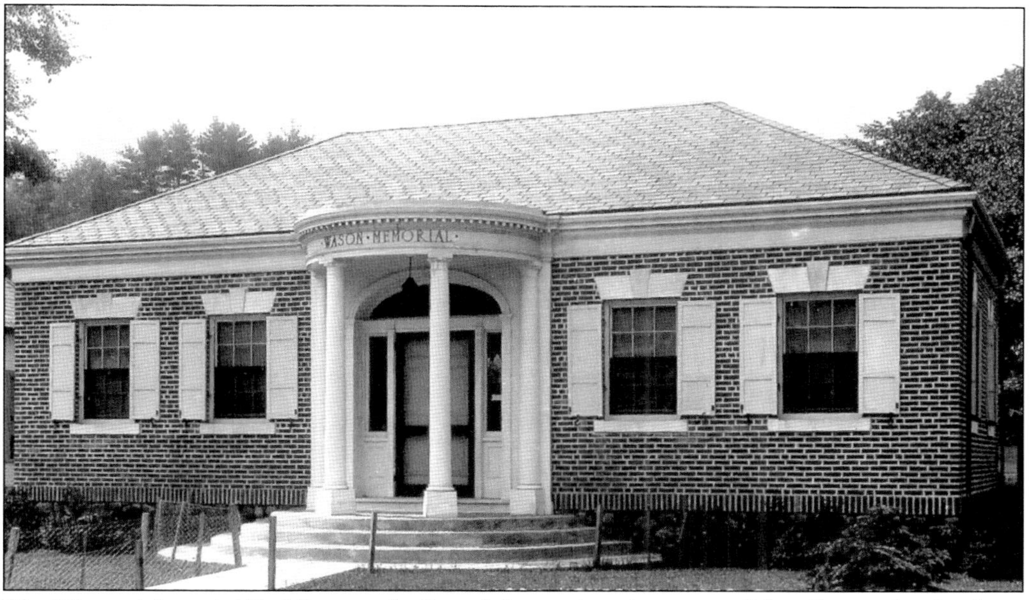

The Wason Memorial Building was built and donated to the town of New Boston by the three sons of George and Clara Wason in memory of their parents. The Whipple Free Library book collection, originally housed in Dodge's Store, was moved to the Wason building in 1927. In 1982, the Hayes-Warren addition was constructed in memory of library supporters Reg and Beulah Hayes and longtime librarian Elsie Warren. The Whipple Free Library remains at this site today.

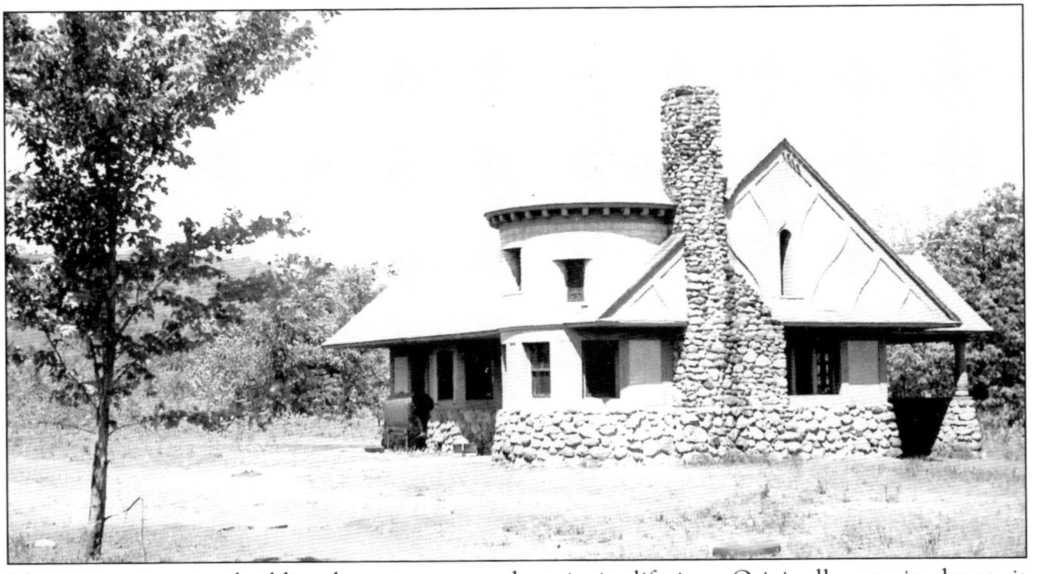

This very attractive building has worn many hats in its lifetime. Originally a train depot, it was constructed in 1893, when the railroad came to town. After the tracks were taken up in 1935, the building was sold to the playground association, which used it as a community house. Later, the Baptist church used the building as its meeting place. In 1977, it was rechristened the Depot, and in 1980, it became the town's police station. Today, it is a private residence.

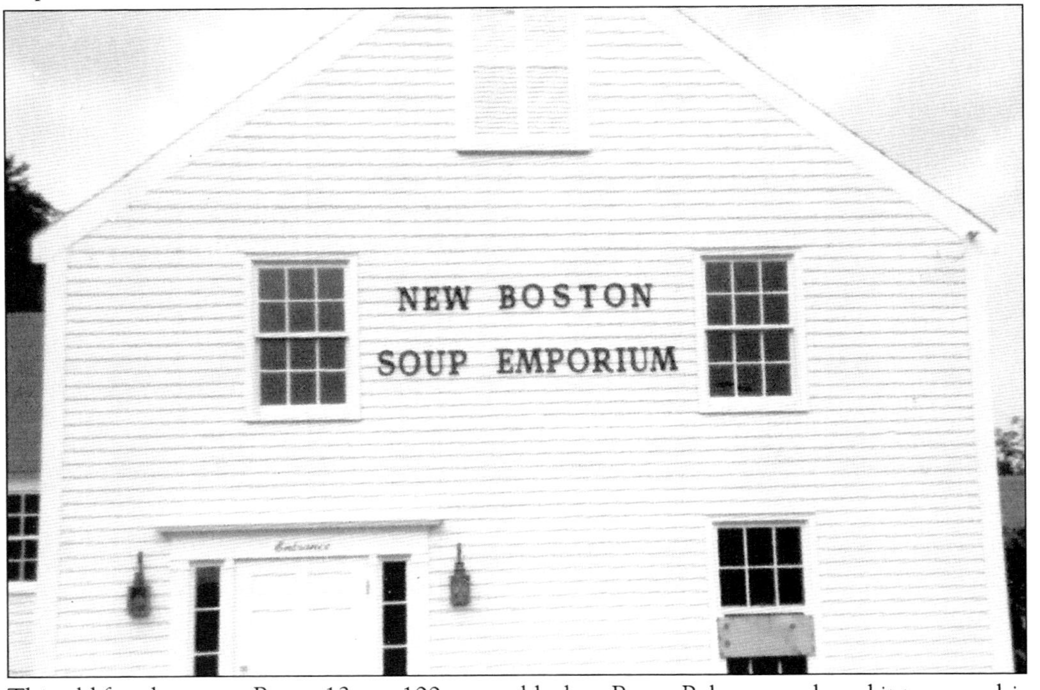

This old farmhouse on Route 13 was 100 years old when Roger Babson purchased it to use as his gravity research headquarters. After Babson's death in 1967, the Gravity Research Foundation left town and the building became the Soup Emporium restaurant, as pictured here. Since 1979, it has been the home of New Boston's fine restaurant the Molly Stark Tavern.

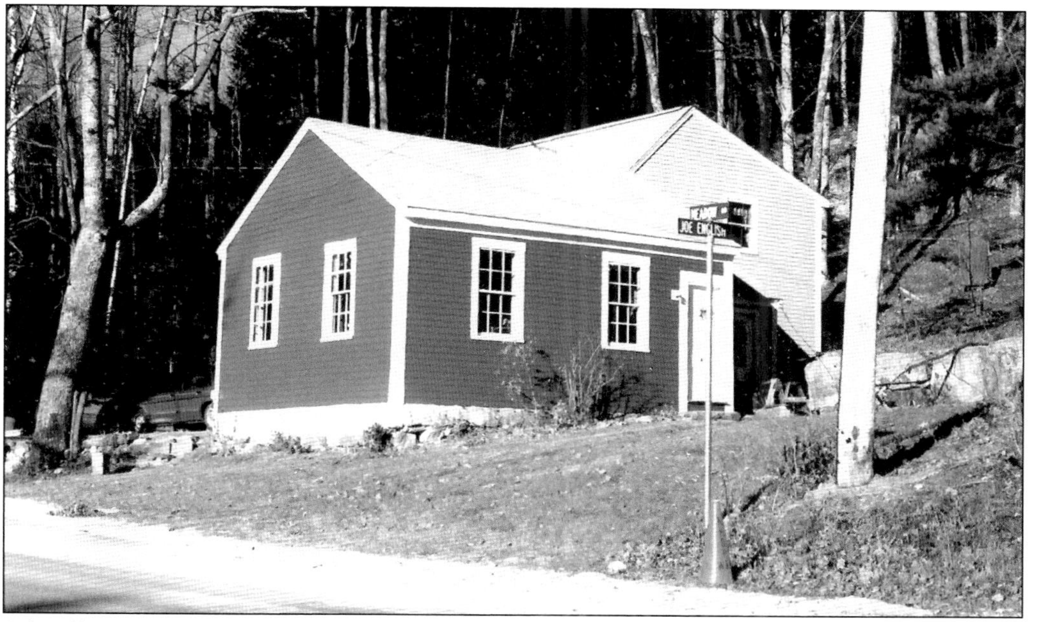

Schoolhouse No. 4, located on Joe English Road, is the only one of New Boston's 18 schoolhouses that still exists in its original location and general condition. Although the Poole family, which has owned the building since the early 1970s, constructed an addition to the structure, the building's original room remains much as it was during its tenure as a schoolhouse, including the raised stage-like area where the teacher's desk sat. (Courtesy of N. Poole.)

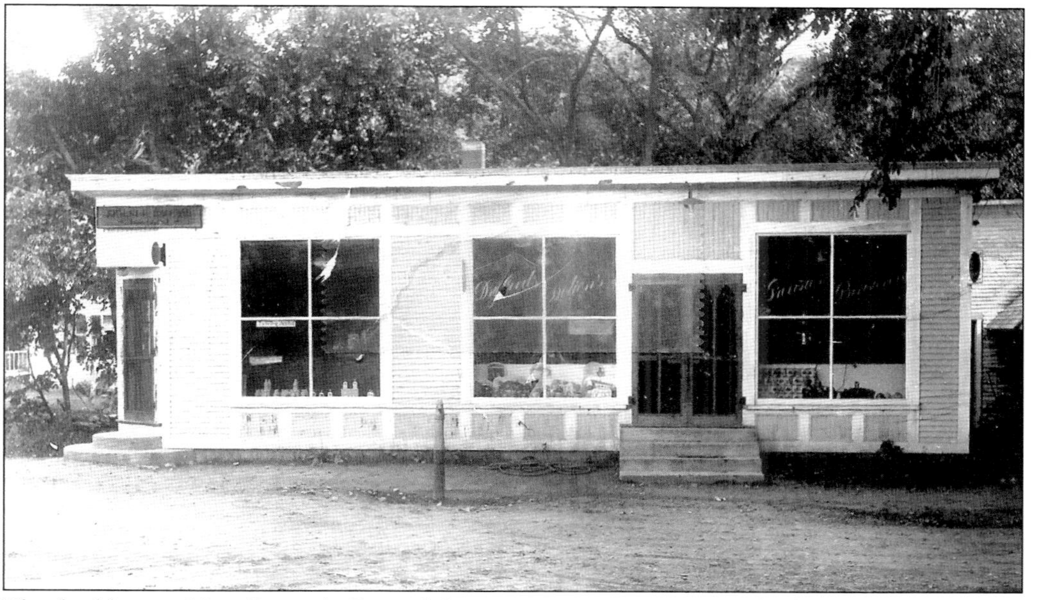

This building in New Boston's Central Square was at various times the home of a pharmacy, café, and antique shop. With the beautiful Piscataquog River running through the town with its bounty of fish, it is no wonder that this tiny village requires its own anglers' supply store. Hunter's Angling Supplies has served the community in this location since 1972.

ACKNOWLEDGMENTS

The book committee would like to thank Sandy Molloy first and foremost for her dedication and the seemingly countless hours she devoted to working on and managing this project. Throughout the project, Sandy kept everyone on schedule and made the whole process a truly enjoyable experience! Also, we would like to acknowledge committee member Tom Lazott for writing the book and chapter introductions and for the extensive research that was required; Dave Chamberlain for scanning and editing over 200 photographs; Jim Hansen for going to extraordinary lengths to create new photographs; and everyone else who helped us with suggestions, support, or photographs. Finally, we would like to thank in advance the future citizens and members of the New Boston Historical Society for any corrections, additions, or other efforts they undertake and complete to carry on the spirit and traditions in which this book was written.

—The New Boston Historical Society Book Committee, December 2003

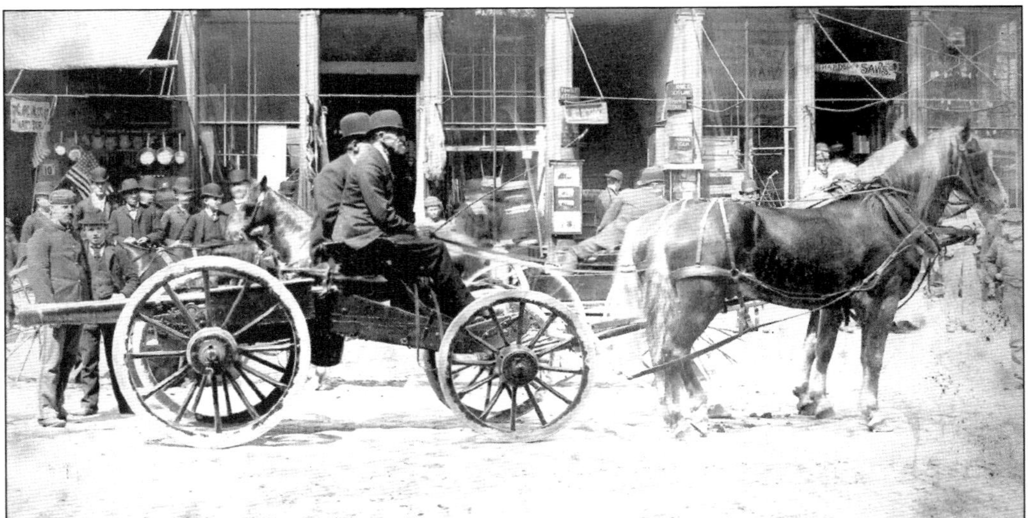

Seen here is the Molly Stark cannon in Manchester *c.* 1897.